THE MAD AND THE BRAVE

THE MAD AND THE BRAVE

THE UNTOLD STORY OF UKRAINE'S FOREIGN LEGION

COLIN FREEMAN

MUDLARK

Mudlark
An imprint of HarperCollins*Publishers*
1 London Bridge Street
London SE1 9GF

www.harpercollins.co.uk

HarperCollins*Publishers*
Macken House, 39/40 Mayor Street Upper
Dublin 1, D01 C9W8, Ireland

First published by Mudlark 2025

1 3 5 7 9 10 8 6 4 2

Map © Collins Bartholomew 2025

A catalogue record of this book is
available from the British Library

HB ISBN 978-0-00-872246-3
PB ISBN 978-0-00-872247-0

Printed and bound in the UK using 100%
renewable electricity at CPI Group (UK) Ltd

This book is dedicated to my long-suffering
partner Jane (who threatened dire
consequences if it wasn't)

CONTENTS

PART II – 'IT'S NOT LIKE *CALL OF DUTY*'
Mykolaiv, Kharkiv, the black site

PART III – ALL BUZZING ON THE EASTERN FRONT
Drones, learning on the job, Kharkiv, Kherson

PART IV – 'BRAVERY IS IN OUR DNA'
Grief and loss, epilogue

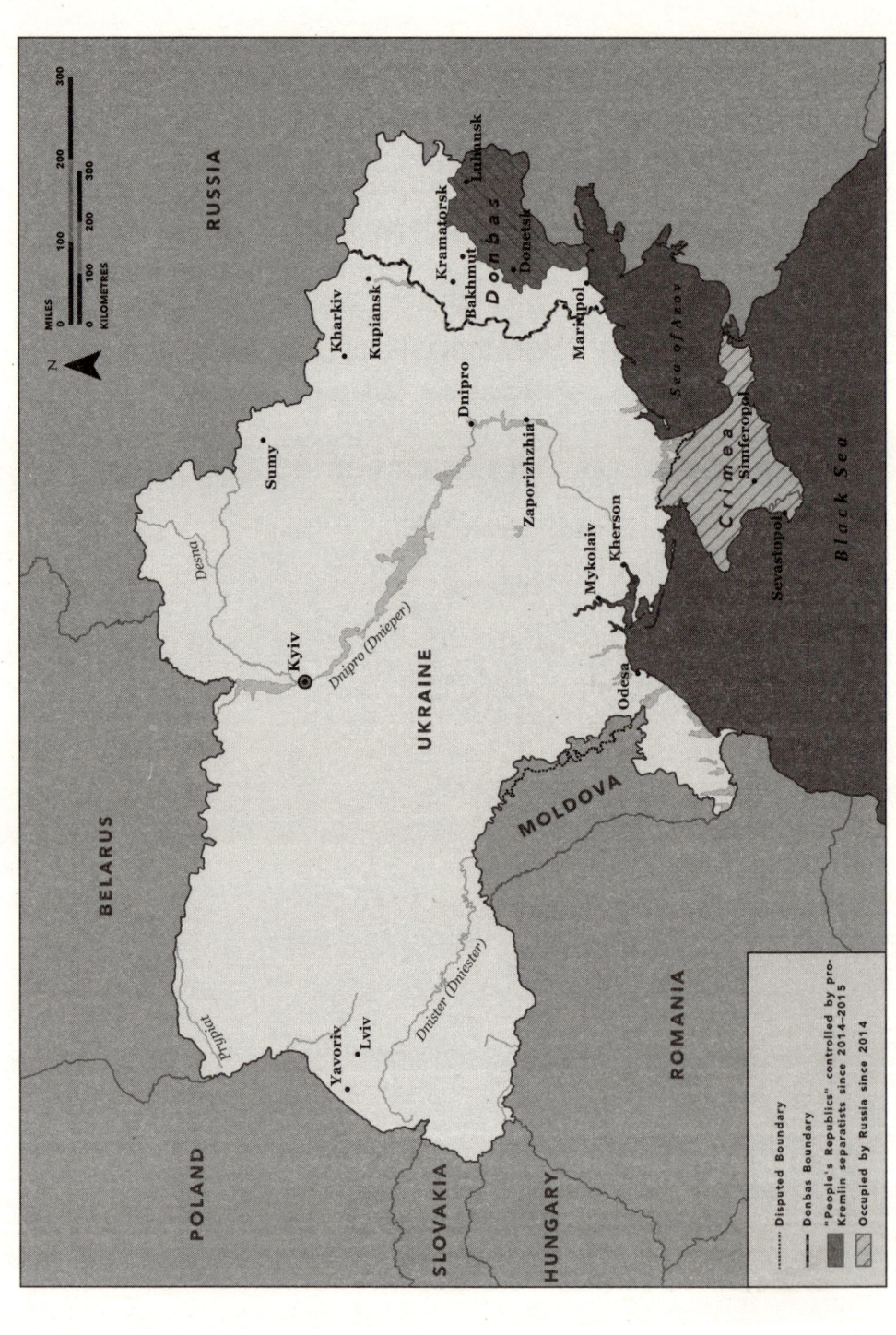

INTRODUCTION

This book is based on conversations with volunteers during the war's first three years. Some I met on the frontline in Ukraine, some in bars, cafés and hospital wards from Kyiv to Kherson. Others I caught up with while they were on R&R back in Britain, with battlefield stories re-enacted in their local pub: 'So imagine the trench is where our table is, and the shell lands over there, where the bar is …' The accounts would go on for hours sometimes, with breaks for cigarettes, more beer, and occasionally the odd tear. We took care to talk out of earshot of other drinkers. Conversations about gunfights with Russians can be alarming if heard out of context.

The volunteers in this book were not picked in any scientific fashion. Rather, they are those who were willing to be interviewed, something many avoid. Partly, this is down to soldiers' usual wariness of nosy journalists. But with the war still ongoing, they also fear being targeted by the Kremlin, even when back home. Nonetheless, I think that the narrative features a wide range of voices. There are those who went to Ukraine as seasoned combat veterans, and those who'd never held a gun before. For some, the main motivation was defending democracy, for others the reasons were more complex and personal.

1

As a British author, I have inevitably focused mainly on British volunteers, but in keeping with the spirit of the International Legion, other voices appear too: Americans, Canadians and Europeans. In an ideal world, I would have limited the number of voices to perhaps just half a dozen, all in the same unit, all fighting together from the start, like a real-life *Band of Brothers*. I soon realised this was not going to be easy in a volunteer force like the Legion, where fighters have relative freedom to move around, often shifting from one unit to another, sometimes only fighting for a few months. As I've also learned through writing about an ongoing war, death and injury sometimes cut stories short. For that reason, the cast in this book is something of a hotchpotch: characters come and go, some playing bigger roles, others with only walk-on parts.

Most chapters are told from one volunteer's perspective at a time, witnessing key events in the invasion, be it the siege of Kyiv, the gruelling trench combat in the Donbas or the horrors of Russian captivity. That way, I hope readers get not just the story of the Legion, but that of the wider war itself. Rather than attempting an exhaustive account of every frontline, I've focused on whichever aspects of volunteers' experiences struck me as interesting, like their time in battle, their motivations for coming to Ukraine or what they did afterwards. Soldiering is generally long periods of boredom spliced with short bursts of action, with many volunteers recalling just a few memorable days per deployment. I have focused mainly on those memorable days, rather than chronicle each volunteer's time in Ukraine from start to finish. Again, this is a reason for more voices rather than less, and where readers may be curious about each volunteer's subsequent adventures, the Epilogue section does its best to tie up their stories.

As well as the volunteers themselves, there is also a supporting cast of others: logisticians and well-wishers who helped them, and also some of the volunteers' families. They may not have been sitting in the trenches, but they often had a war all of their own, worrying constantly about their loved ones, and having to cope if they were captured or killed. Some interviewees, because of concerns about their own security, appear under pseudonyms, with minor biographical details also changed to protect their identity.

In return for their speaking to me, I've tried to tell the volunteers' stories as best I can, although I make no claim to have done so perfectly. If there is one thing I have learnt while researching this book, it is that battlefields are far more chaotic and complicated than they look in the movies. One volunteer likened firefights to very bad dreams: terrifying, hard to explain and unique to the individual involved. One person's recollection of events, therefore, can be substantially different from another's. And when things go wrong in war, there's often a tendency to blame someone else. Nor, despite its heightened sense of life and death, is a battlefield necessarily where great insights into the meaning of existence are acquired. Observations while under fire tend towards the profane rather than the profound. And when reflecting later, not every soldier is a Siegfried Sassoon or Wilfred Owen, even if they have spent just as long in cold, muddy trenches.

Besides, most of us are lucky enough never to experience the more hideous ordeals outlined in this book, which means the vocabulary available to describe them is sparse. Often, when I asked volunteers what it was like to be shot, shelled or tortured, to put into words extremes of fear or pain, they would shrug, reach for a cliché or simply say: 'It's indescribable.' At times I have left it at that, rather than fill in the blanks. What I have tried to do, however, is to convey some sense of what those battlefields are like in Ukraine, and why so many from around the world chose to risk their lives there.

Finally, a quick word about 'frontlines' – a word overused in war reporting, and which needs some context. When journalists like myself talk about being on Ukraine's 'frontlines', we seldom mean literally right at the front, with bullets flying everywhere. It usually refers to somewhere a few kilometres back – close enough to hear gunfire and watch the odd explosion, but not so close that a safe exit isn't possible. The real frontline in Ukraine – also known as 'the zero line' – is a different place altogether, where artillery roars, drones buzz and bodies lie rotting on open ground because it isn't safe to collect them.

Or so I'm told. The zero line isn't a place I ever really went to much in Ukraine. To reach it would require soldiers to risk their lives escorting me there, and to go there simply to see it would be voyeuristic (I'm as much of a war tourist as any other reporter, but not at others' expense). I rely, therefore, on second-hand accounts, which are terrifying enough in themselves. One Ukrainian medic I interviewed, who regularly visited the zero line to pick up dead and injured, summed it up thus: 'The fear there is so intense, you want to vomit, shit and cry at the same time.' And he only went there during lulls in fighting.

In other words, the zero line is frightening even when it's quiet. Yet this is where the volunteers in this book would spend much of their time. Many, by their own admission, are flawed characters, sometimes with troubled pasts, whose motives for fighting in Ukraine were not always just the pure and the noble. But to do what they did still takes guts. And besides, the war didn't really care why people came to fight, only that they did so. On which note, not all of those who feature in this book are still alive. It is dedicated to their memory, and the sacrifice they made.

Colin Freeman
London, January 2025

The Combatants

* indicates name changed at interviewee's request. Pseudonyms are also generally used for minor characters referred to by interviewees in passing.

Daniel Burke from Manchester, England. Ex-Parachute Regiment.

Douglas Cartner from Castle Douglas, Scotland. No previous military experience.

Alex Drueke from Alabama, US. Ex-US Army.

James Durose from Middlesbrough, England. No previous military experience.

John Harding from Sunderland, England. Ex-Parachute Regiment.

Andrew Hill from Plymouth, England. Ex-Duke of Lancaster Regiment.

Andy Huynh from Alabama, US. Ex-US Marines.

Richard Johnson* from London, England. Ex-British Army officer.

Jack Knight from London, England. Ex-Royal Engineer.

Hiu Le from California, US. Ex-US Marines.

Christopher Perryman from County Durham, England. Ex-Royal Fusiliers.

Henry Stevens* from US, living in Germany. Ex-US military.

Stephen Wilson from Rochester, England. Ex-Royal Engineer.

Others

Freddie Ickenham and his son David*: part of the British
  volunteer network that supplies Ukrainian forces.
Fatman, Uniform Man, Moustache Man and Dead Eyes:
  interrogators in Kremlin 'black site' prison.
Damon Adams: owner of army surplus store in
  England.

Glossary of terms and abbreviations

Note: Some foreign volunteers serve in the Legion's own battalions, others are attached directly to the Ukrainian military. In
this book, 'Legionnaire' is used as a generic term for all foreign
military volunteers.

The International Legion – umbrella organisation for foreign
  military volunteers in Ukraine, created by President
  Zelensky in February 2022

APC – armoured personnel carrier
BMP – armoured fighting vehicle used by both Ukrainian and
  Russian forces
Casevac – casualty evacuation
dead ground – patch of low-lying ground hidden from enemy
  view
DPR – Donetsk People's Republic. Breakaway pro-Kremlin
  region in Ukraine's eastern Donbas region
Himars – High Mobility Artillery Rocket System
HUR – Ukrainian military intelligence directorate
IED – improvised explosive device

Javelin – US-made anti-tank missile supplied to Ukrainian forces

KIA – killed in action

OP – observation post

PKM – belt-fed machine gun used by both Ukrainian and Russian forces

PoW – prisoner of war

RPG – rocket-propelled grenade

treeline – line of trees along the boundary of a field, often used as cover by advancing/retreating troops

YPG – Western-backed Kurdish militia that fought Islamic State in Syria

PART I
A CALL TO ARMS

Mobilisation, the Siege of Kyiv, Mariupol

'This is the beginning of a war against Europe, against democracy, against basic human rights. Anyone who wants to join the defence of Ukraine, Europe and the world can come and fight side by side with the Ukrainians against the Russian war criminals.'

President Volodymyr Zelensky,
Sunday 27 February 2022

1

'TELL HR I'M OFF TO WAR'

South-east England, 24 February 2022

Most shoppers at Damon Adams' army surplus store were not kitting themselves out for combat. His customers ranged from paintballers and hikers through to school cadets and anglers, browsing his budget camouflage gear and outdoor kit. But aside from a few oddball survivalists busy prepping for Armageddon, very few were stocking up for war. Then, last week, Vladimir Putin had invaded Ukraine, since when his phone had been ringing off the hook. Had he got boots, helmets, uniforms? What about body armour and medical kits? How much could he supply?

At first, the callers were mostly Ukrainians living in Britain. 'Procurers', they called themselves. Buying kit for Ukraine's under-equipped armed forces, funded by whip-rounds in towns and villages back home. They were ringing every military surplus store in Britain they could find. Adams' shop was particularly popular because it was handy for the cross-Channel ferries.

The invasion had started at dawn on 24 February, a Thursday morning. Adams worked round the clock that weekend, helping Ukrainians stuff their vans and cars with kit. Some were heading direct for the ferries and the 1,000-mile drive to Ukraine's Polish border, where millions of refugees were fleeing the other way.

Then, from Monday onwards, Adams noticed a new kind of customer browsing in the shop. This time, they were Brits, although they wore the same preoccupied, shopping-in-a-hurry faces as the Ukrainians. He could guess why they were there. Over the weekend, Ukraine's president Volodymyr Zelensky, holed up in a bunker somewhere in Kyiv, had issued a plea for foreign volunteers to help defend his country. A new 'International Legion' would be formed.

As a former soldier himself, Adams sympathised with anyone who wanted to help. At 52, he had memories of the last time Europe had felt scared of Russia, during the Cold War. Of being terrified by that film *Threads*, a 1980s BBC drama depicting a Soviet nuclear strike in Britain. Of asking Dad if everything was going to be okay, and not feeling totally reassured by the answer.

Then that sense of relief when that nice Mr Gorbachev came along, with his talk of peace and *perestroika*. Adams had joined the army in 1987, just as the Soviet Union was collapsing and Moscow no longer seen as a threat. Now, with Putin's tanks rolling into Ukraine, the bad old Russia was back.

Keen to do his bit, Adams was already offering discounts to the Ukrainian procurers. A few unscrupulous army surplus stores were hiking their prices, and flogging dodgy kit – boots that fell apart, antique body armour from 1970s Belfast. He now extended his discount to any British customer answering Zelensky's call.

As long as they sounded like experienced professionals, he told himself. Fighting in a war wasn't for amateurs. As he served the Brits coming into his shop, Adams tried to strike up conversation. Some talked knowledgeably about tours of Iraq and Afghanistan. Others sounded like the only fighting they'd ever done was playing *Call of Duty*. He grilled them gently, seeing if they knew what they were getting themselves into.

Been in the military before, mate? Where? Ever been under fire? No? Sure you're going to cope? What do your family think about all this?

A few he actually turned away – telling them, as politely as he could, that real-life war was not like playing a video game, and that with all due respect, they'd be more of a liability in Ukraine than a help. Yet even among the seasoned players, there were some whose motivations seemed personal rather than professional. Sure, they talked the noble talk of defending democracy. But they also mentioned marriage break-ups, lack of stimulation in work and life, depression. One said he didn't really care if he came back.

Adams wasn't a therapist. But he did know one thing. Going to war made life seem very much simpler, putting all other problems into perspective. He remembered his own days serving in Northern Ireland, being blown up in his army Land Rover in an IRA stronghold in South Armagh, and then going back happily for more. Being close to death made you feel very alive.

Combat was a drug, a rush like no other. You got hooked on it. Those who'd already tasted it in Afghanistan or Iraq probably wanted another fix. And those who'd never fought, yearned for the chance to try it, to sample that raw, potent cocktail of fear and adrenalin. To see if they could handle it.

* * *

HS2 MAINLINE BUILDING SITE, HIGH WYCOMBE, BUCKINGHAMSHIRE, FEBRUARY 2022.

'Paedo! Bigot! Fascist!'

I hate this job, thought Christopher Perryman.

High Wycombe, a leafy Buckinghamshire market town, lay on the proposed line for the new High Speed 2 railway, linking

London with the West Midlands. The line was being blocked by eco-protesters, sceptical of HS2's claims to be the route to a new, greener Britain. They were particularly upset that woodlands around High Wycombe were being destroyed to make way for it. Perryman, along with hundreds of other private security guards, had been hired to stop them disrupting the building work.

The activists might well have had a point, Perryman thought. But for folk whose stated tactic was civil disobedience, they weren't very civil. On TV, they came across as very cuddly – posh, dreadlocked hippies, earnest students, off-duty vicars. Up close, it was rather different.

In the last 20 years, he'd served as a sniper in Iraq, tracked war criminals in the Balkans and worked as a bodyguard in Somalia. The people he was normally paid to worry about were usually trained killers like himself. Which, in terms of job satisfaction, made them much preferable to his new adversaries in Britain's commuter belt. Rather than bombs and bullets coming his way, he now had fireworks, bricks and plastic bags filled with urine and faeces. Plus, every insult the protesters could think of – anything to provoke a reaction, which they'd then film. Any security guard who retaliated risked finding footage of themselves on social media, portraying them as the snarling, hard-hatted face of the Establishment. Not great for the CV. Which you'd be needing the following day, after getting the boot for losing your rag.

He'd never really liked civilian jobs anyway. Having joined the army at 16, he'd become accustomed to its regimented ways. Discipline, punctuality, orders. Being told when to eat and sleep, when to have a haircut, when to have a beer.

After leaving the army in his early thirties, he'd tried everything from farming to delivery driving to highways maintenance. None had really suited him. Frankly, civilians drove him slightly nuts. They turned up late for things. They didn't always appreciate his dark army humour. And they tended to whinge, as if unaware of how nice Britain was compared to somewhere like Iraq or Somalia.

Hence his relief, a few years ago, when a pal had got him onto the bodyguard and close protection circuit. Lots of ex-soldiers did it, guarding VIPs in places like Iraq and Afghanistan, earning ten times what they'd got in uniform. A dividend of the 'War on Terror'. Perryman had worked in Mosul first, then Mogadishu, finding a new home in a fraternity of fellow warrior-nomads. Military routine and banter again, generous R&R. Work hard, play hard.

All of which then got screwed by Covid and lockdown, which forced every expat back to their home country. Since then, the only reasonably paid work he'd found was at HS2. He'd been so desperate to escape from it, to get back abroad again, he'd considered some daft ventures.

Like last year, when Kabul had fallen to the Taliban. A pal in the ex-military networks knew a commander in the Northern Alliance, the Afghan militia that helped America topple the Taliban's rule after 9/11. The commander was recruiting foreign military veterans to help the Alliance overthrow the Taliban again. This time, though, there'd be no US military to help. It was risky, to put it mildly. But Perryman had been so bored, he'd been on the point of signing up. The plan fell through when the commander was himself captured by the Taliban.

With hindsight, the whole enterprise was madness. He'd have stood every chance of ending up in an orange jumpsuit, awaiting beheading. Meanwhile, though, he was still stuck here at HS2. Dressed, as it happened, in an orange jumpsuit, plus a hard hat as well. And being abused by people who'd clearly seen nothing of the world. Who else, after all, would really think that a security guard in hi-vis gear was a fascist?

Paedo. Bigot. Nazi!

Then, just last week, fascism had raised its head for real. Not in a hard hat, nor a steel helmet with swastikas. But fascism all the same – a fanatic, ultranationalist dictator trying to take his neighbour's land by force. President Vladimir Putin of Russia sending his tanks into Ukraine, starting Europe's first major land war in 80 years.

Perryman had followed the invasion on the news, watching with a professional eye. It wasn't how a professional army was supposed to act. There were hospitals and homes getting bombed, civilians getting killed. Sure, soldiers made mistakes during war. During the invasion of Iraq, which he'd taken part in, innocents had died sometimes. But not on this scale. This was far too much to be explained away as 'collateral damage'.

Then, a few days into the war, another ex-military mate had rung. Had he heard the latest from Ukraine's president, Volodymyr Zelensky? Yeah, the guy in the t-shirt and stubble? He'd just appealed for foreign volunteers to defend his country. All ex-soldiers welcome. Just register with your local Ukrainian embassy, and get yourself to Ukraine's Polish border. They'd pick you up from there.

Straightaway, Perryman was tempted. This wasn't some ramshackle militia like the Northern Alliance. This was an elected, legitimate government, wanting help against a bully. A breed of person he'd always despised, be they in a children's playground or a president's office. And Poland was just an EasyJet flight away. Better to be fighting fascists abroad, than standing around being called one at home.

He was due a week off anyway, which he spent looking into it. Half of his old military network seemed to be going, or thinking about it. A pal had worked with some Ukrainians as part of a Nato training programme. Spoke highly of them, reckoned volunteers would be well looked after.

Others urged caution. This wouldn't be like fighting Iraqi insurgents or the Taliban. Russia was the world's second superpower. It had a proper army, plus tanks, jets, spy satellites, hypersonic missiles. And, if it came to it, nuclear weapons. The Ukrainians were underdogs in this war. Fighting alongside them would be like fighting for the Taliban against Nato. No calling in air strikes if it got tough. No helicopters to whisk the wounded to hospital.

Perryman's years in the military, though, had convinced him there was no point fretting about when his time was up. The way he saw it, he was as likely to die in some mundane mishap at home as in a warzone abroad. Run over on the way to buy a pint of milk, or a random victim of knife crime Britain. Stabbed in the pub by some kid trying to be a gangster.

True, there was also his son to think about. The lad was 10 years old. Perryman wasn't with his mum anymore, but saw him when he could. He could imagine already what some people would say. Why fight in someone else's war, when you've got a kid back at home? Nobody's forcing you to go, are they?

No, they weren't. But that was a civilian view of the world. Perryman was from a military family. Most of his relatives had served, going back to World War II and before. And if every father back then had refused to fight, Britons would now be speaking German.

Besides, there were plenty of Ukrainian fathers now out fighting. They didn't have a choice, even though many had never picked up a gun before. He'd done 16 years in the Royal Regiment of Fusiliers, was a trained sniper. Fighting was what he'd spent his life learning to do. What good was it if he didn't use those skills when someone cried out for them? His son would either hate him for his decision, or he'd understand.

*　*　*

CASTLE DOUGLAS, SCOTLAND, FEBRUARY 2022. Zelensky's call for foreign military volunteers didn't seem to have reached the staff at Ukraine's consulate in Scotland. When Douglas Cartner knocked at their door in Edinburgh, there was no grateful military attaché waiting to register him for duty. Instead, an overworked-looking diplomat handed him an email address to write to, and disappeared back inside.

It was perhaps just as well. Had anyone grilled Cartner there and then, the answers might not have sounded very impressive.

What past military experience do you have?

'None.'

What made you volunteer?

'*I was having a beer and watching Netflix when something came on the news about it. Just seemed like a good idea.*'

How do your next of kin feel about your decision?

'*They think I'm fucking daft.*'

Cartner was from Castle Douglas, a town in Scotland's remote Dumfries and Galloway region, where he still lived on his parents' farm. He was 26, a qualified tractor engineer, with a decent job and a girlfriend. Give it another few years, and he'd probably be able to afford his own place too. But it wasn't the life he'd wanted.

Ever since he was a kid, he'd dreamed of being a soldier. At 17, he'd gone to the Commando Training Centre in Devon to take a pre-qualifier course for the Royal Marines. Three days of press-ups, pull-ups and obstacle courses, with a one-in-two failure rate. He'd trained hard for it, only for his shoulder to lock up during one of the press-up marathons. A doctor looked at it later, spotted an old fracture from an accident on the farm. When the Marines found out, they said it meant he could never join them.

After that, he'd lapsed into serious depression. Doctors had got involved. That, in turn, had scuppered his chances of joining other army regiments. Half a dozen had turned him down after seeing the mental health notes on his medical record. The army wasn't big on neuro-diversity back then.

By his mid-twenties, he'd finally accepted that soldiering was not to be, and had done a college course in agricultural engineering. Plenty of work on the farms around Dumfries and Galloway. He now had a job, a partner and a future – everything in life, that was, except any sense of adventure. Other people his age went on gap years, travelled the world. But if you'd set your heart on being a Commando, going off to find yourself in India wasn't really a substitute.

Hence the twin stab of hope and fear he'd felt one Sunday night, while having a beer and a TV dinner. He'd been browsing Netflix for something to watch, and getting distracted as usual by the latest news from Ukraine. Normally he didn't follow current affairs closely, but the invasion was another matter, a drama not even Netflix could compete with. An old-school land-grab, on Europe's doorstep in 2022. And now, as the Russians circled Kyiv, here was Ukraine's president, appealing for military volunteers.

Shit. Is this what I am going to do? Shall I sign up?

No. Didn't you hear the man? He's said he only wants people with military experience.

Well, yeah … but …

He'd started looking into it the next day. If he was ever going to fight in a war, this was the right one. A despotic, nuclear-armed bully, beating up on its smaller, democratic neighbour. Not some messy religious or ethnic conflict. If he couldn't actually fight, perhaps he could do humanitarian work. Even if it was just handing out sandwiches at an aid station.

A few days later, he got an email back from the Ukrainian consulate. His services, they said, were not required. Not even as a sandwich man. If he wanted to help Ukraine, the email politely advised, he could do some fundraising at home.

His parents, when he told them of his plans, took the same view. In rather less diplomatic language. Don't be so bloody silly, said his dad. You've got a job, a girlfriend, a future. You could get killed. Are you insane?

The arguments in the Cartner homestead raged back and forth for days. Sensible parents versus impulsive youth. Cartner tried quoting history at them. Remember the Spanish volunteers in the International Brigade? He'd be following in a noble tradition.

At the time, he could see his parents' point. It was, by any normal reckoning, a daft idea. And much as he wanted to go, part of him was undecided. Every moment his mind was racing, chewing it over.

Driving home from work one day, he asked for a sign. He didn't believe in God. Or Fate. So he asked Spotify instead. Put his playlist on shuffle. A thousand songs at least. Everything from the Rolling Stones and Credence Clearwater Revival to Britney Spears and Johnny Cash. Let's see what come up first.

Jesus. 'Seven Nation Army' by the White Stripes. Surely, that was a sign. Of all the songs to come on …

Granted, it wasn't the most rational way to make up his mind. Then again, going to Ukraine wasn't the most rational thing to do anyway. What he would have done if Britney Spears had come up, he wasn't sure.

The next day, he announced his plans to his baffled bosses at Cornthwaites, suppliers of tractors to south-west Scotland and the Borders. They weren't used to employees disappearing off to fight for democracy. When he asked if they might keep his job open until he came back, they said they couldn't guarantee it.

So he scribbled a resignation letter out on top of an oil drum, and used a work laptop to type a will and funeral plans. Then he downloaded them onto a memory stick, which he stuck in a bedroom drawer and marked with a coloured tag.

'IF NOT HEARD FROM IN THREE MONTHS, READ THIS.'

* * *

ROCHESTER, KENT, FEBRUARY 2022. Stephen Wilson saw Zelensky's appeal while watching TV at his flat in a housing block set aside for ex-soldiers. The Kitchener Memorial Home in Rochester was built in honour of the general who'd led a previous military recruitment campaign in Europe a century before. Lord Kitchener was the finger-pointing, handlebar-moustached figure in the 'Your Country Needs You' posters, urging fellow Britons to do their bit in World War I.

One of the most famous campaigns of all time, its themes of duty and honour had featured in British Army recruitment patter ever since. Yet when Wilson had signed up as a young squaddie in 2005, that had only really been half the story. As much as fighting other people's battles, he was joining up to get away from his own.

He'd been raised on a council estate in Slough, born to a Scottish mother and a Romany gypsy father. Burning the candle at both ends, as he used to put it. From the age of seven he'd fought other kids in bare-knuckle boxing contests on gypsy sites around southern England. Not so much a gypsy rite of passage, more just a way for others to make money. Bets would be had on the outcomes. Sometimes people would even bet on him to lose.

Wilson was a disaster at school, a cheeky, aggressive little shit, never out of trouble. Part of it was the gypsy in him, taught never to back down. But mostly, he was the bully, not the bullied. Expelled aged 13, then sent to a Pupil Referral Unit. Around that time, he'd refused to carry on fighting for his dad. But there'd been plenty of other punch-ups on his estate in Slough, where there was no shortage of kids with a point to prove. He'd left school barely able to read and write, drifting round town, smoking weed and drinking, life going nowhere.

Around his 18th birthday, he'd decided to join the army. He'd always vaguely fancied it, thought it might suit the warrior in him. Plus it might impose discipline in his life, get him out of Slough, off the booze and weed.

It had been the making of him. He'd been accepted into the Royal Engineers, working as a lorry driver. Not exactly the SAS, but as good as he was going to get with his lack of qualifications. Like many other young soldiers who'd been failures at school, he'd finally mastered basic numeracy and literacy, with the help of army education classes. No opportunity to mess around in them.

The army felt like the family he'd never had. He took up boxing again, won some army trophies. Did a sapper's course in the Royal Engineers' Explosive Ordnance Disposal unit, studying bombs and how to defuse them. Life was finally coming together. At a pal's wedding, he met a girl. Soon he was a father too. Then came Afghanistan.

In 2010, just after his first daughter was born, the Royal Engineers were sent to Sangin, one of the toughest spots in

Helmand Province. As a sapper, he went out with infantry patrols, checking routes for improvised explosive devices (IEDs), the booby traps that were killing British soldiers every day.

His time in Helmand was nothing particularly special by the standards of some people's tours. But he'd been shot at and bombed enough times, and was near the scene when a helicopter was shot down. Saw the crew burn alive. Some PTSD around that, which he hadn't really addressed at the time.

Things went downhill after he left the army in 2013. He'd drifted through jobs, spent time homeless. He felt constantly angry, at everyone and everything. Angry at his old man for his lousy upbringing. Angry at his missus and kids. Angry that the Nato mission to Afghanistan – the one time he'd felt proud of himself – was starting to go downhill. All those lives wasted. Angry at himself too, for acting like a selfish dickhead. He was drinking far too much, cheating on his partner, ruining his relationship with her and his kids.

He went back to lorry driving, and for want of anywhere else to stay, ended up back with his dad, now in a caravan on a traveller site. It was a rowdy place at times. Wilson would come home after a day on the road, have a few hours' sleep, get woken up to help his dad out in some punch-up, then go back to driving lorries all day. Not ideal health and safety practice. After a couple of years at his dad's, half the knuckles in his right fist were broken.

Then, sometime around 2019 – it was all a blur really – he'd started to confront his mental health issues. Got in touch with an army mental health charity, found a bit of inner peace, anger management. Stopped blaming everyone else, stopped seeing himself as the victim. Decided that from now on, he was in charge of his own fate.

By 2022, he was the happiest he'd been in a decade. But when he watched TV footage of the Russian invasion, and saw Zelensky making that announcement, it was a lightbulb moment. Sure, there wasn't much wrong with his life at that point. He had his bachelor pad in Rochester, a job with a decent lorry firm, visiting rights to the kids. Ukraine, though, would offer a sense of purpose, which was what men needed. Men like him, anyway.

He was no crusading hero, for sure. He still saw himself as a bum, who'd treated people badly. Not many higher ideals in him. But Ukraine was a good cause nonetheless – even if the motives for going were mostly personal, to ride some redemption arc. Besides, if you had issues with anger, why not direct it at someone who deserved it? Nor was he the only one thinking about it. As he mulled things over, he got a message on WhatsApp.

'Yo Steve, you fancy going to Ukraine with me?'

* * *

OCADO DISTRIBUTION WAREHOUSE, SOUTH-EAST LONDON, FEBRUARY 2022. The WhatsApp message to Wilson was from Jack Knight, an old pal from his days in the Royal Engineers. Knight had also served in the bomb disposal squad, and, like Wilson, credited the military with being the making of him.

He'd wanted to be a soldier since he was a boy, lying about his age to get into the Army Cadets at 11. Other kids in his old south London neighbourhood had laughed, thought running around in uniform was naff. But it had kept him straight, when some of them had gone astray.

He hadn't just learned how to shoot guns, he'd learned basic life skills too. Punctuality, cleanliness, tidiness. Say what you like about old school spit-and-polish, most women he'd ever dated liked a man who could make his own bed, and wash and iron his clothes.

Unlike Wilson, Knight's unit in the Engineers hadn't been sent to Afghanistan. A big disappointment. Soldering was probably the only job in the world where you could train for years, and never get the chance to put your skills into practice. Like being a pilot who never got to fly, or a surgeon who never operated. That wasn't the only reason, though, why he'd then quit.

The army had gone soft. When he'd first signed up, there was drill and discipline. If someone messed up, the instructors would make them do press-ups as a punishment. It kept everyone fit, like in *Band of Brothers*. By the time he'd left, it felt like a youth club, the instructors forbidden to be tough anymore. But if recruits couldn't handle being shouted at, how were they going to handle a battlefield?

Knight saw it as the decline of a once-great institution, one that his own family had a proud history in serving. His great-great-grandfather, William Young, had won the Victoria Cross during the Battle of the Somme in World War I. Rescued a wounded comrade from no man's land, despite being shot twice himself in the process. There was still a street named after him in Preston. Quite a thing to have in the bloodline as a soldier.

Knight had left the army in 2016. Like Wilson, he'd struggled to adjust at first. Spells of depression, poor mental health. For a while, he'd fallen in with old friends from south London who were dealing drugs. Some had ended up behind bars. A new girlfriend had helped him settle. Thanks to the training he'd had in the Engineers, he'd found work as an electrical technician at Ocado, the online delivery firm.

Right now he was working at one of their giant warehouses, supervising an automatic production line that loaded up the nation's shopping. The job was well-paid, and he got on well with his bosses. Funnily enough, they quite liked people who knew how to obey orders, who didn't gob-off like they were owed a living, which a few of his workmates did.

But as a calling in life, keeping Britain supplied in groceries wasn't quite up there with defending the realm. For all that the army might have gone a bit soft, he missed the camaraderie. He sometimes also felt out of step with modern-day Britain in general. Too many people out protesting about stupid things, mouthing off on social media, then getting offended at what someone had said. It was in Britons' DNA to fight, had been for centuries, but now with no wars to wage, people just turned on each other, arguing about anything. They were too mollycoddled, demanding safe spaces at school and college where nobody could offend them. When he'd been at school, if someone offended you, you answered back and, if necessary, punched them in the face. Not the right answer for every situation, granted. But if you were being bullied, sometimes you had to stand up for yourself. Like Ukraine was having to do against Putin.

He'd been on shift at Ocado when he'd heard about the war. Someone asked him whether he'd get called up as a reservist if Nato got dragged in. If that happened, it might end up being settled with nuclear weapons. But if Ukraine put up a good fight, other countries wouldn't have to get directly involved. And now Ukraine's president was appealing for foreign fighters to help.

A moment of reckoning had arrived, and with it a chance to play a role. A chance he thought had gone, to see if he could live up to his great-great-grandfather's example. *This is the shit I missed out on, this is the shit I wanted to do.*

His family didn't quite grasp the grand historical narrative. His mum thought he was just seeking attention, told him to stay at work. He himself began to dither. He decided to force his own hand, by handing in his notice at Ocado. Otherwise, he knew, he'd spend forever mulling it over, and the next thing the war would be over. If he quit a well-paid job, and told everyone he was off to the war, he'd have no choice but to go. Or look very silly indeed.

His shop-floor bosses were supportive, if somewhat surprised. They told him to take a couple of days off to think it through while they spoke to HR. Who knew, they said, perhaps HR might give him a sabbatical. A week later, he was summoned for a meeting in some posh executive suite. Two people were there from the HR department at head office. Very smooth, full of praise for what he was doing. But no, sorry, they couldn't give him a sabbatical. Ocado couldn't be seen to be involved in politics. Subsidising staff to fight Vladimir Putin counted as a political activity, no matter the rights and wrongs.

Knight wasn't impressed. If he'd asked for a sabbatical to travel the world, or take a six-month yoga and wellness course, or some other bucket-list dream, he'd have probably been fine. He tried arguing the point, then gave up, shook everyone's hands and walked out. The next day, he said his goodbyes to his workmates, and handed in his notice.

* * *

As they packed their bags, bade farewells and put their affairs in order, one emotion played on the nerves of even the most combat-seasoned volunteers. Loneliness. Normally, when soldiers mobilised for war, they were accompanied by comrades from their own unit, people they'd often known for years. The volunteers would be travelling to Ukraine on their own, joining a Legion full of strangers. If anyone else turned up at all. Nobody could dismiss the feeling that the entire venture could be folly, that they might turn up to an empty barracks.

Yet rightly or wrongly, Zelensky's appeal had captured the imaginations of people everywhere, be it to defend democracy, or take part in some global, militarised version of *Fight Club*. Volunteers from all walks of life were now heading for Ukraine, leaving worried families, baffled HR departments and hastily written wills in their wake.

Down in Plymouth, Devon, Andrew Hill was handing in his notice as a scaffolder. A former infantryman with the Duke of Lancaster's Regiment, he'd been sent to Afghanistan in 2013, just as the action was winding down. The nearest he'd got to combat was a stint a few years ago as a nightclub bouncer.

Up in Middlesbrough, Teesside, James Durose was quitting his job as a welder, the trade he'd learned since turning his back on a life of crime. A former courier for a drugs gang, he'd spent much of his early twenties in trouble with the law. He had no military background, and his only experience of guns was transporting a firearm in the boot of a car, for which he'd served a jail term. Ukraine, for him, was about atonement.

In Manchester, ex-soldier Daniel Burke was quitting his concreting business and preparing for his third war in 15 years. After serving with the Paras in Afghanistan, he'd taken up arms again after the Manchester Arena bombing, when an Islamic State suicide bomber massacred pop concert goers in his home city. He'd spent a year with a Kurdish militia fighting Islamic State on the ground in Syria.

In Alabama, US army veteran Alex Drueke, 39, was gambling on Ukraine as a kill-or-cure for the PTSD he'd suffered in Iraq a decade before. It would, he hoped, be shock therapy, a chance to confront his demons.

In Colombia, a Vietnamese American and ex-US army veteran named Hieu Le had just set up home. He'd fallen in love with the place while on a backpacking tour, and had just opened his own Vietnamese restaurant in downtown Medellin. But it didn't feel right, as a young, fit, 30-year-old ex-soldier, to be sitting around making Pho soup and pancakes, when Ukraine needed all the help it could get.

In Germany was Henry Stevens*, a softly spoken American IT consultant who looked more like a Silicon Valley hipster than a warrior. A former computer operator in the US military, he'd spent the last two decades working round Europe as an IT consultant. He lived in the countryside in an off-grid cottage that he built himself, complete with solar panels, a hand-pumped well and his own beehives.

At 46, he was older than most volunteers, with no great desire to leave his well-paid job, his cottage or his eco-bachelor lifestyle. But if Russian tanks went into Ukraine unopposed, they might one day roll into the safe, comfortable corner of central Europe in which he'd made his home. Germany had seen quite enough fighting in the twentieth century. Besides, he figured, if something happened to him, the only living things he'd leave behind would be his bees.

* * *

On the South Bank of the River Thames near Parliament stands a modernist sculpture of four bronze figurines, their hands clasped together. Like many abstract works of public art, it is ignored by most sightseers, who usually walk straight past en route to the London Eye or Big Ben. But those who look closer will see that in their clasped hands, the figurines carry a fifth, wounded companion. They represent a previous generation of volunteers who, 80 years before Ukraine, also went to defend democracy in a distant land. In three brief sentences, the sculpture's plaque tells the story of British members of the International Brigade, who fought against Franco's Fascists in the Spanish Civil War.

'*In honour of over 2,100 men & women volunteers who left these shores to fight side by side with the Spanish people in their heroic struggle against fascism 1936–1939. Many were wounded and maimed. 526 were killed. Their example inspired the world.*'

It was a noble cause, and a lost one. After four years of war, and nearly half a million deaths, Franco's forces – backed by Hitler and Mussolini – overthrew Spain's elected, left-leaning Republican government. Franco's dictatorship did not end until 1975. But as the sculpture claims, the International Brigade did indeed inspire the world.

Around 40,000 volunteers from 52 countries went to Spain, including 5,000 North Americans, and 15,000 from France, Germany and Italy. Others came from Poland, Ireland, the Baltics and Scandinavia, all keen to stop a young democracy being snuffed out by fascism's spread. The cause attracted idealists and progressives of every sort: trade unionists, anarchists, South Wales miners and Clydeside dockers, intellectuals who'd realised that the pen wasn't always mightier than the sword.

Thanks to the presence of so many writers in the trenches, it was one of the few wars where history wasn't written by the victors. Eric Blair, better known as George Orwell, served on the Republican side, recording his experiences in *Homage to Catalonia*. Ernest Hemingway went as a war correspondent and cheerleader for the Republican cause, experiences later dramatised in his novel *For Whom the Bell Tolls*.

The International Brigade's members had been celebrated in popular culture ever since, iconised as freedom fighters in the same way as Che Guevara and Nelson Mandela. Even pop musicians, for whom war is generally considered uncool, make an exception for the Brigade. The Manic Street Preachers eulogised Brigade members from their native Wales in their first No 1 single, 'If You Tolerate This Your Children Will Be Next'. The Clash song 'Spanish Bombs in Andalucia' recalls the 'trenches full of poets'.

Yet at the time, the British government took a less romantic view. British officials feared being dragged into the Spanish conflict, and threatened to jail anyone who went to fight in Spain. They also knew that most volunteers were members of their local Communist parties, which did much of the recruiting. The security services, nervous about social unrest in the Depression, worried about battle-hardened left-wing radicals coming home to agitate.

In practice, there were no prosecutions of International Brigade members, many of whom returned to heroes' welcomes. With Hitler on the rise, anyone who fought Fascists was seen as being on the right side of history. But the memorial on the South Bank was not put up until 1985, as one of the dying acts of the Greater London Council, whose old County Hall HQ overlooks it. The following year, Margaret Thatcher shut down the GLC, as part of her war on 'loony-left' councils and their gesture politics.

* * *

If Britain's government felt uneasy about freelance freedom fighters in the Spanish Civil War, it was no more certain by 2022. Ministers gave out mixed messages in response to President Zelensky's call for volunteers. Three days into the war, Britain's then Foreign Secretary, Liz Truss, said she 'absolutely' supported Britons who went to Ukraine to fight. The day after, she was slapped down by Downing Street, which urged all Britons to stay at home instead. A memo also went out to all serving soldiers, reminding them to stay put too. The stakes, Whitehall feared, were much higher than the odd Briton killed in action. If UK volunteers were caught by Russian forces, Vladimir Putin could use it as an excuse to start World War III.

The problem was that by then nobody was listening. A week after Truss made her comments, Kyiv's government said that some 20,000 volunteers worldwide had already offered their services. It was the biggest international mobilisation since the Spanish Civil War.

As well as Britons and Americans, Canadians and western Europeans, there were large contingents from the former Warsaw Pact countries and the Baltics, which feared that if Ukraine fell, they would be next. While British officials fretted, some governments actively encouraged anyone who was game for the fight. Latvia's parliament passed a vote endorsing the right of citizens to go. Denmark's prime minister, Mette Frederiksen, described it as 'a choice anyone could make'.

In fact, as they weighed up whether to go, most volunteers were less concerned about what their governments said, and more about what friends and family thought. The world of 2022 wasn't like the world of the 1930s. Back then, going to war was a rite of passage for young men. Orwell's ever-dutiful wife Eileen followed him out to Spain, and even visited the trenches during a Fascist bombardment. Most Spanish Civil War volunteers also belonged to their local Communist parties, who encouraged members to go.

Seventy years later, with Western nations grown used to peace and prosperity, the peer pressure was the other way around. If there was one thing that the volunteers for Ukraine had in common – be they veterans or amateurs – it was that nearly everyone else thought they were crazy. Friends, family and colleagues questioned not just their judgement, but sometimes also their mental health. The tone would go from scolding to soft, concerned. Never mind Ukraine, what was this *really* about?

The scepticism was understandable. After all, why give up a safe, comfortable life to fight in someone else's war? What if they got killed or badly injured, leaving others to look after them or their children? It was all very well for the Manic Street Preachers to sing 'If You Tolerate This Your Children Will Be Next'. Right now, the war hadn't gone beyond Ukraine's borders, and if it did there were regular armies who could step up.

The naysayers were right, the Russians weren't threatening to land on the beaches at Dover. Britain had known no serious external threats since World War II. But that was precisely why many volunteers felt drawn to Ukraine. In their eyes, the West no longer prized old-school-warrior values – or, worse still, labelled them as 'toxic masculinity'. Nor did they have much time for the cosseted attitudes of generations who knew nothing but peace. Indeed, the problem with modern life was that it was too comfortable, too sanitised, too lacking in the kind of mortal challenges that previous generations had faced. Ukraine – a country facing Europe's worst bloodshed since World War II – was just the place they were looking for.

2

THE SCREAM FACTORY

Yavoriv military training base, western Ukraine, March 2022

'So, you are Special Forces, right?'

The young Ukrainian corporal on registration duty nodded at Stephen Wilson. His words sounded more like a statement than a question.

'Er, no, not Special Forces. Regular army. British Royal Engineers. I …'

'Yes, you're Special Forces,' interrupted another corporal. 'You said on your registration form that you had combat experience, right?'

'Er … yeah, sort of, in Afghanistan.'

'Yes, so here in Ukraine, you'll be Special Forces.'

'Er, okay …'

It didn't take a trained military recruiter to spot that Wilson wasn't quite Special Forces. Since leaving the army in 2013, years of drinking and truck driving had left him several stone overweight. In his new military fatigues, he bulged in all the wrong places – dressed for the barracks, built for the bar. He wouldn't pass SAS selection by any means, unless they needed someone to go undercover as a boozy lorry driver.

Yet here at the Yavoriv military training base, the clearing house for all new foreign volunteers, they didn't seem too fussy. He'd shown them his old military ID, as proof of his past service record. Judging by the cursory glance they gave it, he might as well have flashed his HGV licence. Nor was the criteria for 'Special Forces' particularly exacting. Anyone who said they had past combat experience was put in that category.

Yavoriv was Ukraine's answer to the British Army's training area at Salisbury Plain – a vast stretch of fields and forest with dozens of empty villages for battlefield exercises. Built by the Soviets during World War II, it covered 150 square miles of land near the Polish border. For the last 20 years, visiting Nato troops had been training Ukrainians there under a 'Partnership for Peace' programme, much to Russia's irritation. The Nato trainers had pulled out just before the invasion started.

Wilson was there with hundreds of other volunteers, who'd arrived in dribs and drabs from all over the world. He'd handed in his notice at the lorry firm in Kent just days beforehand, then he'd set off carrying about 70 lb of kit. With Ukraine's airspace closed, the only way to get there was across the land border from Poland. He'd flown in on a budget airline, the kind that normally ferried Brits into Poland on stag parties. A Polish humanitarian volunteer had taken him to a refugee centre near the frontier, where he'd spent the night.

The centre had been a wake-up call – thousands of people who'd fled their homes, mainly women, elderly and children, grab-bags on their shoulders, tears on their faces, scrolling anxiously on their phones. All heading the opposite way to him. For the first time, it had dawned on him that he might not come back alive. On the other hand, watching the misery made him feel needed. Like he wasn't some complete loon.

That could not be said for some of the other volunteers. Despite Zelensky saying that he only wanted those with military experience, all kinds of people were turning up. Many, by the looks of it, eminently unqualified for civilian life, let alone military life.

Regular soldiers had nicknames for such characters: Screamers, Paintballers, Instagram Warriors. People who'd watched too many episodes of *SAS: Who Dares Wins*, who thought the Legion was going to be like an episode of *The A-Team*. An alarming number had found their way to Yavoriv, undeterred by warnings from the likes of Damon Adams, the army surplus store boss back in England, that their mission was foolhardy in the extreme.

The Screamers stood out because they nearly always sported brand-new combat kit, or berets with insignias that nobody recognised. Plus, while Wilson was trying to tell the Ukrainians that he *didn't* have a Special Forces background, the Screamers tried to convince everyone that they *did*. To a man, they were all ex-SAS, Paras, US Navy Seals and other units too hush-hush to mention.

Stories about the most spectacular and delusional bullshitters were doing the rounds on volunteers' WhatsApp groups. One American arrived with a CV saying he had fought for 'Qween (sic) and Country'. Another claimed to have a list of people he wanted to kill back home, and was here in Ukraine simply to get some practice in. Others boasted of carrying out sensitive Special Forces' missions – which, if true, would have remained strictly classified forever. A few claimed God himself had sent them to Ukraine. Already, some volunteers began nicknaming Yavoriv 'The Scream Factory'.

Most were harmless enough, and in awe of anyone who'd actually served. But they were called Screamers for a reason: the moment any shooting started, they'd just panic. They were the last people anyone wanted to be alongside in a gun battle, a danger to themselves and others.

Fortunately, the Ukrainians were making at least some effort to stream everyone. Recruits with combat experience – aka the Special Forces – were separated off on their own. Wilson was in an English-speaking team of about 20, made up of Swedes, Poles, Brits, Americans, Canadians and Georgians.

The Ukrainians issued them with supplies and weapons. The quartermasters were surprisingly well-supplied – courtesy of all the Nato kit that had been flooding in during the run-up to the war. Wilson got a Kalashnikov, a pistol and six grenades. It would have been very easy, he thought, to filch the lot and flog it to some gang back over the border.

Wilson's team tried to get to know each other. Normally, soldiers had years to bond with their comrades before going near a battlefield. Here, they'd be fighting alongside people they'd never met before, whose combat qualities and personalities were unknown.

They did fitness and first aid drills, nominating more experienced soldiers as team leaders. They swapped kit, snacks and back stories. They set up a guard roster around their section of the camp, with a muster point in case of attack. At night, the base had no lights on, so everyone had to be able to find it in the pitch dark.

In a sense, the war didn't feel too close here. Yavoriv was nearly 400 miles west of Kyiv, where the nearest Russian troops were. But there'd been sporadic missile attacks across western Ukraine, and the air raid sirens regularly warned of enemy aircraft in the regional airspace. The Ukrainians were also worried that Russian saboteurs had infiltrated the base, planning to strike at any time. The other security risk came from the volunteers' own ranks. Many of the Instagram Warriors filmed everything they did, posting it on social media as if they thought some TV company was going to hire them as the new Ant Middleton.

Just before dawn on 13 March – Day 18 of the war – Wilson clambered back into his sleeping bag after doing the 4–5 a.m. guard duty slot. As usual, he slept in his uniform, with his boots, body armour and rifle nearby. He was just nodding off when he heard what seemed to be a plane approaching. It sounded like an airliner coming in to land, the noise of jets and turbines. Then an almighty bang. Louder and bigger than anything he'd ever heard in Afghanistan. He felt the blast wave pass right through him.

He leapt from his sleeping bag. Boots. Body armour. Helmet. Gun.

This is it. You're in a warzone now, buddy.

Outside, a massive blaze was raging through a nearby accommodation block. Flames lit up the night sky. Panicking, silhouetted figures were running in every direction, some in shorts and flip-flops, one fellow butt naked. Debris was strewn all over the place. Whatever had just landed was far more powerful than a mortar round or artillery shell.

Wilson ran to the muster point in the woods. The only other person there was an American, an Iraq veteran, wearing just his boxer shorts. No gun, no body armour. So for much for all those attack drills. Another missile ploughed into a building, shaking the ground, lighting up the night sky. Then another.

Other random stragglers appeared, most looking shellshocked, one chomping a cigar like he was General Patton. More missiles were hitting distant parts of the camp. They could hear other soldiers charging around in the dark, shouting commands in a dozen different languages. Nobody seemed to be in charge.

Eventually, a team leader arrived, relaying what he said were instructions from the Yavoriv camp commander.

'Kyiv has fallen, and Zelensky is dead,' he said. 'Russian para-troopers are coming here in helicopters. They're saying it's going to be a fight to the death.'

His words were met with baffled stares. Most volunteers had now switched their phones off, terrified they were being tracked, so hadn't checked the news. But given that half of Yavoriv had just been reduced to rubble, anything seemed possible. Especially a Russian paratrooper assault. Specially despatched here to wipe out the Legion at birth.

The volunteers were instructed to head to the helicopter land-ing site, where it was thought the paratroopers would land. Nobody thought that was a good idea. One well-aimed missile and they'd all be massacred. The camp was full of bunkers, trenches, choke points and other good places to hole up in. Let the paratroopers come to them.

As dawn broke, firefighters were still tackling blazes, while rescue workers tried to reach dead and injured. A number of volunteers were throwing down their weapons, threatening to quit altogether. They weren't even near a frontline, yet already the Kremlin had them in its sights. Some spy must have given their location away. Or, less glamorously, some dickhead doing a TikTok tour of the camp.

The Ukrainians, sensing the unease, lined everyone up.

'Right, those who want to fight, stay here and fight. Those of you who don't, drop your weapons. We will get you back to the border.'

The non-combatants were told to gather together. Later that morning, a bus arrived to take them back to Poland. Wilson watched it pull away, crammed with about 100 miserable-looking souls on board, many sporting cuts and bandages. It looked like a Club 18–30 holiday gone wrong.

He and a few others were planning to stay, though not at

Yavoriv. While it now seemed unlikely that Russian paratroopers were about to land, whoever was in charge here didn't know what they were doing. Plus the camp was half-destroyed, and might well get missiled again.

They handed in their weapons, and arranged transport to Lviv, where Wilson planned to have a 'Condor Moment'. A bit of British Army slang, passed down by grizzled sergeants of a certain age, borrowed from some 1980s TV ad for Condor pipe tobacco, where a chap sat puffing away contemplatively.

The idea was to snatch a moment of calm during a crisis, to mull the options over in peace. What was probably called 'mindfulness' these days. He'd find somewhere to doss in Lviv, have a Condor Moment and work things out from there.

* * *

The bus to Poland dropped the departing volunteers at the frontier, where waiting media greeted them as they trudged over the border. They were a bedraggled sight, with bandaged heads, arms in slings and dazed faces. On their way into Ukraine, many had been happy to publicise their cause to passing news crews. On the way out, few even stopped to speak, scared that some all-seeing Kremlin eye was tracking them. For once, the Instagram Warriors didn't want their photos taken. They headed off in search of beds for the night, and a bottle to toast dead comrades with.

Also raising a glass was the Kremlin. It hailed the Yavoriv strike as a targeted strike against 'foreign mercenaries', a due warning to outsiders to stay out of Russia's wars. If these veterans of Iraq and Afghanistan thought they knew about fighting, let them taste grown-up warfare. News reports claimed that Moscow had unleashed its new hypersonic missiles for the attack, capable of travelling at four times the speed of sound. At least 36 people were reported to have been killed, among them three ex-members of Britain's Special Forces, despatched to Ukraine on some undercover mission.*

Some reports said the Kremlin had identified the site because of the huge numbers of foreign mobile signals. Others pointed out that with thousands of volunteers streaming across the border in response to Zelensky's well-publicised appeal, it wouldn't have required more than an educated guess to figure that they might head to Yavoriv, the nearest Nato training base to Poland.

It would later turn out that most of the deaths at Yavoriv were Ukrainians, not foreigners, the missiles having narrowly missed one of the Legionnaires' main accommodation blocks. Still, the missile attack was a wake-up call – a reminder to the volunteers that in this war, they were the underdogs, facing a superpower's wrath. Moscow's defence ministry also warned that if captured, foreign legionnaires would be treated not as members of Ukraine's armed forces, but as 'common criminals', bereft of the protections of the Geneva Convention. While nobody expected the Kremlin to respect the Geneva Convention anyway, they didn't want to find out what Russia's equivalent of Guantanamo Bay would be.

* * *

Wilson and a dozen other volunteers left Yavoriv on the first transport they could find. Their lift didn't take them as far as Lviv, but some town halfway, dropping them off amid a sprawl

---

* This was never officially confirmed. Given how many volunteers at Yavoriv claimed to be ex-Special Forces, it may have just been a rumour.

of tatty Soviet housing blocks. They stood there in their uniforms, surrounded by large kit bags, trying not to feel paranoid.

They were still all in shock from the missile attack, scared to turn their phones on for fear they were being tracked. As they'd left Yavoriv, there'd been talk that Kyiv was now a bloodbath, with Russian machine-gunners hosing down civilians as they tried to flee. It was surely only a matter of time before some passing Russian saboteur team would spot them loitering round the tower blocks, and see that all of them were now unarmed. They now tried their best to look inconspicuous.

'Don't look at people. And keep your voices down! We don't want them realising we're foreigners.'

'Stick your masks on, hide your faces!'

'Actually, don't do that, we look like terrorists …'

The locals weren't fooled. No matter how much they tried not to, 14 uniformed men on a street corner aroused a certain curiosity. As word spread that some foreign soldiers were in the neighbourhood, locals came up to offer tea, snacks and messages of thanks for coming to help Ukraine.

'Don't eat or drink anything!' warned the team leader. 'It could be poisoned.'

Eventually, they'd been given shelter for the night in the basement of a chemist's shop. Despite the locals' hospitality, some had had enough. The next day, the team leader and a few others headed back to Poland, while Wilson and the rest headed on to Lviv. There, the fog of war lifted. They learned that Kyiv had not in fact fallen, and that the nearest Russian troops were still 500 miles away.

Wilson also learned that shortly after the Yavoriv attack, a pro-Russian social media channel had published a list containing the full names, dates of birth and passports of every volunteer there. The channel claimed there was now a 200,000 rouble (£2,000) bounty on each one of them. Already he was on someone's kill list. And he wasn't even near a frontline yet.

3

SUBURBAN WARFARE

Irpin, outside Kyiv, mid-March 2022

In any other circumstances, it would have been a nice place to stay: a modern, two-storey house, built in the style of a Mediterranean villa, with whitewash walls and terracotta roof tiles. A big garden, overlooking a landscaped park with a playground, amid glades of pine trees.

Irpin was a posh commuter suburb of Kyiv, where people came to escape the capital's Soviet-era sprawl. Inside the villa were reminders of the family that had fled in the weeks before. A kid's bedroom with toys in it, photos of Mum and Dad on the walls. Young professionals, by the looks of it, doing well for themselves.

For the soldiers inside, the villa offered other comforts. A six-foot-high fence that skirted the garden, with a lockable gate. A basement to take cover in. And from the first-floor bathroom, a good observation point, with a clear view over the park. Normally it would have been full of parents and kids, messing around on the swings, playing hide-and-seek in the trees. The soldiers, up in the bathroom, had their own version of the game. Watching the park from their hidden vantage point, round the clock, in case Russian troops tried to sneak through.

British military volunteer Andrew Hill, newly arrived from Plymouth, shivered as he took his turn on observation duty.

Explosions and gunfire sounded in the distance. This was his first combat mission in Ukraine. Although if he ended up using his weapon, things would have gone badly wrong. The point of an observation post – or OP – was to observe unobserved. The moment you opened fire, you gave your position away.

Already, Russian forces were on Irpin's outskirts, pounding it with artillery. Apartment blocks that had once graced the front cover of estate agents' brochures lay in rubble. The park in front of the villa had taken several hits, leaving giant molehills in the grass. The villa's bathroom window had been blown out by shrapnel – not that the soldiers went too near it anyway. A face at the window could be spotted by a sniper or a drone. Hill stayed several feet back, his breath forming clouds in the icy March air.

They'd been led to the villa by a Ukrainian military scout, sneaking through gardens and back alleys. Like most other homes in Irpin, the electricity and the water had been cut off. Visits to the bathroom involved buckets and pails. Downstairs were the rest of his team, led by Mark*, a fellow Briton. Unless they were on watch, they stayed in the basement. Below ground was always the safest place to be from artillery, which showered shrapnel everywhere. Sure, if the house suffered a direct hit, the basement might get buried under the rubble, along with everyone in it. Round here, those were the best odds on offer.

It felt good to be finally here on the frontline, doing what he'd come to do. Especially after the journey that morning into Irpin, where the sniper had nearly got them. Only now, as the adrenalin wore off, there were urgent discussions going on in his head. The adventurous Andrew Hill – the freedom fighter who'd come to Ukraine to defend democracy – felt in the right place at the right time. The other Andrew Hill, the professional infantry-man, who'd been trained to plan carefully for every contingency, was worried.

They had no maps, no radios, no night vision goggles. And, frankly, no real idea of where they were. Only that they were somewhere in this place Irpin, in what would soon be the pitch dark. None of the streetlights were working, and without night vision they'd be blind. What the hell would they do if they got attacked?

* * *

Three weeks earlier, Hill had been back in Plymouth, Devon, the city where he'd grown up. After a standard West Country boyhood, much of it spent surfing and skateboarding, he'd joined the Royal Navy at 17, following in a local and family tradition. Plymouth had been the home of the Royal Navy since the days of Sir Francis Drake, and Hill's grandad had been a career submariner.

Five years in, he'd switched to the army, serving with the Duke of Lancaster's Regiment. He'd gone to Afghanistan in 2013, just as the mission there was winding down. While previous Lancaster deployments had been in the thick of it in Helmand, Hill had never got beyond the wire of Camp Bastion, the vast rear operating base.

He'd left the army in 2019 because of the strain it was putting on his wife and kids, only for the marriage to end anyway. Then he'd spent the next three years as a scaffolder back in Plymouth. Scaffolding wasn't a bad life for an ex-soldier. Plenty of exercise, lots of lads' banter. But even after he'd settled down with his new partner, Candice, he still missed the army life, the routine, the comrades.

Before the invasion even began, he'd told Candice that if Ukraine asked for foreign military volunteers, he'd put his hand up. It wasn't just about putting himself to the test. Morally, it didn't feel right to sit at home doing nothing. And unlike his old mates still in the regular army, who'd been warned of court martials if they went AWOL to fight in Ukraine, he was now a free agent, with nothing to prevent him going. So no excuses.

Candice hadn't stood in his way, although she'd drawn the line at helping him look for his passport, which he spent several frantic days hunting for. To convince everyone he was aware of the risks, he'd gone through his will with his family, just as he'd done before deploying to Afghanistan. This time, it felt more than just a formality.

In mid-March, he'd crossed the Ukrainian border, where Legion representatives had driven volunteers to a barracks and quizzed them about their past military records. They hadn't asked for any proof, but about half had been told to go home. Hill hadn't felt sad to see the back of some of them. Like that old South African guy, dressed in slacks and shirt and dragging a wheelie suitcase, as if on a business trip. Claimed to have been a scout in South Africa's bush wars, said he could operate as a solo assassin behind the Russian lines.

Once the others had been sent packing, there'd been about 40 of them left: Brits, Americans, French, Danes, Israelis, plus a Latvian, a Lithuanian and a Moldovan. Hill was given a Kalashnikov, 1980s-issue, but straight out of the box. Old-fashioned iron sights, rather than a laser-dot system, and much more kick than the SA80, the British Army's standard assault rifle. But very robust, and less prone to jamming if it wasn't judiciously cleaned. After an hour of practice on the range, he was happy with it. A weapon was a weapon, really, and a good soldier worked with what he was given.

Then they'd been bussed to Kyiv overnight, an 11-hour journey with no headlights on. Rather than a barracks, they were taken to what looked like a student hall of residence. Information was on a need-to-know basis. All they were told was that they'd be in at the sharp end. Their base was shared by some volunteer units from Georgia, who were just back from a mission in Irpin. Two had been killed.

* * *

After a night in the student hall, Hill and a dozen others had been driven by minibus towards Irpin. En route, he got his first proper glimpse of Kyiv. Big Soviet-era housing blocks, stretching for miles. The streets largely empty except for soldiers and armed civilians. Crates of petrol bombs piled up at junctions, there for anyone to use. At major intersections, there were sandbagged checkpoints and concrete chicanes. Some checkpoints had rows of 'Czech Hedgehog' anti-tank traps – metre-long girders, welded together into huge jacks. It looked like a newsreel from World War II.

Irpin lay north-west of Kyiv, separated from the city by a belt of pine forests and the River Irpin. Much of it was newly built, Nordic-style apartment blocks, like a flat-pack IKEA suburb. The Russians had swept in from the Belarusian border, 50 miles north, first attacking Irpin's neighbouring towns of Bucha and Hostomel. Hostomel had a cargo airport, which they planned to commandeer for landing giant troop transporter planes, bringing in reinforcements for the capture of Kyiv itself. Also heading towards the capital from Belarus was an immense Russian armoured convoy, a line of tanks and artillery vehicles nearly 40 miles long.

Already Russian snipers, scouts and armoured units had footholds in Irpin, while Russian artillery teams pounded it from afar. As the minibus reached the pine forests on the Kyiv side of the river, Hill heard explosions in the distance. A Ukrainian scout picked them up at the forest's edge. Amid the trees, tanks sat covered in brushwood, ready to ambush any Russian forces that pushed through.

They'd just entered the woods when the first artillery landed. Rounds crashing in through the trees, some only 100 metres away, everyone diving to the ground. It felt unreal, like watching himself in a war movie.

To reach Irpin, they'd have to cross the river, which wound through a half-mile-wide plain of marshy scrubland. Across it ran a dual carriageway with a bridge, which the Ukrainians had blown up to slow the Russian advance. Underneath the bridge's mangled remains was an improvised wooden footbridge made of a few slippery planks. To reach that, they'd have to break cover from the woods and make their way across open ground.

The scout warned that Russian snipers were operating out of the apartment blocks in Irpin on the river's far side. The blocks were maybe half a kilometre away, but a good sniper could hit people at twice that range.

One by one, Hill and his team made the run for the bridge, trying to keep a distance from each other. A big group would be an easy target. In front of Hill was Mark, his fellow British volunteer. Halfway to the bridge, Hill heard a sniper's bullet go between the two of them, a whizzing sound as it cut through the air.

Fuck! Head down. Run. Run!

He charged forwards, catching up with Mark.

'Mark, you need to run! There's a sniper!'

'I know!'

They dashed on, finally reaching the bridge's concrete flyover. Its underbelly offered some protection from artillery, and had become a stop-off point for civilians fleeing Irpin. On top of the bridge was a long tailback of abandoned cars, left there by residents who'd driven blindly down it before realising that it now led nowhere. Some had their windscreens shot out, others were burnt-out husks, peppered with shrapnel holes. Several had handwritten signs in the back windows, saying, 'Children inside. Don't shoot.'

Half an hour later, when reports of a marauding Russian helicopter gunship came to nothing, they pressed on, hugging an earth bank skirting the side of the dual carriageway. When they reached Irpin's outskirts, the scout took them to a rendezvous point at a block of flats, where they were introduced to the Legion's local Ukrainian commander, a man called Taras. Curt and businesslike, he told them to head to the OP in the villa overlooking the park. Hill's first proper tasking in a war: staring at a children's playground, waiting for something to happen.

*　*　*

By the second night, the artillery was getting closer. Mark, who was acting as team leader, reckoned the OP was being targeted, and wanted to pull the team out. Hill reckoned it was best to just stay put. True, a heavy artillery barrage could be the prelude to an infantry assault. But retreating to the rendezvous point under fire could be even riskier. Best just sit it out in the basement. Besides, abandoning the OP might not go down well with Taras, their Ukrainian commander.

Mark insisted. Didn't want anyone dying on his watch, he said. They crept back through the back alleys, mortar shells landing in nearby gardens, spattering them with mud and earth.

Taras hadn't been happy to see them back, demanding to know why they'd left their positions. To add to their embarrassment, Jorg*, a Danish volunteer who'd been with them, then remembered that some weapons had been left behind in the OP.

They had to retrace their steps and retrieve them. When they got back to the rendezvous point at the apartment block, they dossed down for the night, wondering if the Ukrainians thought they were blundering amateurs.

The next morning, as they prepared to leave Irpin, Jorg was missing from the morning headcount. Eventually, Taras appeared, dragging him by the hair. He'd found the Dane lying drunk in an empty flat, having raided the absent owner's drinks cabinet.

'Your fucking soldier's pissed!' Taras snarled at the other Legion members. 'What the fuck? This is not acceptable.'

The day got worse. Heading back out of Irpin towards Kyiv, Mark slipped on a muddy track, just in time for a passing vehicle to run over his foot. He had to stagger the whole way back on a broken ankle. Then, when the Legion bus took them back to base that night, they were all ordered to stay on the coach. They were let off one by one, their weapons confiscated, their breath smelt for alcohol and their bags searched.

The search turned up another bottle of booze in Jorg's bag, and a MacBook laptop in a bag that Hill recognised as belonging to Sam*, a fellow Brit. A Ukrainian commander held the laptop up. It wasn't the kind of thing you took on a combat mission.

'Did you steal this from one of the apartments in Irpin?' he asked Sam. 'Someone fucking did. And if they don't admit to it, everyone's getting sent home.'

Sam and Jorg had their passports confiscated and spent the night under armed guard. The next morning, they were gone. Hill was mortified. The foreigners' first mission, and it had ended in drunkenness and theft. Both Sam and Jorg had seemed like decent guys. It was a reminder that none of the Legionnaires really knew who the others were.

The whole unit was tarnished now. There was every likeli-hood that they'd never be trusted for any decent taskings. Instead it would be guard duty round the barracks – or, worse still, missions the Ukrainians didn't want to risk their own troops on, where they'd just be cannon fodder. Not that the foreigners would probably realise until it was too late. That was the problem, fighting other people's wars.

4

THE BODY

Irpin, March 2022

Andrew Hill wasn't the only volunteer harbouring doubts about some of his fellow Legionnaires. At the Legion's base in Kyiv, an ex-US army soldier named Hieu Le had been feeling uneasy ever since arriving on a minibus from Yavoriv, where he'd been camped out in a tent during the Russian missile attack. Of the 23 volunteers he'd been billeted with, all but seven had opted to head back to Poland afterwards.

The minibus journey from Yavoriv to Kyiv had itself been a further test of nerve. The route went through countless make-shift checkpoints, many manned by jumpy citizen militiamen, some clutching guns for the first time in their lives. Rumours abounded of Russian units staging ambushes. Le saw a man tied to a telegraph pole, being questioned on suspicion of spying.

It had all got too much for one of Le's fellow Legionnaires, a fellow American, who'd been jittery ever since the missile attack. By rights, he should have been on the bus back to Poland. En route to Kyiv, he'd panicked, saying 'something bad' was going to happen. Le had given the guy a talking to. A soldier's skill was to keep his fear under control, not spread it.

'You're not set up for this,' he told him. 'My advice to is to leave Ukraine as soon as you can.'

When the minibus had finally pulled into the Legion's make-shift base in the hall of residence in Kyiv, the Ukrainians asked if anyone wanted to change their mind. Nobody did, not even the jumpy American. By the following day, though, Le himself was having second thoughts. This time it was nothing to do with the Russians.

They'd gone to a depot to be issued with some extra kit, and on the way back had shared a bus with some fellow Legionnaires, who'd been zeroing their weapons at a rifle range. Three in particular stood out: two Americans and a Brit. Big, hulking fellows, with the top-heavy build of men who spent a lot of time in the gym.

The Rambo Special Forces look, you might call it. Plenty of them in Afghanistan. Or, what he called Special Forces 'Wash-outs'. Guys who'd tried to qualify, but didn't quite make it.

They certainly acted like they were ex-SAS or Delta Force. A certain know-it-all swagger, as if they'd spent the morning on the frontlines in Irpin, rather than shooting at paper targets. They blanked Le and the others, as if talking to rookies was beneath them. But there were glances in their direction, sniggers, muttered asides about the newcomers looking out of shape and out of their depth. One of the Americans sounded like he was spoiling for a fight. Le wondered if he was having a bout of 'roid rage, those temper swings that steroid abusers suffer from. Certainly looked the type.

Le pretended he hadn't heard. He was here to fight Russians, not fellow Americans. He was glad, though, when the bus finally pulled into the Legion base. Less glad to see the Wash-outs getting off there too. The base was a big place, and hopefully, their paths wouldn't cross again. But no way did he want to end up fighting alongside pumped-up fools like that. They'd be as likely to put a bullet in you as the Russians were. For the first time, he began to wonder if he should have got the bus back to Poland after all.

* * *

Le was from a family that knew all about being uprooted by big-power conflict. His parents had come to the US as refugees from the Vietnam War in 1975, fleeing the Communist takeover. His mother had been on the US airlift out of Saigon as the North Vietnamese Army closed in.

He'd grown up in San Francisco: better than life in Communist-run Vietnam, but still not that easy. His parents had split, and some of his childhood had been in high-crime public housing projects. After high school, the army had been an obvious choice for a kid from a low-income family. It offered training, career options, the chance to do college without running up a heap of debt.

In 2012, he'd been deployed to Kandahar Province in southern Afghanistan, the Taliban's birthplace. Le worked as a radio and comms expert in his base's operations centre, not getting out beyond the wire that much. He wasn't too bothered. The times he did spend on patrol were enough to teach him that in Taliban country every mission sucked.

Most of the time, the enemy never showed. But danger still lurked with every step, courtesy of the IEDs that the Taliban planted everywhere. It was a lousy soldiering experience, wandering through fields and villages, waiting to get blown up by an enemy that one seldom even got to see, let alone shoot back at. In Le's unit, three soldiers had died and several others lost limbs.

After Afghanistan, he'd decided to travel the world, only to fall in love with Colombia, the first place he'd set foot in. Maybe anywhere looked nice to someone who'd come from a US military base. He'd set up a Vietnamese restaurant in the city of Medellin, serving up recipes from the old country.

By 2021, it was hailed on Tripadvisor as one of Medellin's best. Which helped take his mind off things when that summer the US troop withdrawal from Afghanistan led to the Taliban taking over again. Like many Afghan veterans, Le took it personally. All that work, all that sacrifice, for nothing? The moment the US had upped stakes, the same old thugs had swept back to power. Like the Afghans didn't want to fight for their country, to preserve the freedoms the US had spent 20 years trying to give them.

He'd felt a similar gloom in early 2022, when Russian troops began massing on Ukraine's borders. Another fledgling democracy facing obliteration. Putin clearly figured that if America couldn't be bothered with Afghanistan anymore, it wouldn't put up a fuss if he snatched Ukraine. Retired US generals were predicting that it would be a re-run of Kabul, that Kyiv would fall in about three days.

The Ukrainians, though, had given the invaders hell. On TV, there was footage of Russian armoured columns ablaze, of grandmoms in the street making Molotov cocktails. Ukraine's president, that Zelensky guy, had refused America's offer to help him flee, saying: 'I need ammunition, not a ride.' Fighting talk indeed. Then came his appeal for foreign military volunteers.

Straightaway, Le wanted to go. Ukraine was standing up for itself, and it deserved help. Sure, if some shrink examined him, they'd probably say it was some attempt to resolve his anger about Afghanistan. But he was 30 years old, combat-trained and single. What right did he have to sit around semi-retired in Colombia, when he had a skill set that could be useful in Ukraine? Someone could take care of the restaurant while he was away.

On his multi-stage journey to Europe, he kept a running diary on his public Facebook page: partly as a way of reaching out to other volunteers, partly for the record in case he never came back alive.

'At the time of this post, the Russians are only 15 miles outside Kyiv,' he wrote on 3 March. 'This thing may be over before I even get there and if I do get there before it ends, I may be literally one of the last men defending the capital.'

* * *

Le's original plan had been to offer himself up as a military comms expert and intelligence analyst. By the time he reached the Legion base in Kyiv, it was clear that most Legionnaires were likely to be frontline infantry. In a war – especially some- one else's war – you didn't get to choose.

His first combat assignment was one that involved neither taking life nor saving it, but was equally important. He and a dozen other volunteers were tasked with retrieving a dead body from no man's land in Irpin. A Georgian volunteer, one of the two Legionnaires killed by shellfire on the evening that Andrew Hill had arrived. It would require a seven-kilometre trek into Irpin, across the bombed-out bridge and through the thick of the fighting, lugging the corpse back on a stretcher.

A lot of risk and effort, for a man already slain. But the Ukrainians did it as a matter of course, and not just to give the bereaved a body to grieve over. Unretrieved corpses could be used as trophies by the Russians, who didn't always respect the dead. Pictures of mutilated bodies were sometimes posted on social media, or messaged to every contact on the deceased's mobile phone.

Le and 11 others were dropped off near Irpin one morning, the sky clear blue, the weather bitterly cold. They went over the makeshift river crossing under the blown-up motorway bridge, past push-chairs, clothes and cuddly toys abandoned by fleeing families. They pressed on across the marshy river plain, where patches of grass were freshly ablaze from artillery salvoes. Ahead, palls of smoke rose over Irpin's tower blocks. At the outskirts of town, billboards still touted new homes for sale in a complex called 'Dream Wood'. Packs of dogs, abandoned by their fleeing owners, roamed past.

Le's team walked five metres apart from each other, led by a Ukrainian guide. They entered a thick pine forest by a housing estate, avoiding marked paths. Landmine risk. Walking through the trees, Le felt a sense of dread, like what a kid got when thinking about the forest bogeyman. The Russians could be anywhere in here. Behind some bushes, in a trench, behind a tree. Up a tree.

Still, he felt like his old training was kicking in. Moving through hostile territory, a standard soldiering job. Just like Afghanistan. Then, as they headed over the crest of a low hill, an urgent order came down the line.

'Find cover! Assume fighting positions!'

The scout, up at the front of the patrol 50 metres in front, had spotted Russians. Le couldn't see them, but dropped prone behind a tree. He readied his weapon, heart pumping. *Shit, this is it!*

Then he heard shouts of 'Slava Ukraini!' Glory to Ukraine.

Huh? They weren't Ukrainians, that was for sure. All Ukrainian forces, his own team included, wore yellow ribbons on their arms. They might be Russian conscripts trying to surrender. Equally, they might be Russian conscripts *pretending* to surrender.

Whoever they were, the guide wanted nothing to do with them. He called their location into an artillery crew and they pressed on, not waiting around to find out what happened. It didn't help Le's confidence. In a battlefield, it helped to at least know friend from foe.

He also realised how dependent they were on the guide. Without being able to speak Ukrainian or Russian, he was fighting deaf and dumb. If he got separated from the patrol, he'd have no idea how to find his way back.

They reached the Georgian's body. A man in his forties maybe, his face concrete-grey, traces of blood round the mouth. Le had never seen anyone dead like that, let alone close up. One of the Georgian's legs had a big shrapnel wound. It had probably severed his main artery. Le couldn't help wondering if his death had been preventable. No sign of a tourniquet having been applied. Without one, he'd have bled out in minutes.

They loaded the body onto the stretcher. There was six of them to carry it, three either side. The other six would maintain the patrol, watching their backs. Then they'd swap around so the stretcher-bearers could rest. Carrying a grown man's body was no easy task, especially when already laden down with a weapon and body armour. Plus the Georgian was a big guy. At least six foot, and easily 15 stone. When Le took his turn at the stretcher, it was far heftier than expected. Even six of them could barely carry it more than ten metres at a time.

After an hour, Lee's clothes were drenched with sweat, and both arms ached. Blisters were swelling on his palms, even though he had gloves on. They'd barely covered more than a couple of kilometres of the seven-kilometre journey back. It was as hard as anything he'd ever done in basic army training, and he was nothing like as fit as he was back then. *I can't do this. I can't keep this up.*

It didn't help that they were using a blanket-stretcher, rather than a rigid one with poles. It was designed for rescues in buildings, where there might be tight corners to get around, and could fold into a back-pack. But it sagged in the middle, requiring extra effort to stop it dragging on the ground. Much of the route was on slippery, muddy paths, hauling the body over ditches, fences and piles of logs. Several times, their dead companion fell from the stretcher while they were negotiating obstacles. Not very respectful. *Sorry, buddy, we're doing our best.*

Eventually, they reached a road, where a hatchback car collected the corpse for the last leg of the journey towards the broken bridge. The Georgian wouldn't fit inside, his limbs rigid with rigor mortis. One arm stuck stubbornly out at an angle. They had to break it at the joint to get him in.

The car dropped the body at the Irpin side of the bridge, where the stretcher party reconvened to carry it across the river. Other soldiers, posted as bridge sentries, looked at the body, the same thoughts doubtless going through their minds.

That's one of ours. That could be me.

Le focused on the task. Now was not the time to drop the body from the stretcher again. They forged the makeshift plank bridge, made one more agonising haul up a steep earth bank and delivered their cargo to a waiting ambulance.

By now it was late afternoon. It had taken nearly seven hours to get him back. The stretcher team bade farewell to the passenger, who now felt like some honorary comrade. A few murmured prayers. One man closed the Georgian's eyes, laying coins on top of them to stop them opening again.

Le went through the deceased's pockets to make a note of his personal effects. There wasn't much there, just an ID. Most soldiers avoided carrying personal stuff around, in case they were taken PoW. Le wrote down the Georgian's details on a piece of cardboard, attaching it to the dead man's uniform. The more clearly labelled he was, the better. Corpses could get lost in war, like anything else.

David Ratiani, aged 53, KIA, Irpin.

The ambulance guys took over. Le didn't like their manner. They were smiling, laughing with each other, like they ferried corpses around every day. Then again, that was exactly what they did do. The team saluted the ambulance as it departed.

Mission complete. A truck was waiting to take them back to the Legion base. Le wandered over, his body aching, his uniform stained with the Georgian's blood. Then he began sobbing, in front of the other soldiers. Super-embarrassing. Nothing he could do.

Not a shot had been fired, yet the mission had been as wearing on his psyche as on his arms. A whole day, quite literally staring death in the face. Ahead of coming here, he'd readied himself for the unexpected. But he'd never imagined this. In Afghanistan, KIAs were usually picked up by helicopter, not lugged for miles. This was old-school warfare. Casualty clear-up wasn't outsourced to someone else.

He was glad he'd done it. But he knew then and there that this first mission would also be his last.

'Sorry, guys, I just can't do this anymore,' he said.

There was a pause. Then someone patted his back.

'No worries, buddy. This mission sucked. You did your bit.'

* * *

Back at the Legion's base, Le told the Ukrainian commanders that he wanted to quit. He'd heard stories about them trying to stop volunteers leaving, of passports being confiscated. But there was no fuss. Just a few days' wait at base while his paperwork was sorted.

In the meantime, Le and a comrade were asked to help a civilian building manager clear out more dormitories in the halls of residence. Le's comrade found a greetings card that had a $100 bill in it, a gift to some student from his grandmother. They'd handed it in and thought no more of it, only to be accused the next day of having stolen it.

It was ridiculous. The pair had both spent thousands of dollars of their own money coming to Ukraine. Why would they then steal some grandmother's $100 gift? All they could guess was that someone else had taken it, and was pointing the finger to cover their own tracks. Whoever the thief was, it seemed they'd been busy. Some other volunteers on another wing of the Legion HQ also claimed to have had property stolen. Word reached them that Le and his comrade were already under suspicion. The other volunteers decided no further investigation was necessary, and confronted them in a corridor. Among them were the Wash-outs. A fight nearly broke out, halted only by the intervention of the Ukrainians, who pulled everyone apart. Barrack room brawls weren't a good idea, not when weapons were close to hand.

The Ukrainians asked Le to take a polygraph test, which cleared him. In the coming days, the Legion's commanders would identify other potential suspects, when the volunteers who'd served alongside Andrew Hill in Irpin were caught looting and stealing drink. By then though, Le was on an overnight train to Poland, starting his journey home. He planned to roam Europe a bit first, look up some old Nato buddies from Afghan days. Physically, he was fine. Inside, he felt like he had wounds on his soul.

The only consolation was a news article about the funeral of David Ratiani, the Georgian. He'd been buried in Tbilisi with full military honours, the Georgian flag draped over his coffins. A photo showed Ratiani's mother, clad in a black mourning scarf, grieving at his coffin. If nothing else, his family could now grieve properly, have a grave to tend to and one day maybe move on.

On his Facebook page, Le posted updates for his followers, explaining why he was now quitting.

'In the time I've been in Ukraine, I survived cruise missile strikes, constant shelling from artillery, moving through hostile territory, cold down to my bones, sickness, hunger, and the anguish of recovering our war dead. I am tired in my bones ... but I feel that I've done my part, and am satisfied that it's more than most.'

He felt guilty, he wrote, about leaving his comrades behind to carry on the fight. But he issued a warning to other would-be Legionnaires to beware men like Wash-outs, who 'live the day high on amphetamines, testosterone, steroids, and who knows what other drugs'.

'Among the many volunteers who come with good intentions in their hearts are those who only come to satisfy a sadistic need to kill and feed their egos ... They claim to be former Special Forces, and maybe that's true, but their behaviour is totally unhinged.'

* * *

Le was just one of many volunteers whose time in Ukraine lasted just a matter of weeks. They came expecting a modern-day *Homage to Catalonia*, and found themselves keeping company with misfits and losers.

It was deeply disillusioning, yet simply history repeating itself, if International Brigade archives from the Spanish Civil War are anything to go by. Old personnel records show that for every Orwell whose bravery was later celebrated on a memorial, others proved a liability, often attracting scathing comments from brigade political officers.

'Weak, cowardly and unreliable.'

'Drunkard. Deserter. Demoralised.'

'Deliberately contracted venereal disease in order to escape frontline service.'

Unlike Spain, however, Ukraine did not have time to employ sharp-eyed commissars looking to eject unsuitable volunteers from the country. From now on, most of those who chose to remain would have made Orwell proud. A minority, meanwhile, might have ticked every box on a commissar's blacklist.

5

SUICIDE MISSION

Irpin, March 2022

Despite the lapses in discipline, the Ukrainians continued to use the Legionnaires on the frontline. A few days after his two comrades were caught looting and drinking, Andrew Hill's unit returned to Irpin. Taras, the local Irpin commander, said nothing more about it. The Ukrainians presumably couldn't afford to be too fussy about manpower.

With Mark out of action because of his injured ankle, Hill took over as team leader. Joining him was a Lithuanian, Darius, who was fluent in Russian. It was the same OP as before, and the same tasking. Sit, observe and stay unobserved.

At times, they felt they were being watched themselves. A surprising number of locals were still around, either because they feared their homes might get looted, or because they had nowhere else to go. Sometimes they'd walk past the observation point, pet dog in tow, as if there was no war going on. One guy, though, kept walking past the villa, then disappearing round the corner. He looked like a 'dicker', as the British Army used to call them in Northern Ireland – a civilian who spied on troops. Just keep an eye on him, Taras said. Doing anything more risked giving their position away.

Then, late morning one day, two kids turned up at the playground, messing around on the swings and climbing frames. No older than 13 or 14. Darius had radioed command, wondering what to do. Adults were free to wander Irpin at their own risk. Kids were another matter. He could have shouted a warning, but it risked giving their position away. One of the other OPs said they'd send a patrol out to get the kids back indoors.

Seconds after that, an artillery barrage had started up. Two shells, right on the playground, just where Hill had seen the kids were. When the smoke cleared, no sign of them. He couldn't go out to look for their bodies, as the Russians were probably watching. And, perhaps, listening. The OPs' radios weren't encrypted. It was possible they'd overheard the talk about sending the patrol out, and had launched the salvo in response.

Christ. Dead children. Killed right in front of him. Nothing they could do.

Enough. Now is not the time.

He tried to process it back at base, on the phone to Candice back in Plymouth. Until now, she'd noticed how upbeat he sounded. None of the gloom and introspection that he sometimes lapsed into back home. That night, his tone had been different. Just matter of fact. When you'd seen two kids get killed, there wasn't much more to say.

* * *

A few weeks later, Hill's team were standing on a street in Bucha, the neighbouring town to Irpin, drinking rabbit borsch soup cooked by the locals. A Ukrainian speciality. And a liberation dinner.

At the end of March, after just a month of fighting, the Russians had given up their siege of Kyiv. The armoured columns that should have been doing victory parades in the city centre were now in retreat. Thwarted by Ukrainian resistance and their own incompetence.

In Irpin and neighbouring Bucha, the guns and artillery had fallen silent. Hundreds of Russian soldiers were dead or captured, their vehicles lying in smouldering ruins. Residents who'd fled Irpin were slowly returning, assessing homes for damage. For some, there wasn't much left to assess. No matter. Many had never expected to see their front doors again.

Putin's plan to capture Kyiv was supposed to have been a pushover, all done in three days flat. Now, a roadshow for the Kremlin's military might had turned into one of the most humiliating battlefield failures of modern history.

Already, military pundits were conducting post-mortems on what had gone wrong. It had been botched from the outset. Captured Russian troops said they hadn't even been told of the invasion plan until just hours beforehand. And once they'd rolled over the border, they hadn't actually expected to fight.

The Kremlin had presumed that Zelensky's government, confronted with an overwhelming show of force, would simply collapse overnight, with the president fleeing abroad. Putin was convinced that most Ukrainians would jump at the chance for rule from Moscow once more.

It hadn't worked out like that. Far from being greeted as liberators, the Russians had been ambushed, shelled and shot at every step of the way to Kyiv. By the time they'd reached Hostomel airport, the airport runway had been sabotaged, rendering it useless for flying in more troops. Hundreds of Russia's best paratroopers had been lost during the assault, after being hit by Ukrainian artillery batteries.

Other Russian forces had got hopelessly lost, having relied on Soviet-era maps. The 40-mile-long Russian armoured convoy that had looked so menacing was more like a bank holiday traffic jam, full of inept tourists stuck on the same main road. Thousands of tanks, APCs and supply vehicles had ended up wedged behind each other, easy pickings for Ukrainian hit-and-run ambushes.

Among the Russians who'd made it to Kyiv, a good number were ill-disciplined rookies. Hill's unit had seen some of the abandoned Russian positions, festooned with litter and discarded ration packs. No good soldier left such obvious traces of their presence. Judging by the amount of empty booze bottles, they'd also spent much of their time on the piss.

That same ill-discipline had also made them dangerous. They'd swept into Irpin expecting people to pose with them for selfies. Instead, the locals had forwarded pictures of the Russian positions to the Ukrainian military, which had bombed them. Very soon, the Russians had seen every resident of Irpin and Bucha as a possible spy. Hundreds had been detained, tortured and murdered. Others had simply been gunned down on sight. When the Russians had withdrawn, they'd left the streets littered with corpses.

Hill himself had passed a dozen bodies on the roadsides as his unit had come into Bucha. Women, kids. An old man lying dead by his bicycle. A leg on its own, an arm, a torso. Some of the bodies had clearly been there a while, untouched for fear they might be booby trapped.

Locals were digging in back gardens and woodlands, unearthing graves containing dozens of corpses. Bodies were being dragged out of the half-frozen earth, some bound and gagged. Bucha and Irpin were now giant war crimes scenes, with leaders calling for Putin to face The Hague.

The Russians were trying to save face, claiming the withdrawal was to give peace negotiations a chance, and that the corpse-littered landscape was a big Ukrainian set-up. They weren't defeated, they insisted – they were just going to concentrate on taking eastern and southern Ukraine instead.

For now, though, the fight for Kyiv was over. In Bucha, Hill and his unit were no longer on guard for Russians, but looters. The locals noticed the little foreign flags on the Legionnaires' uniform patches, realised they were international volunteers.

Thanks for coming, thanks for helping with the liberation.

Liberator? Him? That sounded a bit grand. All he'd done, really, was sit in an OP, soaking up artillery fire. But that was how war went. You didn't get to choose what to do. Not everyone got to be a hero. The important thing was just to turn up and stick it out.

* * *

MYKOLAIV, APRIL 2022. The village of Oleksandrivka lay on Ukraine's Black Sea coast, on the marsh plain between the shipbuilding ports of Mykolaiv and Kherson. At the start of the invasion, Kherson had fallen within a week, making it the first major city to come under Russian occupation. But when the Russians advanced west to Mykolaiv, 40 miles along the coast, they were beaten back. The territory between Ukrainian-held Mykolaiv and Russian-held Kherson, most of it flat farmland, was now an ever-shifting frontline. Villages like Oleksandrivka could change hands like pieces in a board-game.

A 60-strong Ukrainian unit were trapped there, outgunned by 200 Russians armed with tanks. They were making a last stand in an empty school, taking casualties most days, running low on food and ammunition. Other Ukrainian units had tried and failed five times to get them out. As a last resort, the Ukrainians invited the International Legion to have a try.

Hill's Legionnaires team had been relocated to Mykolaiv in early April, just after the end of the siege of Kyiv. A few had quit then, saying they'd had enough, but for the rest it felt like things were looking up. They'd had time to bond as a unit, and they'd been issued with new assault rifles, Czech-made Bren 2s, which fired Nato-standard 5.56 mm ammo. Not so powerful as the 7.62 mm Kalashnikov, but more accurate and less kick. Being given decent kit was a sign, hopefully, that the Ukrainians now recognised them as competent operators, not drunken looters.

They also had a good new team leader, Grady Kurpasi, a former US Marine who'd served three tours of Iraq. He'd left the military in 2021, only to be turned down for a planned university course, leaving him directionless. Ukraine had filled that gap.

Kurpasi put together a team of 20 volunteers for the rescue mission. The plan was to pummel Oleksandrivka with heavy artillery fire, creating a diversion for trapped soldiers to escape from the school. They'd then have to run to the village's outskirts, where the volunteers would be waiting at a rendez-vous point.

The escape route to the rendezvous point was about a mile, and went past several Russian positions. A rolling Ukrainian artillery barrage would clear the way, hitting each Russian posi-tion at fixed times. While the Russians in each position were hunkered down, the Ukrainians could hopefully slip past, after which each Russian position would be hit again. The escaping troops would have to time their runs carefully to make sure they didn't get hit in the barrages themselves.

It was a long shot, but the plan was duly approved by Ukrainian high command. Just before midnight, the rescue unit sneaked through the no man's land to Oleksandrivka. Then, at 2 a.m., the main artillery barrage started.

An hour later, Ukrainians started reaching the rendezvous point, arriving a few at a time. Some were wounded, others stretchered in dead comrades. By 4 a.m., 52 of the 60 trapped Ukrainians were out. The other eight died in firefights on the way. As rescue operations went, that counted as a success. The freed Ukrainians tugged hard on cigarettes that the Legionnaires handed out, haggard faces breaking into grins. Judging by the hugs and handshakes, they hadn't expected to get out alive. Hill was grinning too. They'd actually saved some lives.

* * *

Like in Irpin, much of life on the frontline outside Mykolaiv involved sitting around in OPs. It felt more like guard duty than combat: the point was simply to be there, static as a CCTV camera, watching enemy movements.

If there were any. On the Aragón front in 1937, Orwell could often see his Fascist enemies in trenches just a few hundred yards away. Here in Mykolaiv, an OP could be miles from the nearest Russian positions. Whoever was manning it might spend days looking out over empty farmland, never laying eyes on an enemy soldier.

The difficulty with OP duty around Mykolaiv was that there was nowhere much to hide. In Irpin, there were tower blocks to take cover behind, alleyways to sneak through, houses to hole up in. Outside Mykolaiv was just flat open farmland, an endless patchwork quilt of wheat and sunflower crops. The only cover was the treelines grown by farmers as windbreaks between the fields, plus a few drainage ditches and farm cottages. The soldiers dug trenches and foxholes, a Flanders on the Steppe. World War I veterans might have felt at home, were it not for the drones that buzzed overhead.

On 22 April, not long after the rescue at Oleksandrivka, several of Hill's comrades were posted to a foxhole right on the zero-line, the closest point to the nearby Russian positions. Among them was another British volunteer, Scott Sibley, a former member of the Royal Logistics Corps. Prior to Ukraine, he'd been working as a truck driver around his home town of Grimsby. But he'd served in Afghanistan with the Commando Logistic Support Squadron, for which he'd done the All-Arms Commando Course, a gruelling infantry course. Fellow Legionnaires saw him as a reliable operator.

At the end of Sibley's team's stint at the OP, a group of Georgian volunteers came to relieve them, attracting mortar fire as they made their way there. A Russian drone seemed to be tracking their movements. Shortly after they reached Sibley's OP, it was hit. The explosion engulfed the insides with a dust cloud. In the confusion, the soldiers ran outside, where a follow-up shell hit Sibley, inflicting fatal injuries to his chest and abdomen. Sibley's team managed to get out alive, taking his corpse with them. Kurpasi then had to inform his family back home in Britain, where he had an ex-wife and a young daughter.

Sibley was the first foreign volunteer known to have been killed in combat in Ukraine. His death made headlines internationally, with old comrades praising his bravery. For his new comrades in Ukraine, however, there wasn't much time for reflection. A more pressing matter loomed: who was going to go back to man the OP?

The Ukrainians wanted troops re-inserted there as soon as possible. As the OP furthest forward into no-man's-land, it could fall into Russian hands if simply abandoned. On the other hand, it was clearly compromised: the Russian artillery squads would now have its coordinates pre-programmed.

The Georgians refused to go back, saying it was a suicide mission. They exchanged heated words with a Ukrainian commander. If you don't want to follow orders, find somewhere else to fight, he'd said. They'd called his bluff, and gone elsewhere.

Keen to show willingness, Kurpasi volunteered to lead a mission to the OP himself. He asked for five volunteers to come with him. Yes, it would be dangerous, but the OP was not one the Ukrainians wanted to surrender. It needed to be done, and they were good soldiers, more capable than the Georgians. On top of that, it would honour Sibley's memory. Hill put his hand up.

They left early one morning, arriving at the OP as daylight broke. Inside, they saw Sibley's discarded body armour, and smears of dried blood. Expecting further attacks, the new arrivals spent the rest of the day digging shellscrapes – coffin-sized trenches just big enough to lie down in. They set up a belt-fed machine gun facing down a dirt track that led towards the Russian lines. The following morning, Russian mortar fire began pounding a Ukrainian OP in a nearby village.

'Sounds like that mortar is coming from somewhere near here,' Kurpasi said to Hill. 'Shall we go out and see if we can get eyes on it? If we can spot the location, we can pass it on to the Ukrainian artillery.'

He and Hill set off as a two-man team, crawling down the treeline parallel to the dirt track. Depending on what they could see of the mortar team, they might put down some harassing fire to shut them up for a bit, or even try to take them out altogether. As they moved down the treeline, the mortars stopped. With no firing sound to guide them, Hill and Kurpasi decided to turn around.

The bullets started coming as they made their way back. Not just the one shot from far away, like that sniper in Irpin, but multiple bursts. Direct fire meant two things. First, someone had spotted them. Second, they were probably near.

Hill and Kurpasi dropped flat on their stomachs. As they crawled forwards through the treeline, Hill saw movement. Then, no more than a few metres away, a Russian soldier appeared. Looking left and right, but facing away from them.

Jesus.

Hill trained his weapon on the Russian, but didn't pull the trigger. Shooting him from behind would have been easy. But it would give their position away. And where there was one Russian, there'd likely be several more.

He and Kurpasi began crawling backwards. Two grenades landed somewhere nearby. It was unclear if whoever had thrown them had actually seen them, or was just trying to flush them out.

'What the fuck do we do now?' whispered Hill. 'There's Russians between us and the OP.'

Kurpasi radioed the OP.

'There's a Russian section pushing towards you! Some are between you and us already. Get the machine gun going, keep them occupied. Then we'll try to come up behind them and take them out.'

It was a plan. It seemed the Russians still hadn't clocked their exact whereabouts. If they got machine gun fire from one direction, and Kurpasi and Hill firing from another, they might think they were outnumbered.

Hill and Kurpasi crawled back up towards the OP. If they got spotted, they'd shoot back to get the Russians' heads down, then make a break for it. For some reason, the OP's machine gun was still silent. *Why weren't they fucking firing?*

Just ahead was a big empty foxhole, built to hide an armoured vehicle. Maybe they could hole up there for now. As they neared it, Kurpasi jumped to his knees and fired half a dozen times. Hill couldn't see what Kurpasi was shooting at, but put some rounds down in the same direction.

Then Hill saw Kurpasi buckle, as at least four or five shots hit him. He flopped face down. No sound, no scream. No doubt he was dead.

Shit. I am fucked now …

He began to return fire. No option now but to fight. As he pulled the trigger, a pain surged through his left arm, like nothing he'd ever felt. He looked down and saw blood everywhere, a hole near his elbow with bone and other stuff coming out. His forearm hung uselessly, like it no longer belonged to him.

And now, standing over him, a Russian soldier. Pointing a gun, yelling.

* * *

'Drop your fucking weapon!' didn't really need translation. With his good arm, Hill pushed his own gun aside. He couldn't use it now anyway.

His wound was spurting. If he carried on bleeding, he'd be dead in minutes. There was a tourniquet in the medical pack strapped to his body armour. Time to appeal to his enemy's sense of mercy. He pointed at the medical pack, urging the Russian to help. *Tourniquet. Tourniquet.*

The Russian did nothing. Then a companion appeared behind him, barked an order. The first Russian slung his weapon and began to help.

He and two others carried Hill to the vehicle foxhole. Mortar fire sounded. The Russians were now targeting Hill's OP, where the other four of his team were. Three other Legionnaires, plus a Ukrainian special forces guy.

Hill felt hot and drowsy, short of breath. The tourniquet hurt as much as the wound, the blood pressure building up against it. He gestured for help to take his body armour off. When he lifted his injured arm, blood spurted again. A Russian sergeant applied a second tourniquet.

A wounded Russian came into the foxhole. Saw Hill, started making hand signals like he was going to shoot him. The sergeant shot him a look. Whoever this lot were, they seemed reasonably professional. Good news for him. Not so good for his team back at the OP. A few minutes later, another Russian came in carrying a silenced pistol. Hill recognised it as one that had belonged to the Ukrainian special forces guy.

Keep calm. Hill pulled out his cigarettes. His captors let him light one and took the rest of the pack, along with his phone. But they didn't search him properly. If they had, they'd also have found that he still had a grenade and a knife.

Should he use them? The grenade would kill or wound a couple of people, no more. Then they'd kill him, without a doubt. Best take his chances in captivity.

A Russian armoured vehicle pulled up and loaded him in. They drove to Oleksandrivka, the village where he'd helped spring the trapped Ukrainian soldiers. Last time he was there as a liberator. Now he was a prisoner of war.

6

THEIR OWN WORST ENEMY

Mykolaiv, April 2022

When Christopher Perryman had told his family that he was off to Ukraine, he hadn't said he was going to fight. Instead, he'd said he'd be doing 'humanitarian work' – a cover story to stop his mother worrying. She'd figure he was teaching first aid, perhaps, or training soldiers at some base far from the frontlines. No more dangerous than doing security work in Somalia, really. And better than being stuck with those eco-protesters at HS2.

He hadn't felt comfortable, lying to his family. And as it turned out, he needn't have even bothered. Rather than getting sent into battle, he'd ended up stuck in Lviv – running, yes, a training programme, teaching civilians basic military skills. The Ukrainians were certainly keen to learn. At gun shops around the city, there were queues of people buying hunting rifles and shotguns. Their enthusiasm outmatched their aptitude.

Perryman's trainees were a Bohemian-looking crowd made up mainly of teachers, librarians and musicians, as if the local art college had signed up en masse. Most had never held a rifle before. All wanted instruction in advanced combat, how to storm buildings and so on. 'Guys, you have to learn to walk before you can run,' he'd told them.

After a week of it, Perryman wanted to run himself. He hadn't come to Ukraine to kid geography lecturers and jazz bassists into thinking they were Andy McNab. Frankly, Ukraine already had quite enough people like that coming in via the International Legion. When he'd first arrived, he'd spent five days at a Legion recruitment centre in Ternopil, east of Lviv. A proper Scream Factory. Full of people telling war stories about wars they'd never actually been in, and folk who tried to give off the vibe of being undercover spooks. Wouldn't even tell people their names, just said call me 'B' or 'C', like they were James Bond's line manager.

The Legion seemed a waste of time, a standing army sitting on its arse, and Lviv was far from the action. So, like many other volunteers, he'd teamed up with some others – friends of friends, plus some of their friends in turn – and had gone off looking for a frontline to serve on, like jobless labourers seeking work.

They'd ended up in Odesa, where their luck had improved. Someone knew Someone who knew Someone, who'd introduced them to a battalion commander. He'd issued them with weapons, and sent them east to Mykolaiv, where there might be recce work on the frontlines toward Kherson.

That would suit Perryman. In the Fusiliers, where he'd trained as a sniper, recce work was central to the tradecraft. You could be the world's greatest marksman, hitting bullseyes at 1,000 metres on the practice range, but on a real-life battlefield the enemy seldom walked obligingly into your crosshairs. Your job was to sneak towards them through no-man's-land, holing up somewhere they wouldn't expect. Even then, you might never fire a shot, just gather information on their movements.

True, the Russian artillery out in those villages towards Kherson sounded fearsome. In Iraq, he'd been based in Amara, an insurgent stronghold, where they'd been hit nearly every night with mortars. But a Russian artillery barrage would make the Iraqi insurgents' mortars look like firecrackers. And if that made him worried, how would the others in his team cope? They were about a dozen in total, most of whom he'd only just met, all with skill sets as yet untested on the frontline.

That is, if they ever got near a frontline. The Ukrainians, despite issuing them with weapons, now seemed reluctant to deploy them anywhere. Perryman's team sat for weeks, getting passed back and forth. He was frustrated, if not entirely surprised. In battle, you relied on other troops to watch your back. If he'd been a Ukrainian commander, he wouldn't have trusted some random bunch of foreigners, who'd only just met, who might not know one end of a gun from the other.

The other problem was the language barrier. While the Legion sounded very romantic on paper, its creator clearly hadn't thought too much about the practicalities of a polyglot force who didn't speak the local tongue. Who might look blank, for example, if someone shouted the Ukrainian for 'Get your fucking head down!' or 'That field is land-mined!'.

That, moreover, was just the basics. Explaining a complex battle strategy, with all its Plan A's and B's, nuances and what-ifs, would be impossible, especially if the translator wasn't particularly good. And in combat, a misunderstood word or phrase could be fatal. The Ukrainians did have English-speaking soldiers, but they were often the more educated ones, whom the commanders were reluctant to detach to a group of foreign upstarts. Perryman's team had their own translator, Iryna*, but the Ukrainians forbade her working on the frontlines, saying she wasn't combat-trained. To add to the team's woes, their paperwork got delayed because the office where it had been stored was bombed. Several times at checkpoints, they had soldiers attempting to confiscate their weapons.

What missions were offered to them were best avoided. One Ukrainian commander invited them to head into the country-side beyond Mykolaiv to look for Russian tanks. It sounded like the sort of big-game hunt every volunteer fancied doing, were it not for the fact that they had no anti-tank weapons. It would be like lion-hunting with an air rifle. They did a few missions searching villages for pro-Russian 'dickers' who were calling in artillery strikes. But it was low-level stuff, not what Perryman had come for.

It was tempting to think the Ukrainians were trying to convey a message. Like *Please fuck off home, things are bad enough without you lot hanging about too.* Other Legionnaires in Mykolaiv were getting similarly daft offers, judging by the stories doing the rounds. One Swedish guy, a sniper like Perryman, had been invited to join four Ukrainians on a mission to take out a Russian sniper post. His fellow marksmen turned out to be four local farmers with hunting rifles, who'd never shot anything more dangerous than a fox. Others found them-selves being asked to guard private shops and warehouses, acting as unpaid security staff. There were even stories of commanders charging volunteers money to come on missions, fleecing them like gullible gap-year students.

It was dispiriting, to give up everything at home to fight in someone else's war, only to be made to feel that one's services weren't required. In most conflicts, the frontline was the place soldiers dreaded. Here, among the eager, up-for-it volunteers, it felt like a military El Dorado, a promised land that nobody could quite find.

In early April, Perryman decided to go home. He hadn't come out here expecting to be paid, but he couldn't afford to just hang around forever. A job offer had come up on the close protection networks, looking after a diamond mine in the Congo.

He'd do that for a bit, get some cash in the bank, then return in a few months. This time get his paperwork sorted properly, and hopefully find an outfit doing proper fighting. Here in Ukraine, that seemed to be the biggest battle of all.

7

'THIS MAY BE THE LAST TIME YOU EVER HEAR FROM ME'

Mariupol, February 2022

If one thing had tempted Putin into thinking that Kyiv's government would fall without a fight, it was the ease with which he'd snatched parts of eastern Ukraine less than a decade before. In 2014, after huge street protests in Kyiv had ousted the corrupt, pro-Kremlin regime of President Viktor Yanukovych, Putin had wreaked vengeance by sending troops to seize Crimea, the diamond-shaped peninsula on Ukraine's Black Sea coast.

Ever since Soviet times, Crimea had been a popular holiday resort for Ukrainians and Russians alike, famed for its sub-tropical temperatures and cheap champagne. For Putin, what mattered was not its beaches and resorts, but the deep-water naval base at the Crimean port of Sevastopol, built in the time of Catherine the Great. Not only did it give access to the Mediterranean, but it was Russia's sole warm-water port, where shipping didn't have to worry about winter seas freezing over.

When the Soviet Union collapsed, and Ukraine got its independence, Russia had agreed to lease Sevastopol's port from the Kyiv government. But Moscow had never felt comfortable having its prized southern naval asset in the hands of a foreign landlord – especially one that had now just overthrown its pro-Kremlin government. Putin decided to snatch Crimea and its port back while he still could.

In late February 2014, not long after Yanukovych fled to Russia, pro-Kremlin crowds had staged demonstrations in Crimea, raising the Russian flag on government buildings. Backing them up were groups of well-armed, disciplined soldiers, dressed in unmarked green army uniforms. They wore no military insignia, and declined to say who they answered to. But the 'Little Green Men', as they became known, left no doubt about whose side they were on. First, they occupied the Crimean Parliament. Then they confronted local Ukrainian troops, ordering them to leave Crimea immediately. Caught off-guard, and wary of sparking a direct war with Moscow, Kyiv ordered its forces to evacuate rather than fight. In mid-March, Putin announced the annexation of Crimea back into Russian hands – admitting, a few weeks later, that yes, the 'Little Green Men' had been Russian troops all along.

It was an invasion like no other, earning Putin a reputation as a master of a new hybrid warfare, where stealth and confusion were the chief weapons. As the Russian leader himself gleefully boasted, Crimea 'had fallen without a shot'. Yet that was only really half the story. The invasion had taken advantage of a power vacuum in Kyiv, when the new government was only just finding its feet. And for all Putin's boasts of not a shot being fired, some very big guns had been brandished. While the Little Green Men had been shooing Ukrainian troops out of Crimea, Russian warships had blockaded the peninsula, leaving Kyiv in no doubt about the consequences of fighting back.

Elsewhere in eastern Ukraine, pro-Kremlin movements met rather more resistance. In the Donbas region, a rust-belt of Soviet coal mines and steel plants, separatists seized the cities of Donetsk and Luhansk, creating the self-declared Donetsk and Luhansk People's Republics. But there, the Russian flag didn't fly unchallenged. Kyiv declared a major military operation aimed at kicking the 'terrorists' out from both statelets, and by the summer of 2014 much of the Donbas was in civil war.

Then, even more than now, Kyiv's forces were the underdogs. The national army that the new government had inherited was an underfunded Soviet throwback, with many of its commanders still loyal to Moscow. The army's rank and file had little stomach for fighting fellow Ukrainians in the Donbas – especially if they were backed by their more powerful Russian neighbours.

Into the breach, however, came thousands of volunteer militia fighters, mostly Ukrainian nationalists. Prominent was the Azov militia, drawn from a far-right group involved in the protests that overthrew Yanukovych's government. That summer, they fought the separatists all over the Donbas and beyond, gaining a reputation for near-suicidal bravery. They particularly distinguished themselves in Mariupol, a port city of 400,000 on the Sea of Azov, fending off two attempts by Russian separatists to capture it.

Not everyone saw Azov as heroes. Some of the militia's founding members had links to football hooligan gangs and neo-Nazi groups. Their original emblem resembled runic symbols used by the SS, and a few members even professed admiration for Adolf Hitler. The charitable explanation was that this was just to wind up the Russians, millions of whom died fighting the Nazis during World War II. But it was still a propaganda gift to Putin, who'd always claimed 'neo-Nazis' were behind Kyiv's drift towards the West.

He'd returned to the theme on the eve of the 2022 invasion, declaring it an operation to 'demilitarize and de-Nazify' Ukraine. High on its list of targets would be Mariupol, with its goose-stepping Azov defenders. Never mind that President Zelensky was himself Jewish. In Putin's eyes, it was all part of a wider anti-Russian conspiracy – one orchestrated, ultimately, by Moscow's old enemies in the West.

As proof, the Kremlin pointed out that years before Zelensky had created the International Legion, Azov had been enlisting foreign soldiers. They weren't many, and most had been recruited only because they had military skills that Azov lacked. But in Moscow's eyes, such men were living proof of the depths to which Ukraine had sunk – hiring foreign mercenaries, dogs of war, doubtless on some CIA or MI6 payroll.

As ever, the Kremlin's image of such men was more Cold War spy thriller than truth. In reality, Azov's foreign hires were men like John Harding, a journeyman soldier from the north of England. He had no interest in Nazism, and his route into Azov three years before the invasion was more by accident than design. He was already nearly 60, and on the eve of the 2022 invasion was about to head back to Britain and retirement. Instead, he found himself in the very eye of the storm.

* * *

Just as Harding didn't fit the stereotype of an Azov Nazi, he didn't match that of a British squaddie either. Raised in Sunderland in England's North-East, he'd joined the army at 16, serving with the Parachute Regiment in the Falklands War. The victory over the Argentine military junta was the making of Prime Minister Margaret Thatcher, hailed as proof that Britain wasn't in terminal decline. But when the Falklands Task Force sailed home, Harding wasn't excited by the crowds of jingoistic flag-wavers. He was a committed socialist, with no great pride in Britain's colonial past. In his mid-twenties, having done his bit for Queen and country, he left the army for university. He started a new career as an engineer, never expecting to see combat again.

Then, in 2015, he'd watched a TV report about Islamic State fighters in Syria capturing a Jordanian air force pilot, whom they imprisoned in a cage and burned alive. Even by the standards of Islamic State, it was spectacular barbarity. Soon after, Harding joined the international wing of the Kurdish YPG, or People's Protection Units, the Western-backed volunteer militia that was fighting Islamic State on the ground. While the YPG's foreign cadre numbered in the hundreds rather than thousands, it was a forerunner of what Zelensky would attempt with the Legion.

Harding's decision to join was a mix of the political and the personal. He didn't think Britain was doing enough to help in Syria, given how much of the region's problems were legacies of the colonial past. More prosaically, he was unhappy at work, and his relationship had broken down. *Sod this*, he thought. *I'll go out there instead.*

He started out as a YPG infantryman, switching to the role of combat medic after spotting it as a weakness in the Kurds' capabilities. They were fearless warriors, who saw death on the battlefield as a chance to meet God. It was one reason why they were a match for the Islamic State. Yet the 'martyr culture' also meant they paid scant attention to battlefield medicine, dying from injuries that shouldn't have been fatal. Harding did his best to change their attitude. Dying for God was fine, sure. Just make your enemies do it first.

Harding thrived in the YPG, whose younger ranks respected his age and experience. As the saying went, beware an old man in a profession where men die young. He became commander of a specialist medical unit, which saved hundreds of lives, kept the YPG combat-effective and, in turn, helped bring Islamic State's rule to an end. But the YPG's foreign volunteers got little credit back in Britain. Harding returned home, only to find that Britons who'd fought for the YPG in Syria were being prosecuted.

While the YPG was Western-backed, it had links to militant Kurdish separatists in Turkey, who classed it as a terrorist group. It mattered not that volunteers like Harding were only helping the YPG fight Islamic State. British officials didn't like the idea of private citizens getting involved in the Middle East's wars, or the guerrilla skills they might bring back to Britain.

Fearing it was only a matter of time before the police knocked at his door, he decided to get out of Britain again. A former YPG comrade mentioned that the Ukrainian army was hiring foreign recruits to keep the separatists at bay. In 2018, Harding was accepted as a combat medic with Azov – whose base on the coast outside Mariupol, he noted, had a nice private beach. True, the Russians might come storming up it one day. But back then, the odds of being thrown in a prison cell back in England seemed higher.

* * *

For the next four years, Harding made Mariupol his home from home. There were worse places to be billeted. The base was in an elegant villa belonging to the deposed former president Yanukovych, a man known for his love of luxury. When not practising their warfare drills, Azov's volunteers could sunbathe, surf, sunbathe and enjoy Mariupol's nightlife.

By the time Harding joined, Azov had been formally integrated into Ukraine's armed forces – partly in recognition of its fighting prowess, partly to sideline its far-right founders. Harding had always felt the extremist tag to be somewhat overstated anyway. Yes, Azov had a few genuine Nazis, but it was a tiny minority. Besides, anyone willing to die for their country was, by default, nationalistic to some extent. Most people were in Azov for the same reason as he was – they had a reputation for being very effective fighters, with the best gear and kit, and they didn't just take anyone.

Frankly, if they'd been true ideologues, Harding himself wouldn't have fitted in. As well being a socialist, he was bisexual, something unlikely to make him welcome in neo-Nazi circles. It wasn't something he made a big deal of, though, and at his age he kept his private life to himself. While Azov's young blades caroused in Mariupol's nightclubs, he spent his spare time touring the city's museums and cultural spots. A favourite was the Czarist-era concert theatre, which put on Vivaldi concertos.

The longer Harding stayed in Mariupol, the more he liked it. The war against the separatists had cooled to what diplomats termed a 'frozen conflict', the two sides sticking largely to demarcated lines. There was ample leisure time, and unlike in Syria a decent glass of red wine was easy to come by. Back in Britain, prosecutions of YPG fighters had been discontinued amid an outcry from the public, who didn't consider it a crime to fight Isis. But he didn't have much to go home to anyway.

By late 2021, though, he figured his time with Azov was up. He'd be 60 at his next birthday. His legs weren't what they were. Better head home to retirement, whatever that would be, than become a liability to his comrades. As with all unpleasant decisions, he kept putting it off, and in the end it wasn't until early February 2022 that he formally asked his unit commander to leave. By then, the Russians were already massing on Ukraine's border. But nobody in Mariupol seriously thought they were going to invade.

'No problem,' Harding's commander told him. 'But why not stay till the end of the month? The paperwork will be easier, and you'll get your full wages?'

Harding agreed. On the evening of 23 February, he'd gone to bed in his dormitory as usual, his kitbags already packed for heading home the following week.

Then, at 5 a.m. the next day, one of his Ukrainian roommates woke him up.

'The Russians have crossed the border,' the roommate said.

'How many?' Harding asked.

'All of them.'

* * *

Less than an hour later, Harding was in full battle kit, sitting in the back of an armoured personnel carrier. It had no windows, so he couldn't see where they were heading, but his guess was Kyiv. If this really was a full-on invasion, defending the capital would be the priority. Then, before they'd even left Mariupol, the APC pulled up at an empty school, which their commander said would be their base for the next few days. That meant they'd probably be fighting a rearguard action here in Mariupol, trying to slow the Russian advance. A last stand, in other words.

Harding didn't dwell on it. A shitshow, yes. But this was what he'd signed up for. No point contemplating 'If only …' scenarios right now. If there was a voice inside him saying *Why the fuck didn't you quit earlier?* he didn't want to hear it. Besides, the other Azov fighters were his comrades. After four years, they were as close to family as anyone else in his life. If he'd been back in the UK with his feet up, he'd have been going spare with guilt for not being here.

Nobody doubted that Putin would hit Mariupol very hard. It wasn't just about settling the score from 2014, when Mariupol's defenders had halted the separatists' march east. The city sat on a stretch of coast directly linking the Donetsk People's Republic – now known as the DPR – to Crimea. Seizing it would help stitch the separatist-held fiefdoms together.

Before the invasion, a strike force of 14,000 Russian troops had massed in the DPR, poised to move on Mariupol. Backing them were DPR separatist units. If you could call them that. They were often just militias of thugs and drunks, motivated mainly by the chances for looting and aggro. As fighters, they were nothing on the Russians. But their very lack of discipline made them dangerous. A good incentive to make a last stand, if it came to that. Better to go out swinging than fall into the separatists' hands alive.

Over the next 48 hours, the strike force advanced towards Mariupol's outskirts from the east. Meanwhile, thousands of Russian marines landed on the coast 40 miles west, creating a pincer movement. Downtown Mariupol was hammered with artillery, vast palls of smoke drifting over the sea.

The invaders were using Grad missile launchers, a crude Soviet-era system named after the Russian word for 'hailstorm'. It was the artillery equivalent of an AK-47, capable of firing 40 unguided rockets in 20 seconds, which would randomly pulverise an area the size of ten football pitches. Grads were designed for use on large, open battlefields, where armies would be spread out. But the Russians had no qualms about using them on Mariupol, despite the risk of slaughtering civilians indiscriminately.

On day three, a Grad hit the school where Harding's unit was based. He was asleep at the time, and woke up covered in ceiling tiles, glass and pieces of metal. He wasn't badly hurt, but his hearing was gone completely for a while. Even when people shouted at him, it was as if the sound was turned down.

The school wrecked, Harding's unit relocated to a supermarket, where they set up a casualty collection point. Wounded fighters were brought in each day, the more serious ones picked up by Ukrainian helicopters, which were still flying in and out of Mariupol. Nobody expected the lifeline to last long.

One day, Harding was stood on the supermarket's roof, seeking a signal for his mobile phone, when he heard bursts of gunfire. He came down to find a car riddled with bullets. A DPR colonel had driven his car right up to the Azov position, having taken a wrong turn somewhere. A gunfight had ensued, in which the colonel had been cut to pieces. Two of his comrades who'd escaped were found dead nearby, both with bullet holes under their chins. They'd shot themselves with their own weapons, death deemed preferable to capture.

There was a risk that before they'd died the militiamen had radioed the Azov location in to their HQ. Harding's commander said the unit would now be splitting up. Harding and his fellow medic Hassan, a Muslim Tatar from Crimea, would be sent to join some other Azov fighters, holed up in the Azovstal Steel Works.

* * *

Built in the 1930s during Stalin's reign, the steelworks was massive even by Soviet standards. It stretched for nearly two miles along the coast, a vast, rusty sprawl of chimney stacks, furnaces, warehouses and cranes, connected by tunnels, gantries and walkways. The plant's antiquated production lines were among Europe's biggest, churning out steel for the Shard in

London, shipyards in Germany, and bridges and condos from Italy to Manhattan.

Now it was Mariupol's last hope. Its labyrinthine layout was a perfect citadel – an endless maze of bolt-holes, ambush points and ready-made sniper nests. It also had huge networks of nuclear bunkers, built during the Cold War, when Mariupol had feared attack from the West, not Moscow. No amount of Grads would be able to reach them.

First, Harding and Hassan had to get there. Azovstal was 20 miles east down the coast, on roads that were no longer safe. The two medics were loaded into the back of a truck, full of weapons and ammo, that would drop them at a rendezvous point on the beach. A motorboat would take them the rest of the way.

They waited until darkness to leave the supermarket, the driver relying on night vision goggles rather than headlights. It worked fine, until the goggles briefly cut out, and the truck ploughed straight into a concrete checkpoint, hurling them forwards and leaving them buried in ammunition boxes. At first, Hassan thought they'd hit a landmine. This was the kind of nonsense that happened in war. When nothing was working as it should, and everyone's minds were on other things, mistakes were made. You were as likely to die in a road accident as on the frontline, a casualty not of combat but a cock-up. A further shambles unfolded at the beach, where the skipper of the motorboat dropped his keys in the sand. They ended up stuck there for a whole hour, dangerously exposed, while the truck driver headed off to a base to locate a spare set of keys. Not the kind of thing you saw in *Dunkirk*.

They finally headed out to sea, the air bitterly cold, the night fortunately moonless. The vessel was a RIB, or rigid inflatable boat, basically a rubberised dinghy with an outboard engine. A few bullet holes and it would sink. The passengers would follow suit, dragged down by the weight of their own body armour.

They couldn't just hug the coast to get to Azovstal. Too much risk of being spotted. The skipper planned to head three miles out to sea, then arc back in. Half an hour out to sea, they heard a Russian patrol boat. They couldn't see it, and it couldn't see them, because both had their lights off. But they could make out its engine pattern. A bigger, heavier sound than theirs, weaving steadily back and forth. Almost certainly trying to track them down.

The skipper cut the engine. They sat motionless in the water, like a surfer hoping to avoid the attention of a shark. Harding pulled the safety catch off his Kalashnikov. Fighting on land was bad enough. Here at sea there was no cover, nowhere to hide. *Any second now. Any second now.*

He hadn't felt so scared since the Falklands. But with the gunboat unable to use its searchlight, they were hard to spot. After 20 of the longest minutes of his life, he heard it heading off.

*   *   *

The boat reached Azovstal via a creek under a bridge. After covering the vessel with camouflage, they got in a truck to the steelworks. The Soviets had designed it as a closed city, with houses for 12,000 people, plus schools, shops and a hospital. It was now home to 2,500 Azov troops. The network of bunkers ran for miles, some of them five floors underground. Two metres of concrete separated each floor. Word had it that they could withstand a direct hit from a nuclear bomb.

The Russians were now hitting Mariupol with everything short of that, unleashing the full shock-and-awe treatment.

Missile strikes and artillery had turned entire neighbourhoods into smouldering wastelands. The scale of the destruction dwarfed that in Kyiv, giving the world some of the grimmest images of the war

Three weeks into the siege, an air strike had devastated Mariupol's maternity hospital. A pregnant woman was photographed being stretchered out over the rubble, her pelvis crushed. Neither she nor her baby survived. A week later, another air strike had hit Mariupol's main theatre building, where Harding had once enjoyed classical concerts. Its basement had been requisitioned as the city's biggest bomb shelter, with more than 1,000 people hiding inside. Up to 600 were killed, the worst civilian loss of life in the war so far.

Four days later, hundreds more were feared dead in a bombing of a bunker at an art school. By then, the city was in such disarray that accurate casualty counts were impossible. One casualty indicator was satellite footage of parklands and waste grounds, showing freshly dug mass graves. More bodies lay uncollected in the streets, chewed by abandoned cats and dogs.

It was a scene of industrialised slaughter, the war's worst carnage so far. Western leaders wrung their hands, comparing Mariupol to the massacres at Srebrenica in the Balkans, Homs in Syria, Guernica in Civil War Spain. It was, they lamented, the kind of warfare Europe was supposed to have turned the page on.

* * *

Harding was assigned to Azovstal plant's hospital. The building itself had already been bombed, so it operated out of a bunker directly beneath. Casualties came in constantly. Harding worked round the clock, snatching sleep between shifts, no longer much aware of the passing of time. Underground, the distinction between day and night faded. So too, as the weeks went past, did the hope of ever leaving alive. There was an unspoken realisation that this would be a last stand.

In one of his nightly addresses from Kyiv, President Zelensky praised the Azov fighters' courage, awarding their commander the title of Hero of Ukraine, the equivalent of the Victoria Cross. It also looked like being a posthumous honour.

Militarily, the siege was working in Kyiv's favour. Thousands of Russian troops who should have been helping with the wider invasion effort were tied up trying to clear the steelworks. Azov's fighters were mounting hit-and-run attacks, emerging out of one set of service tunnels before disappearing back into another. The Russians were wary of following them inside, knowing that booby-traps were waiting. By late April, even Putin appeared to realise the difficulties involved. In a rare show of consideration for the lives of his troops, he told them to starve Azovstal rather than storm it, ordering them to seal the plant off so that 'not a fly can get past'.

The fighting, however, carried on around the steel plant. Ukrainian helicopters continued near-suicidal missions to resupply the Azov fighters, skimming the coast at just 20 feet above ground to weave through the Russian anti-aircraft defences. Then someone posted footage of one on Facebook, and the next time a helicopter flew in it was shot down, bringing the resupply missions to a halt.

From then on, medical supplies ran low. Wounds went gangrenous, requiring amputations. Increasingly, they had to be done without anaesthetic. Harding was part of a six-strong team that assisted the surgeons, using brute strength to restrain amputees as they writhed on the operating table. An amputation above the knee required two people each side of the patient, and one more to muffle his screams. The surgeon didn't want other patients frightened.

Amputating the main leg bone, the femur, was the hardest. With no pain relief, speed was key. A good surgeon, armed with a sharp hacksaw, could do it in a couple of minutes. But it wasn't simply a case of lopping the limb off. First, the flesh had to be peeled back from the bone, creating flaps of tissue that could be stitched together into a stump. Muscle might also need removing. All Harding could offer to comfort patients was a piece of wood or leather to bite on, and a warning to prepare themselves. *We're going to cut your leg off, mate, it's going to fucking hurt.*

*   *   *

By May, the fighters were running low on food too. As bunker-buster bombs continued to pound the plant, the Azov commanders decided to turn their suffering to their advantage. Using a Starlink satellite terminal that let the plant communicate with the outside world, they sent out photographs of the amputees. Some hobbled round on crutches to support missing legs. Others raised bandaged stumps where their arms used to be. A few defiantly raised grimy fingers in victory salutes.

The idea was to show that, despite three months of siege, the Ukrainian fighting spirit was undaunted. But it was also a plea for help, the commanders hoping that international pressure would grow on Russia to show mercy. Eventually, with Turkey acting as broker, Kyiv and Moscow struck an agreement to surrender the Azov fighters into Kremlin custody. They'd be taken to a separatist-run jail in the DPR, held under the terms of the Geneva Convention, and exchanged for Russian prisoners of war in coming months.

The deal satisfied nobody. In Moscow, hardliners were outraged that the Azov fighters should be getting anything other than the gallows. In the steel plant, the Azov fighters doubted the Kremlin would stick to its promises about the Geneva Convention. Many wanted to fight to the last bullet, rather than risk a sticky end in the DPR's torture chambers. Especially Harding, who rated his chances of clemency even lower than the average Azov fighter. The Kremlin had already said that anyone who wasn't Ukrainian would be treated as a mercenary. And in the DPR, being a mercenary was a capital crime.

Orders, though, were orders. On 15 May, buses escorted by Russian armoured vehicles arrived outside the steel plant, ready to take Azov fighters off to the DPR. Before getting on, Harding made one final visit to the plant's Starlink hotspot, writing a message to a friend on Facebook.

'This may be the last you ever hear from me.'

PART II
'IT'S NOT LIKE *CALL OF DUTY*'

Mykolaiv, Kharkiv, the black site

8

'FREE MEAT'

Lyubomyrivka village, outside Mykolaiv, May–June 2022

For proof that Ukrainians were made of sterner stuff than most Europeans, all anyone had to do was visit the frontline villages outside Mykolaiv. They lay deep in the no-man's-land towards Russian-held Kherson, down an empty, shell-cratered highway where the sounds of artillery exchanges grew louder with every mile. Many had been half reduced to rubble by Russian artillery, yet despite a steady stream of casualties, not everyone had done the seemingly sensible thing and fled. In most villages, a hardcore of about 10 per cent of the population remained – ignoring pleas from local officials to get out while they were still alive.

Some of the remainers were local drunks, too busy necking their home-brew vodka to worry about anything else. But others were just reluctant to leave – some because they had nowhere else to go, some out of stout-hearted patriotism, and some out of sheer stubbornness. Visiting army evacuation teams would knock at their cottages, expecting them to jump into their arms, only to be offered tea and excuses.

My vegetable patch needs tending.
I have to look after my dog.
I have to look after my neighbour's dog.
Thanks for offering, but I was born here and I'll die here.

Many were pensioners who'd lived through World War II and Stalin's era, and regarded the latest hostilities as barely more than a nuisance. Occasionally they'd feature in some visiting TV crew's broadcast, looking entirely unfazed as shells landed around them, asking reporters why they were wearing those silly flak jackets. Then, as the TV crew dived for cover, they'd saunter off to water their marrows. They made Europe's biggest land war since 1945 feel like an episode of *The Archers*.

Their unflappability impressed Stephen Wilson, who was now stationed on the Mykolaiv frontlines. Clearly, a people who valued their vegetable patches more than their lives weren't going to give up their land easily. Not the sort of grit you'd find in Britain anymore, despite all the talk of the Blitz spirit. During Covid, when all most Brits had to do was sit on their arses and watch Netflix, there'd been a national panic just because there was a toilet roll shortage.

Here, the older and more frail someone looked, the tougher they seemed to be. There were stories of old Ukrainian *babusyas*, or grandmothers, hurling insults at Russian soldiers, and sometimes rotten vegetables. In Lyubomyrivka, where Wilson was now fighting, word had it that some old boy with a knapsack of explosives had blown up a telegraph pole where the Russians had mounted a CCTV camera, killing himself in the process. Proper suicide mission. Could have just been Ukrainian propaganda, of course. But very believable.

Still, it was one thing for the Ukrainians to have a cavalier disregard for their own lives. It was another when they showed that attitude to the volunteers. Some commanders saw them as simply thrill-seeking 'volun-tourists', who were therefore expendable. Wilson couldn't forget the way his unit had been introduced to one Ukrainian officer when they'd reported for duty.

'The Free Meat are here for their safari, commander,' some underling had said. 'Where do you like them to go?'

The underling had spoken in Ukrainian, assuming the Legionnaires wouldn't understand. It was only later that a friendly interpreter had explained.

'They call you Free Meat because there's no repercussions for them if you die,' he told Wilson.

It wasn't gratifying, to be dismissed as some pith-helmeted Western trophy hunter. Worse still, Wilson didn't really blame them. The Ukrainians had already had a lot of volunteers who were gung-ho idiots, who'd lied about their military capabilities. And some *did* act like they were on safari. They wanted to shoot a few Russians, or missile a tank, then post it on YouTube and go home.

Wilson and his team had been in Mykolaiv for a couple of months, having been transferred there from Kyiv. Mykolaiv seemed to be where the Legion sent all the volunteers that it didn't quite know what to do with. They were now one of several 'Have gun, will travel' volunteer groups in town. All trying to make themselves useful around the frontline. All trying to persuade the Ukrainians that, no, they weren't just there to bag some Russian's head to mount on their living room wall.

With their previous commander having gone back to Poland, Wilson now found himself in charge of a small group of volunteers, including Jack Knight, his old comrade from the Royal Engineers. They were based outside Lyubomyrivka, a hamlet nestling in wheatfields about 25 miles east of Mykolaiv. Like most other villages in the area, it was like something from the set of *Fiddler on the Roof*. Rows of vine-canopied cottages with water wells. Gardens full of chicken coops, fruit trees and beehives.

At least that's how it looked from a distance. The village was currently in Russian hands, so the closest Wilson had got was a kilometre from its western edge, doing recon from Ukrainian OPs. Much of the recon work was about establishing 'pattern of life' – tracking the enemy's regular movements to work out who they were and what their plans were. Even fleeting glimpses of enemy activity could add to the intelligence picture. A pickup with an escort might mean some high-ranking figure was visiting to plan an attack. A Russian taking a shit in some woods might signal a shift changeover – a time when the outgoing troops might be half-asleep, and therefore vulnerable.

By June, Wilson's team had done numerous recon jobs, and joined in the odd battle, where a few Russians had been killed during small arms engagements. Just the kind of thing a trophy hunter might want to brag about, although that wasn't really how it worked. In gunfights, the enemy seldom lingered in the open long enough for anyone to get a clean shot at them. All one often saw was muzzle flash from a hedge several hundred metres away, or a flurry of movement in some woods, at which point everyone returned fire in the same general direction. With all guns blazing at once, it was often impossible to work out who'd fired the fatal shot. They had a Danish sniper with them, Jens*, who reckoned most of the kills were down to him. But usually, everyone was putting down such a wall of fire that nobody could really pinpoint who got who.

* * *

In early June, Wilson's team were assigned to ambush a Russian recon patrol outside Lyubomyrivka. The plan was to hole up in some nearby woods overnight, and lie in wait. The ambush would then initiate a bigger attack to try to capture the village. It would be the fifth time the Ukrainians had tried.

Wilson's team headed out mid-morning. Just reaching the ambush point was a challenge in itself, avoiding open ground wherever possible. There'd be long belly-crawls through treelines or drainage ditches, keeping an eye out for anti-personnel mines. Mines were usually laid where people were most likely to walk, in gaps through hedges or near a plank straddling a ditch. The safest route was often the least appealing – down a culvert full of stinking rubbish, or a ditch full of cow dung and flies. Not the kind of thing they showed on British Arny recruitment videos. But preferable to having a foot blown off.

Once they'd reached the ambush point, Wilson placed Jens and another sniper 30 metres apart. Knight took a separate position to the north-east. The Russian recon patrol wasn't predicted to come past until first light, so they settled in to wait, concealed in a treeline. Then, around 6 p.m. that evening, Russian artillery began landing around their position.

At first, it wasn't clear if they'd actually seen them. The Russians had such vast artillery stocks that they often just fired random salvos. Some rounds hit the trees, setting them ablaze. But slowly, it got closer. First it was just standard, par-for-the-course close. Then very close. Then *very fucking close indeed*.

Gunfire you could run away from, or fire back at. Artillery forced you to just lie down and passively accept your fate. The only option was to wait it out and hope you didn't wake up in Heaven.

Or … Sandgate Beach? Suddenly, Wilson was down on the south Kent coast, not far from his home in Rochester. With his kids, playing on the beach. Doing the dad thing, slapping his hand on his thighs and asking: 'Who wants ice cream?'

What the ... was this a dream? No, surely not. He could feel the warmth of the sun on his skin, the seagulls crying.

No, hang on, who the fuck was this? Some dude with a rifle, yelling at him, slapping him. Jens the sniper. What the fuck was a Danish sniper doing on Sandgate Beach? Did he want an ice cream too?

Suddenly, the beach vanished. Wilson was back outside Lyubomyrivka again. Blood was trickling down his face. His head hurt. He was covered in dust and soil. Jens, the Danish sniper, was slapping him again.

'Steve, Steve, speak to me! Do you know where you are?'

'Yeah, yeah. I'm in Ukraine?'

'Thank fuck! You're alive!'

'Eh? Uh? What kind of ice cream do you want?'

A pebble-sized piece of shrapnel from a very close shell blast had hit Wilson's head. It would have caved in his skull, had his helmet not got in the way. The impact had concussed him, and shoved his helmet down over his face so he couldn't breathe properly. He'd been lying senseless, issuing a slow, rasping sound like he was snoring.

Wondering why his commander had chosen to have a nap during an artillery barrage, Jens had run over and yanked Wilson's helmet back up. When he'd seen that Wilson was insensible, he'd done the 'Alert, Voice, Pain' routine, dragging Wilson's dazed, confused brain back to reality after its little out-of-body day trip to Sandgate Beach.

Right now, he was still somewhere in between. As they crawled towards a deeper trench, Wilson was back on Sandgate Beach again. This time he was dragging himself along the pebbles utterly exhausted, barely able to put one hand in front of another. He continued oscillating between south Kent and southern Ukraine until he reached the trench, where his comrades pumped him full of painkillers. They helped him stagger back to the rear lines, where he was loaded into an ancient Soviet-era Lada that ferried him to hospital. Even with pain relief, every bump in the road felt like being kicked in the head.

He'd been familiar with concussion ever since his days as a child boxer. But this felt different – a proper, full-on near-death experience. Like those ones he'd seen people talk about on some TV documentary, where a celestial light guided them up to Heaven. Apparently the body produced some hallucinogenic chemical to stop cells dying when oxygen was low. Hence the feeling of a mystical encounter, teetering on some cosmic boundary between life and death.

Hence also the unfamiliar masked figures now gathered solemnly around him. And yes, a lone light, shining in the dark. Could this be it?

Ow! Fuck off!

Once again, he wasn't in Paradise. The Lada had dropped him off at a Ukrainian hospital in Mykolaiv. Medics were now trying to put a drip in his arm, guided only by a light from an iPhone because of a power cut. And struggling to find a vein. Either it was darker than he realised, or they weren't doing it right.

No, not like that. Or that! No, hang on. Here, let me show you ...

In the end, he took the needle off them and put the drip in himself.

* * *

State Hospital No 4, Odesa, June 2022. Plenty of people had called Wilson a lunatic during his lifetime – sometimes, he had to admit, with good reason. Now, after two weeks in a Ukrainian hospital, he actually looked like one. His hair and beard had grown long and unkempt, and as an after-effect of his head injury, he'd developed an uncontrollable shake and a wild, lopsided grin. Combined with all the medication the nurses were pumping into him, he looked like some lobotomised extra from *One Flew Over the Cuckoo's Nest.*

He was, according to his comrades, lucky not to be in the morgue. Jack Knight, who'd been pitched up a few hundred metres away when the Russian artillery attack began, had filmed the bombardment on his phone. The footage showed Wilson's position engulfed with Grad explosions, black smoke billowing everywhere.

X-rays had shown severe blunt force trauma to the vertebra at the base of his skull. Some temporary swelling, also, to the frontal lobe of his brain, with possible tissue damage. The kind of standard battlefield injury that tens of thousands of Ukrainian soldiers were now suffering as a result of artillery blasts. Whether there'd be any long-term effects was hard to say. But short-term, frontal lobe trauma could shrink the brain's band-width, affecting motor skills, as well as speech, judgement and social interaction. Just about everything that made one human, in other words. Hence him shaking like a madman. As Jack Knight had kindly diagnosed when he'd come to visit: 'You're even more of a fucking retard than you were before, mate.'

About the only thing his shrapnel-pummelled, drug-addled brain had been able to work out was that he'd rather be anywhere else than the ward. Ukrainian hospitals were doing a heroic job in looking after the war wounded, but in terms of creature comforts, they hadn't moved on much since Communist times. The food was awful, the surroundings gloomy and the staff were old-school Soviet-stern. Nor was there any way to pass the time, except lie in dread every time some nurse bore down upon him with a big needle, the insertion technique often inflicting yet more blunt force trauma.

Several times Wilson had tried to escape, only to get lost in the stairwells like some Alzheimer's-stricken geriatric patient. He'd been dragged back to his bed by the burly hospital guards, who seemed accustomed to unruly patients. The Ukrainian soldier in the bed next to him claimed to have been duffed up for messing around with his IV drip.

After about three weeks, when the shaking had eased off, the hospital let him leave. Beds were in short supply in wartime. If the idiot Brit wanted to go before he was medically fit for discharge, that was his problem. Presumably he thought he could get better care back in his own country.

But that wasn't where Wilson was headed. Yes, the sensible thing after serious head trauma would have been to go straight home and get every possible check done on the NHS. Instead he headed back towards Mykolaiv. His comrades were younger than him, even less experienced. He felt he'd let them down by getting injured. Besides, right now, there was no other place he'd rather be. Even it risked another trip to Sandgate Beach.

9

THE ORCHARD

Lyubomyrivka village, outside Mykolaiv,
July 2022. Assault attempt No 11

Ukrainian command hadn't expected to see Wilson again. Their assumption was that most foreign fighters would leave Ukraine once they got injured, having acquired sufficient scars and bragging rights to prop up a bar back home for years. He was still on various hospital medications, and feared that the commanders might not sign him off as fit to fight. However, his body seemed to have mended from his injuries surprisingly quickly. He put that down not to the tender mercies of the staff at Hospital No 4, but to the little vials of liquid that he kept stashed in his kit bag.

Human growth hormone, or HGH, injected twice a week. Illegal back home without a prescription, easy to acquire here in Ukraine. And very popular with soldiers – not just the Rambo types, but anyone trying to get themselves in shape for the front-lines. Sure, unregulated use of HGH had health risks, such as heart attack and diabetes. So too, though, did fighting Russians.

Jens the sniper had retrieved the lump of shrapnel buried in Wilson's helmet, which he presented to him as a keepsake. It was the size of a walnut, with jagged edges. Wilson wore it round his neck like a pendant. Not so much as a souvenir, but an ever-present reminder of just how close he'd got to getting both himself and the rest of his team killed that day.

Their next job would be to hole up near Lyubomyrivka again, ahead of a planned major assault by a Ukrainian armoured unit. It was, by his count, the 11th attempt to take the village, which didn't speak volumes for the competence of Ukrainian command. However, the latest operation was being run by a new officer, call-signed Kilo*, who seemed better prepared than most.

Wilson attended Kilo's battle plan meeting, which could have been from a Nato textbook. Maps, route planning, coordinated strikes, the lot. Much better than the usual fag-packet stuff. What also marked Kilo out was that he'd allowed for the possibility of it all going horribly wrong, with casevac (casualty evacuation) and contingency strategies factored in. He obviously knew the old military saying that 'no battle plan survives contact with the enemy'. One of the wisest combat maxims ever, yet plenty commanders were so cocky that they ignored it.

Wilson's role would be to lead his team to a rendezvous point near an orchard north of Lyubomyrivka. From there, they'd press through the orchard to its eastern edge, which overlooked a road. Hidden in woods on the road's far side were three firing points for Russian armoured vehicles, which would likely come out guns blazing once the main Ukrainian assault got underway. If and when they did, Wilson's team would be waiting for them with anti-tank missiles. It was a dangerous mission, with the likelihood of full-on combat, but it seemed viable. Wilson's team would also have cover from a second Ukrainian flanking team, who would already have recce'd the orchard.

The team – Wilson, Knight, an interpreter called Sasha and two other foreign volunteers – headed out one hot morning in late July. After the usual crawl through aqueducts, overgrown ditches and treelines, they reached the orchard's edge. Orders came on the radio that the attack would soon start. But there was no sign of the Ukrainian flanking team.

Not good. First, their absence meant the orchard might not have been recce'd properly. Secondly, there'd be nobody to provide covering fire for them if they needed to extract quickly. Which, if they'd just tried to incinerate an enemy tank, was likely.

With Sasha interpreting, Wilson radioed his concerns through to command.

'Er, can you tell us where the flanking team is?'

'What flanking team?'

'The one that is supposed to have recce'd the woods.'

'There's not one. Just carry on with the mission anyway.'

'What do you mean, there isn't one? We can't do the mission without it.'

'Just carry on. Don't be cowards about it.'

Cowards?

'Sasha, can you make sure what I am about to say next is translated exactly, please? Tell them that if they think we're cowards, they can pick up a gun and come here and do this mission themselves. Otherwise they can get fucked. Please tell them that word for word.'

Sasha didn't look too keen. But he did as he was told, judging by the explosion of angry Ukrainian invective that came from the handset.

Stuff them. If they hadn't sent in the flanking team, what else might they not have done? What other surprises might be lying in wait?

A new voice came on the handset. Some other Ukrainian unit, who'd been listening in to the conversation on the radio.

'Don't worry, Command, we can handle this mission. No problem.'

Wilson had seen the group earlier. Like his own team, they were configured as an anti-tank squad. But they were only carrying small calibre rocket-launchers, the kind that would only be any use against soft-skinned vehicles. Did they know what they were doing?

It didn't look like it. While Wilson's team had taken cover in 'dead ground' – a hollow in the fields, where the enemy couldn't see them – the Ukrainian group suddenly appeared atop a knoll at the orchard's edge. Not crawling, but standing up, looking round to get their bearings. Silhouetted clearly against the horizon, for all the world to see.

Maybe they knew something he didn't. Maybe they'd cleared the orchard, and were confident it was safe. No matter. He wasn't sending his own team an inch further. If this Ukrainian group wanted to show that they were real men, and that the foreigners were a bunch of cowards, let them go ahead.

The Ukrainians disappeared into the orchard. Fifteen seconds later, two shots rang out, one after another. Screams followed. Then a burst of fire from what sounded like a belt-fed machine gun. More screams. Then a Russian artillery salvo came in. And another. Then more.

On the radio, Sasha was trying to make sense of it. It seemed the Ukrainian team had walked straight into some Russians. Two had been killed. A third was wounded. Their comrades were trying to give him first aid, while radioing for help.

Fucking hell, what did they do now? The artillery barrage was getting heavier, hammering their escape route down the treeline. In between, they could hear Russian voices coming from the woods, maybe no more than 100 metres away. Laughing, celebrating, the way soldiers did after a kill. And yelling 'Fuck you!'. In English.

Why English? Did they know there were Western Legionnaires here? They were a high-value prize, dead or alive. As per the bounty that that Russian social media channel had put on his head. That, though, was just some bunch of keyboard warriors. If the local Russian command knew they were here, they might come for them mob-handed.

Sasha was looking freaked, staring into space. One minute he'd been chatting to the Ukrainian team over the radio. Now two of them were dead. Wilson saw Knight giving him a pep talk.

'Don't think about that now, Sasha, nothing we can do. Just focus on the mission.'

Time for a Condor Moment. They tried to go forward, to set up a firing line to give the Ukrainian team some cover, but then cluster bombs dropped nearby. They also knew they risked heading into exactly the same ambush that had awaited the Ukrainian team. But if they pulled back, they'd likely be spotted, either by the Russian troops or drones above. Best just stay put for now in the dead ground. If nobody knew they were there, maybe nobody would come looking for them.

Besides, he didn't have a clue what else to do. They were a five-man anti-tank team, not a mob of infantry bruisers. Led not by Andy NcNab, but by an overweight ex-squaddie, who'd spend too much of his army days brawling and boozing to become a really good soldier. And who was now shit-scared. The most scared he'd ever been.

Drones were buzzing overhead. The artillery was landing closer, scattering soil from the fields over the team's position. There was every possibility that some drone had spotted them, and was guiding it in. That was if the Russian infantry didn't find them first. All it would take would be for someone to creep up with a couple of grenades.

Keep it together. You're supposed to be in charge. Keep your-self busy. And the team. Don't let minds wander.

He ran the team through some emergency drills. They checked weapons and coordinated firing arcs. They rehearsed casualty drills, and what route to take if they needed to extract. They kept drinking and eating, to keep blood sugar up. Anything to occupy the mental space, to stop the fear flooding in.

An hour passed. The barrage continued. Then another hour. Somewhere to the south, there was what sounded like a tank battle. No sign, though, of the big Ukrainian assault on Lyubomyrivka. That would at least have shaken things up, maybe created a distraction for them to get out.

Light began to fade. They had no night vision goggles. A night spent rough in this dead ground would leave them even more fatigued.

'We need to get out,' Wilson told the others. 'It's just going to get worse. It's now or never.'

The only option was to retrace their route in via the treeline, parts of which were now ablaze from endless Russian shelling. A long hike, laden with kit. Knight was carrying a belt-fed machine gun and ammo, which alone weighed 15 kg. Plus they were all already worn out, the adrenalin rush giving way to fatigue.

Knight passed round a small ziplock bag full of Jack3D, an energy-boosting fitness supplement that he used for workouts. Like the human growth hormone that Wilson had been using, it was banned in the UK. But it produced a great energy rush, better than a dozen cans of energy drink. A gym bro's crystal meth.

They had a large spoonful each, washing the raspberry-tasting powder down with swigs of water. Twenty minutes later, they set off through the treeline, parts of which were still burning. From the fields either side, Wilson could hear voices: Ukrainian or Russian, he didn't know. In this chaos, with the battleplan having gone to pot, either side might shoot at them.

After what seemed like hours, but was actually no more than about 40 minutes, they got back to Ukrainian-held lines. They sat there, feeling like badly scared kids who wanted their mums.

'What are you lot doing sitting around back here? I thought you were up out front?'

It was Jake*, a Canadian volunteer and a pal of Wilson. An experienced soldier, who ran his own casevac extraction team, specialising in pulling dead and injured soldiers from no-man's-land.

'We've just got back. What are you doing here?' Wilson asked.

'We heard there were casualties. Thought it might be you. Turns out you've been sat here all this time?'

'Er, no ... not exactly. Let me explain ...'

Jake had heard about the mission in advance, and had had reservations about it. Sensed it wasn't as billed. He'd even texted Wilson warning him not to go, but the messages had arrived too late. He'd come expecting to be retrieving Wilson's body.

Wilson's fear began to turn to anger. Why hadn't the flanking team been there? Why were there Russians waiting in the orchard? And why were they shouting at them in English? Had they been set up? Maybe the shell-shock and Jack3D had impaired his judgement. But right now, it seemed hard to conclude anything else.

Either way, it had been a fiasco. At least two Ukrainians dead, and a third wounded. And if he hadn't dug his heels in, it would have been him and his team instead.

I am fucking fuming. I am going to kick that fucking commander's head in.

* * *

119

They drove back to HQ and went straight to the commander's bunker. He was stood outside, smoking a cigarette and laughing with a colleague.

Wilson handed his rifle to another of his team and walked straight up to him. He poked him in the chest.

'Get inside that bunker. We need to talk.'

The commander looked at him. Laughed.

Wilson took off his helmet and dropped it on the ground. As the commander's gaze followed it, Wilson punched him in the face, knocking him to the ground. He followed it up with a boot to the head.

Not fighting fair, to kick a man when he was down. So fucking what. The old Wilson was back, the one who didn't give a shit who he hurt in his life. Let them court-martial him. Let them shoot him.

Before he could think about landing another blow, three of the commander's underlings pushed him away. The commander disappeared into his bunker. Sasha, the interpreter, followed him in, trying to explain.

'Sasha, tell him they fucking lied to us, they set us up!' Wilson yelled. 'These cunts deserve to lose this fucking war, if this is how they treat the fucking people who come to fucking help!'

As Wilson ranted, he noticed the commander's underlings had their hands on their pistol holsters. Any one of them would have been justified in putting a bullet in his head, or breaking his nose with a pistol whip. So far they hadn't moved.

Maybe it was because they didn't really know who was to blame. Or maybe it was because they were rear echelon guys, who knew that men who'd come straight from the front, sweaty and wild-eyed, might just fight back.

Or, looking down, it might have been the grenade he was holding in his right hand.

Eh? When had he picked that up?

In his blind rage, he hadn't noticed he was holding it. It was likely, though, that the commander's underlings had.

It snapped him out of his rage. He'd made his point, as it were. If the commander wanted to come out and carry on the argument, he was happy to settle this one with fists. No need to wave a grenade around too.

'Sorry, er, would you mind holding that just now?' he said, handing the grenade to his team. Like he was asking them to hold his jacket.

The commander stayed in his bunker. The guards did nothing except block the door. Suddenly, Wilson began to feel very tired. He turned to the team.

'Fuck it. Let's go home.'

They drove back to a friend's place in Mykolaiv, where the Ukrainians would be less likely to find them. Got blind drunk, swilling vodka like it was water. Someone produced some weed too. Wilson hadn't smoked the stuff since his youth, but toked away.

When he woke up the next morning with a gruesome hangover, it all came back.

Shit, I punched a commander.

Shit, I kicked him.

Shit, I pulled a grenade.

Fuck, where is the water and the aspirin?

Over the next few days, he lay low. Word went round that the Ukrainians were threatening to chuck him in jail, or to kill him. He still didn't care. He'd protected the lives of his men in the field. He wasn't proud of hitting the commander. But someone had to show that the foreigners were prepared to stick up for themselves.

The Ukrainian arrest squad never came. Perhaps they'd forgotten about it. Frontlines were busy places, some new horrible problem every day. Besides, these kind of punch-ups were common. Albeit not necessarily with people pulling grenades as well. In his defence, he hadn't pulled the pin out.

Eventually, wanting to get things over and done with, he went back to the base, found Kilo and apologised. He even got Sasha to teach him the words in Ukrainian. It came out rather mangled, but Kilo seemed mollified. Made some joke about his black eye giving him night vision. They shook hands and agreed to say no more.

That was the advantage of fighting in a real war. If he'd punched and kicked a superior in Afghanistan, he'd have been on his way home under armed escort, bound for military prison. Here in Ukraine, though, there were bigger things to worry about. Soldiers were in too short supply to be carted off to jail. Everyone in uniform was valuable. Even, it seemed, the Free Meat.

10

HERDING CATS IN BATTLE

By the summer of 2022, the Legion's ranks had thinned considerably. Ukraine's government, which had gleefully trumpeted that 20,000 had signed up in the first fortnight, was rather less vocal about how many had left, refusing to give any updated figures. But on the volunteers' WhatsApp groups and Facebook pages, many made it clear that life in the Legion fell somewhat short of following in Orwell or Hemingway's footsteps.

The exodus was fuelled by the growing number of cautionary tales from the battlefield. The death of ex-Marine Scott Sibley and the capture of Andrew Hill and John Harding showed that even well-trained soldiers could come unstuck. They were reminders that for all its romantic allure, taking up arms for a noble cause did not guarantee a dignified end. As Orwell himself once wrote, frontlines were where 'bullets hurt, corpses stink, and men under fire are often so frightened that they wet their trousers'.

That was if they got a chance to fight at all. The Legionnaires had arrived well aware that they'd be fighting for an underdog army, less than Nato-standard in terms of command and control. But they did at least expect that mobilisation would be straightforward: report for duty, do some training and then off to the frontline.

Instead, many languished for months in rearward base camps, sleeping in muddy tents, dining off lousy Ukrainian military food, stuck among the Instagrammers and Screamers. Covid was rampant, as if strains imported by volunteers from far and wide had formed their own battalion. There'd be promises of deployment one week, red tape the next, courtesy of Ukraine's military bureaucracy, which hadn't changed much since Soviet times. As volunteers' money ran low, so did morale. If they were going to risk their lives in defence of democracy, they wanted to at least get on with it, not sit around indefinitely under starter's orders.

As time dragged on, many side-stepped the Legion altogether, forming their own mini-units and heading direct to the frontlines to tout their services. While some nations might have baulked at bands of freelancers roaming around, it didn't raise too many eyebrows in Ukraine. Volunteer militias were already well-represented on the frontlines, be it the combat-hardened professionals like Azov, the Georgians or the Dad's Army Home Guard units that had taken up arms since the war.

One such foreign freelance unit that sprang to prominence were the British-led Dark Angels. In June 2022, they crept into the no-man's-land toward Kherson and fired a Javelin missile that destroyed a Russian tank. It was the first time a British-led team had spilt Russian blood in the area since the Crimean War. A few hours later, they were back celebrating with beers in Mykolaiv, uploading smartphone footage of their mission onto social media. The minute-long clip, showing them nonchalantly waving to the camera before firing, made them the envy of many other volunteers.

The Angels weren't some elite group of ex-SAS and US Navy Seals, but a kind of international Dirty Dozen, some with no military experience at all. Among their ranks were a former

New York fashion photographer, a one-time pizza delivery man from France and an ex-convict, Mark Ayres, discharged from the British Army after a conviction for armed robbery. En route to Ukraine, he'd told a TV crew that he didn't want to be 'an old git living in a rented room' at home.

At the centre of the Dark Angels' success story was their commander, a 35-year-old ex-Para named Daniel Burke. As one of the British Army's best infantry units, ex-Paras had a reputation for being sniffy about who else they worked with. Burke, though, had no hang-ups about soldiers of lesser standing, and was happy also to recruit rookies. For all the talk of Ukraine not being a warzone for amateurs, he believed it was possible to learn on the job – something many Ukrainian volunteers had to do anyway.

'People can serve in the military for twenty years, and still be shit because they don't listen or learn,' he'd tell recruits. 'Some amateurs handle themselves in battle better than many professionals I've worked with. All that's important is that you want to fight.

'Besides, when the rounds start coming in and it all starts going to shit, you only remember about ten per cent of what you've learned anyway. It's like your IQ suddenly drops, and you make it up as you go along.'

Burke's willingness to give others the benefit of the doubt reflected the ups and downs of his own military career. Raised in Wythenshawe, a giant housing estate in south Manchester, he'd joined the Paras aged 20, fulfilling an ambition he'd cherished since boyhood. He'd served in Afghanistan during one of the war's most violent periods, returning with PTSD that led to heavy drinking and a brawl. He'd left the army in 2009, drifting through a series of jobs, struggling to replace the sense of purpose he'd found in his childhood dream.

In 2017, inspiration finally came in a dark form. An Isis suicide bomber blew himself up at a concert by the pop singer Ariana Grande at the Manchester Arena, killing 22 people and injuring more than 1,000 others. It was the terror group's deadliest attack on British soil, with many of the casualties teenage girls. Burke had had a cousin in the crowd. The following day, he filled out an online form to join the Kurdish YPG forces fighting Isis in Syria.

Joining the Kurds in their fight against Isis was every bit as daunting a prospect as fighting the Russians in Ukraine. Isis fighters didn't have air power or tanks, but they did have legions of willing 'shaheeds', or martyrs, who'd charge at the Kurdish lines wearing suicide vests, or drive at them in truck bombs covered in makeshift armour plate. Captured Westerners could expect prolonged torture and then beheading.

In one battle during his nine-month tour, Burke and a handful of other YPG fighters were besieged in a house for 17 hours by Isis fighters. They ran low on ammo, food and water, and an RPG round set part of the house ablaze. At one point, he and a comrade contemplated having to use their 'shaheed' (martyr) rounds, a bullet each fighter kept for themselves to avoid being captured alive.

Burke left Syria soon after, exhausted and skint. But he felt like he'd played his own small part in history. Like many of the foreign volunteers, he'd sensed an *esprit de corps* out there, which had parallels with some of Orwell's depictions of workers' revolutionary Spain in *Homage to Catalonia*. The YPG was run on egalitarian, socialist principles, with women allowed to fight as well as men. In Burke's eyes, it was a welcome challenge to the Middle East's conservative Islamic politics, which had nurtured Isis's rise in the first place, and led to outrages like the Manchester Arena bombing.

Unlike Spain's Republicans, the YPG also won their war, playing the main ground role in destroying Isis's Syrian caliphate. Victory cost nearly 12,000 YPG lives, among them at least a dozen of the 400-strong cadre of international volunteers. Burke and his ilk saw themselves as torchbearers of Orwell's freedom-fighting tradition, taking on a foe every bit as malign as 1930s Fascism. But when he returned home, his own government had treated him not as a hero, but as a criminal.

* * *

In late 2019, Burke was leaving the UK for a holiday when he was stopped at Folkestone ferry port by British counter-terrorism police. At first, he'd thought it was a formality. Like most YPG volunteers such as John Harding, he was already used to them questioning him as he came in and out of the country.

He knew why the police were interested. While the YPG itself wasn't listed as a terrorist group in the West, it was mentored by the PKK, or Kurdistan Workers' Party, which was. The PKK had run bombing and kidnapping campaigns that had killed thousands of Turks since the 1980s. In the cops' eyes, Western YPG volunteers could be learning all sorts of terror tactics that the PKK had passed on. Burke understood their concerns. But he also felt he should have the freedom to fight in Syria if he wanted, as long as he hadn't broken the law.

The shifting sands of Middle East politics meant it was no longer quite that simple. In the time since Burke had left the YPG, Turkey had launched a big cross-border military operation against Kurdish forces in northern Syria. It led to direct clashes with the YPG, with a few of the group's British volunteers getting involved. The Turkish government, which viewed Kurdish separatists in much the same way as Britain had viewed the IRA, had made its displeasure clear to Downing Street.

Burke was confident that he'd done nothing wrong. He hadn't even been in Syria when Turkey had launched its invasion. He also pointed out that in his time with the YPG, he'd made a point of trying to help the British police, handing over thumb drives that he'd found in captured Isis positions.

His interrogators, though, had still found something to pin on him. It involved his friend Dan Newey, a fellow YPG volunteer. Burke had bought Newey a cheap plane ticket to Spain, so the two could spend some time holidaying together. But from there, Newey had made his way back to Syria to fight the Turks. In the cops' view, that meant Burke had helped fund Newey's journey. They'd also spotted various text messages he'd sent Newey when pissed, which said things like 'Fuck the Turks' and 'I hate Turkey'. Just stupid drunken rants, but the police had taken it seriously.

They'd held him for 18 straight days in some secret facility in the Midlands, used for quizzing terror suspects. On one trip out of the cell for exercise, he'd bumped into another suspect, a fat man with a long beard, an Isis supporter by the looks of it. His 'terrorist' opposite number, as it were. The cops had hastily dragged them out of sight of each other.

Eventually he was charged with three counts of terrorism, facing potentially up to 15 years behind bars. Prosecutors opposed granting him bail, fearing he was a flight risk. At Westminster Magistrates Court, he was told he'd be remanded to Wandsworth Prison, one of London's roughest jails. A cramped Victorian shithole. Postcode wars. Drug barons. Muslim gangs.

He was driven there in a custody van with other defendants, several of them ranting, threatening violence. Then, in some reception pen at the prison, he'd seen the fat Isis guy who'd been at the anti-terror unit in Coventry, who was grinning at him, thinking he'd met a fellow traveller.

'Hey, I saw you in Coventry, we are brothers, *inshallah*!'

'I am not your fucking brother, mate, get the fuck away from me!'

Burke was scheduled to be held on D-wing, which contained a number of Islamist terror suspects. Any one of whom, he feared, might try to kill him once they found out why he was in there. One of the guards had noticed his wristband for Help for Heroes, the ex-soldiers' charity. When Burke had explained why he was wearing it, they'd shifted him into another wing for his own protection.

He still felt terrified. The only time he dared go out of his cell was for trips to the exercise yard, which didn't soothe his nerves. Dodgy characters everywhere. Several of the guards sympathised with his plight, and introduced him to a few other inmates who were ex-Forces: a bank robber from Preston and an arms dealer to the London underworld. Not his natural choice of company, maybe, but in jail, there was strength in numbers.

The guards warned that he was still potentially a target. C-wing wasn't full of terrorists, but it did have Muslim inmates. Luckily, one of them was a British-Libyan career criminal, who wielded some clout on the wing. The man said his grandfather had been killed by Isis in Libya, and admired Burke for going to fight them.

Burke spent seven months on remand, just about coping, far from convinced that he could handle a further 15 years. Then, just as he was preparing to face trial, the case against him was abruptly dropped at the Old Bailey.

The prosecution gave no explanation why it had suddenly changed its mind, beyond saying that the 'legal test for a prosecution could no longer be met'. Burke's legal team claimed, however, that the case had been dropped after they had sought a disclosure order about whether the government brought the prosecutions to appease the Turkish government, which had been threatening to sever trade links.

Burke thought he had simply been made an example to deter others. He exited Wandsworth's giant front gates the following day, giving his remaining stash of food to the arms dealer and the bank robber.

After his release, he returned to Manchester, working in a concreting firm with his brothers. Thanks to the publicity around the court case, the Wandsworth One was now something of a local hero, which proved a mixed blessing. Every time someone came up to shake his hand was a reminder of how easy it would be for some Isis fanatic to do the same.

But he retained fond memories of his time with the YPG, whose emblems were tattooed on his forearms. It had never been about the bragging rights anyway. What he'd loved was the adventure, the sense of purpose – a band of volunteers from across the globe, united against a genocidal enemy. In a world of moral grey areas, it was a black and white cause, as righteous a war as one would ever find, and a chance that probably wouldn't come along again. Until, that was, Putin sent his tanks into Ukraine.

*　　*　　*

Unlike most volunteers in Ukraine, Burke hadn't come out planning to take up arms. He was, he told people, still 'burnt out' by Syria. Instead, he'd started out by doing aid deliveries in his black SUV, which had inspired the name for his unit, the Dark Angels. He'd spent his first few weeks helping to supply a children's orphanage in western Ukraine. But after reports emerged of the Russian atrocities at Irpin and Bucha, he'd changed his mind. Already well-versed in fighting other people's wars, he brought a certain nous to bear. In a world where others were wondering why things weren't better-run, he was a leader of men: a natural organiser, who knew how to schmooze the local military command and to make the Dark Angels useful.

The seasoned ex-soldiers respected him as a combat veteran. The novices liked the fact that he was friendly, approachable and not standoffish. All too often, ex-Paras or Green Berets in the Legion's ranks wouldn't give the time of day to combat virgins. His only condition for taking on apprentice Angels was that they heeded his advice, and understood what they were letting themselves in for. Among those who joined the Dark Angels was Sam Newey, the younger brother of Burke's old YPG friend Dan Newey. Burke had advised him to train first as a medic, to see if he could handle the wounded, the dead and stress.*

He also reminded volunteers that fighting other people's wars involved using other people's kit. Just as Orwell wrote of Spanish volunteers making do with nineteenth-century rifles that fell apart, Burke felt that Legionnaires should accustom themselves to equipment that was borrowed, broken or blood-ied.

'Some people come here expecting Gucci-level body armour and rifles, but the first gun I was given here had grass and blood on it, and the second one I had the trigger fell off,' he'd tell other volunteers. 'Of course you're going to get fuck-all. I've already spent £15,000 of my own money here. We're here to help, not just pose around in smart kit on Facebook.'

---

* Sam Newey would later be killed while fighting in eastern Ukraine in August 2023.

Some volunteers were sniffy about Burke's operation, dismissing it as a military creche. But many newcomers found him a useful source of help and inspiration. Among them was Michel Arnaud, a French volunteer, who typified the more idealistic, altruistic side of the volunteer fraternity. His day job was as a pilot with Air France, ferrying Boeing 787 passengers across the Atlantic. But he'd never forgotten watching *Land and Freedom*, the British film director Ken Loach's romantic depiction of Spain's International Brigades.

When the invasion had begun, he'd seen WhatsApp groups from Polish air traffic controllers appealing for help to relocate Ukrainian refugees, and went to the Polish border to offer whatever help he could. He'd bumped into Burke there, and helped him do aid runs into Ukraine from Manchester. When the Dark Angels then took up arms down in Mykolaiv, Arnauld had followed suit, playing a rearguard role in some of the frontline missions.

The Angels' base in Mykolaiv was an abandoned children's hospital, which became a hub for both military and humanitarian volunteers, who'd meet there for evening barbecues. At times, Arnaud felt it was recreating the spirit of *Land and Freedom* – people from all over the world, coming together to defend liberty and values. It took energetic, charismatic figures like Burke, though, to galvanise them, to give them the confidence that they could learn as they went.

Yet of all those who'd gather at the Dark Angels' HQ each evening, the one who often looked least relaxed was Burke himself. Being in charge of a unit could be a thankless task, much of it devoted to humdrum admin issues. He seemed to spend as many hours fixing toilets as fighting Russians. He was on the phone constantly, hustling 24/7. Why had his latest recruit's paperwork not come through? Could someone please tow that truck that had broken down? Who the fuck had recommended those cheap Chinese tourniquets? Yeah, the ones that snapped if they were tightened too much?

On top of being part diplomat and part quartermaster, he was part social worker, sorting out personal issues and squabbles among his troops. Unlike in a regular army, where a commander's word was law, here it was like herding cats in battle. The volunteers, as a whole, were not life's natural conformers. For every Dark Angel who deferred to his authority, others deemed it strictly optional. Some, if bored, would try to go Rambo by planning solo missions behind his back – an easy way, Burke warned, to go home in a body bag.

'I am fighting two wars here,' he'd tell anyone who'd listen. 'One is against the Russians, and the other is just trying to form a unit in the first place. Sometimes that seems like the harder battle.'

11

AN OFFICER AND GENTLEMAN

From his home in north London, Richard Johnson had watched TV coverage of the first days of Ukraine's invasion with as much anger as anyone. What upset him was not just the fleeing refugees and burning buildings, but the footage of Ukrainians fighting back. Yes, they were brave, yes they stood their ground. But anyone watching with an informed eye could see them making mistakes everywhere. Who had sited that defensive position on a forward slope, easy for the advancing Russians to see and shell? Why did that commander have his armoured vehicle blocking that bridge, when it should have been out of sight, ready for ambush?

The list in his head went on and on, and those were just the ones he spotted from TV clips. God only knew what bigger, strategic errors were being made. There was no point in the West cheering Ukraine on if its gallant defenders were going to be slaughtered en masse for lack of decent commanders. Sure, Ukraine had willing footsoldiers aplenty, but in large-scale, mechanised warfare it was good officers who'd really count, who'd make the difference between spirited resistance and outright victory.

Johnson considered himself such a man. Not a Montgomery, Rommel or Henry V, just a former British Army captain, who'd

lived and breathed the military since he was a kid. A graduate of
the officer training course at Sandhurst, he'd served in Northern
Ireland, run jungle warfare schools and been the British Army's
youngest rifle company commander. Plus two years in Germany,
training for high-intensity armoured battlegroup operations.
He'd quit the military nearly 20 years ago, having failed selection
for the SAS, and had become a high-level private security consultant. He'd trained the Singapore Police, looked after blue-chip
businesses in Iraq, evacuated foreigners from a civil war in
Africa.

None of which, he knew, would make him Ukraine's knight
in shining armour. But in his view, even the most bog-standard
British Army officer was still a world-class warrior. People
thought Sandhurst was just some posh military finishing school,
churning out 'Ruperts', as officers were nicknamed by the lower
ranks. Nonsense. Sandhurst was the Oxbridge of combat –
tough to get into, tougher still to graduate from, designed to
produce commanders who were the better of anyone, including
their own troops. They knew weapons and fieldcraft inside out,
did the hardest physical training, could complete a complex
battleplan after three days without sleep. All to help them lead
by example, so others would follow them into danger.

Within days of Zelensky's appeal, Johnson emailed the
Ukrainian embassy in London, and was invited in to meet its
defence attaché. He was better qualified than most volunteers
and, unlike some, was not going to Ukraine to address some
void in his home life. He led a comfortable life in London, had
a decent income and, at 48, no great desire to test himself to his
limits in battle. But he didn't have family, was between work
projects and – frankly – was at his best when things were going
to shit, when others started to get fed up. Call it the arrogance
of the officer class. Or call it just being good at the job.

*   *   *

Johnson arrived in Ukraine in early March, bringing with him a small green ringbinder given to him as a parting gift by an old army pal. A Tactical Aide Memoire – the British Army's answer to the Bible, covering everything from how to man a roadblock through to techniques for fortifying a street or house. It was an old one from the Cold War era, packed full of information about how to fight the Russian military in a European land war. How they'd advance, what weapons they used, how to thwart their clunky top-down command-and-control systems. Everything he'd need in Ukraine.

Everything, that was, except a chapter titled: 'What to do if half of your fellow soldiers are idiots.' Which he could have done with when he'd reached the Legion training base at Yavoriv. He'd known Zelensky's appeal might attract a few unsuitable candidates, but not on this scale. In his dormitory next to him were three ageing members of a biker gang, sporting leather jackets, long grey hair and beer bellies. Barely fit for a charity bike run, let alone combat. Somewhere else he'd met a Scandinavian sniper, who claimed to have worked as a mercenary for a drug cartel in Latin America. Worrying enough if he was just making it up, even more worrying if true. And then there were the TikTokers. All over the bloody barracks, people skipping up and down the corridors with their smartphones: 'Look, I'm in Ukraine, I've come to fight the Russians!' No concept of signals security whatsoever, putting everyone's lives at risk. He'd read the riot act to some of them, as had a few other old salts, but there were far too many to deal with. Globally, #Hanging@CampYavoriv was probably trending by now.

On his second night there, he'd raised the matter with the colonel in command of the camp, whom he'd already tried to establish a rapport with. Officer-to-officer, as it were.

'Colonel, you've got to get a grip on this – either take people's phones off them, or block the signal. Your electromagnetic signature here is going to be off the scale.'

The colonel, a decent enough fellow but clearly run off his feet, had shrugged.

'What can I do? That's beyond my powers.'

'Well, if you don't do that, then get some anti-aircraft batteries in here, or some short-range missiles up on the rooftops. Because I'm telling you, you're going to get some attention, without a doubt.'

'As I say, what can I do about any of that?'

'You're the *fucking commanding officer*. You can do what you want. It's your camp.'

The following day, Johnson organised a trench-digging detail in the woods, constructing three big foxholes to take cover in, should the base be attacked. A few onlookers had sniggered. *Look at the British Army captain, playing his wargames, ordering everyone around.* They sniggered less when the missiles had landed two nights later, 500 kg of explosive each, the loudest bangs any of them had ever heard. After that, they'd been cramming into the trenches, fighting each other to get in.

He didn't want to say: 'I told you so.' But the fact was, he bloody had. In fact, as everyone milled around afterwards, realising what a narrow escape they'd had, he'd realised something else. He was enjoying himself. He was in his element.

* * *

After the Yavoriv fiasco, Johnson had become the de facto leader of a team of volunteers, their original leader having announced that he was heading back to Poland. When Johnson had said he was pressing on to Kyiv, most of the others had followed him. It wasn't hard to figure why. The Legion had not attracted many trained officers, to put it mildly, and the alternative was being commanded by a Ukrainian of unknown provenance. Besides, in Johnson's experience, whatever the average soldier might think of officers, it was to them they always looked when things got diffi-cult, when life-or-death judgement calls had to be made. If only so they could blame the stupid Rupert afterwards if it all went wrong.

Luckily, he'd found a good ex-Royal Marine, Greg*, as his second-in-command, who also liked things done by the book. Like the set of movement orders Johnson had drawn up when they'd moved south from Kyiv, setting out destination times, stopping points, emergency procedures. Just a bunch of notes pinned to a wall, but better than just piling down there in a minibus and hoping for the best. Made his deputy's day. 'Yes, now we're talking. British officer in charge ...'

Like nearly every group of volunteers down in Mykolaiv, they'd had a mixed reception. Pulling rank, Johnson had gained an audience with a local brigade commander, only to be given the world's most inept briefing about the wider threat picture. Whether the commander didn't trust foreigners, or was just plain incompetent, wasn't clear. What *was* clear was that Ukrainian command was far from Nato standard. Far too many top brass, far too many of whom seemed to be someone's uncle or brother. Like that idiot who'd dug a load of trenches right next to a village gas mains. Perfect for being burned alive in when a Russian shell landed.

Then there was just the lack of attention to planning and detail, the boring stuff that actually mattered. As the old military saying went: 'Infantry win battles, logistics win wars.' During mission briefs, there were no battle plans, written orders, combat estimates. Nobody even taking notes. Instead they just nodded their heads, trying to remember everything, then wondered why it all came undone later.

The only one who really impressed Johnson was a local commander called Roman Kostenko, who doubled as an MP. Plenty of Ukrainian politicians had taken to posing in military kit since the invasion began, but Kostenko was the real deal. A career special forces soldier, he'd fought the separatists in 2014, and ran the national security committee in the Kyiv parliament, where he was tipped as a future defence minister. When Mykolaiv had come under attack, he'd swapped his suit for his military uniform, helping to push the Russians back. His office in Mykolaiv had become a makeshift weapons dump, stacked high with munitions. Among them were British-supplied anti-tank missiles, for which he made his gratitude clear to Johnson.

In late March, he'd enlisted the help of Johnson's team to defend Oleksandrivka, a village overlooking the estuary south of Mykolaiv.* The Russians wanted to capture it for use as a staging post for another assault on Mykolaiv itself. It was an insight into how severely outgunned the Ukrainians were. Around 90 Ukrainian troops were based in the village, armed with a few anti-tank weapons but not much else. Parked up outside Oleksandrivka on three sides was a Russian motor rifle regiment with about 60 pieces of armour. From midnight one night, the Russians had pulverised the village for three hours non-stop. Heavy artillery, mortars and Tornado missiles, a souped-up version of the Grad, spraying vast areas with cluster

---

* The following month, Andrew Hill would help rescue 60 Ukrainians from Oleksandrivka, and later be taken PoW there.

bomblets. The bombardment had been so intense that an old lady in the village had had a heart attack.

Johnson, too, had felt his heart briefly flutter at dawn the following morning. While manning an OP on Oleksandrivka's outskirts, he saw a set of white flares go up from the Russian lines. It was a scene straight out of his Tactical Aide Memoire, the prelude to an old-school Soviet mechanised assault. Then the sound of heavy engines revving, tanks and fighting vehicles on the move, the ground shaking. An entire armoured column, heading their way. They wouldn't stand a chance. *Fucking hell, I'm going to die.*

Then, just as two of the tanks were nosing their way towards the village, Kostenko's troops showed some class. Speaking deliberately on an open radio channel, soldiers manning two different positions staged a frantic conversation.

'Fuck, the Russian tanks are coming right at us! How many Javelins have you got? I've got five.'

'Me? I've got seven.'

'Okay, I'll bring mine over to where you are.'

It was nonsense. They had no Javelins whatsoever, just a few ageing RPGs. But the Russians, whom they knew would be listening in, thought they'd be driving into a well-prepared ambush. The two tanks stopped, fired off a couple of rounds, then pulled back. The attack stopped. All thanks to two smart Ukrainians and a cheeky ruse on an elderly, unencrypted army radio. A classic piece of military deception. Not something he'd seen mentioned in his Tactical Aide Memoire.

Terrifying as it was, it was also an insight into how tactically poor the Russians were. He'd expected better from the great Cold War foe. They'd shelled until 3 a.m., then not attacked until 5 a.m. Why the delay? The whole idea of an artillery barrage was do it just minutes before an assault, dazing the enemy troops and charging in while they were still tending to their casualties. Also, why signal their attack with a flare, broadcasting their intentions to all and sundry? Couldn't the commander just set a time in combat orders, and make sure everyone synchronised watches? Come to think of it, why wait until it got light at all, rather than use their night vision capabilities?

He'd left Oleksandrivka with a new appreciation for the ingenuity of Ukrainian forces. They'd stood their ground, and outfoxed a far bigger enemy. Then, later, he'd bumped into one of Kostenko's men, who'd told him that out of the 90 soldiers supposed to have been protecting the village, only 19 had actually been there. The other 71 had left because of the intensity of the shelling, while two infantry companies who were supposed to have turned up had decided to stay out of town altogether. So not a glorious day for either side, really, except those smart Ukrainians bullshitting over the radio.

* * *

He and Kostenko got on well. Like Johnson, Kostenko had wanted to be a soldier since he was a kid, and was a military history buff. At his home in a village near Kherson, he had an entire military library, now looted by the Russian troops who had occupied the city. He struck Johnson as a natural leader – firm but not arrogant, always trying to learn. At the end of one lively frontline recce with Johnson, he'd given his own troops what appeared to be a mild dressing down. When Johnson had asked what had been said, one of Kostenko's comrades replied: 'You all think you are Special Forces, but if you want to know what a professional soldier looks like, then look at Richard and go on a patrol with him.' He'd felt a surge of pride, even if it did come at the cost of a few dirty looks from Kostenko's men.

He wasn't doing anything special, really. Just standard British infantry recon stuff, pushing it that bit further than the Ukrainians. Like the time he'd gone up to take a peek at a large Russian position in one village, crawling through irrigation ditches full of brambles, as thorny as anything during jungle warfare training in Belize. The only way to do it was super-slowly, to avoid giveaway rustles or movement, which meant it took two hours to move just a few hundred metres. But it got him 50 metres from the Russians, close enough to watch a bunch of them sitting around getting pissed. 'That's how close you need to get,' he'd told the Ukrainians. 'Then you need to stay out there, all day, overnight, keep proper watch.'

Not every Ukrainian commander was receptive to his wisdom. He did his best to be diplomatic, offering polite advice, writing up battle plans if requested, sticking his oar in where he felt he could. But for every Kostenko who welcomed his input, others saw a smart-arse Brit trying to tell them their business. Much as the Ukrainians had guts as a nation, they also had pride, and that stopped some of them being willing to learn. Which saddened him, especially when they made mistakes that cost lives.

Some of the volunteers in his own command weren't eager to learn either. On the one hand, it was great to work with people who'd come to Ukraine of their own free will, who wanted to fight. On the other hand, every army in the world, professional or voluntary, had its problem children, who chafed under authority, They thought they were SAS-style mavericks, who didn't need to do things by the book. They weren't. They were just dicks, who didn't realise that procedures were there for a reason.

Most of the time, he let it go. No point in trying too much spit and polish, especially when they knew he had no formal authority. But that was no excuse for sloppy habits, like going out on patrol without a helmet, not carrying enough water, not cleaning weapons or taking regular showers. Out in the field, where he generally knew best, they tended to fall in line. Every so often, though, he'd had to lay down the law, and occasionally it had nearly come to blows. He'd offered to fight any one of them, if that was what they wanted.

As time went on, however, it grew harder to turn the other cheek. One day in June, they'd been at an OP near the Russian lines, to provide flank protection for an attack the following morning. Just him, his second-in-command Greg, and a Polish volunteer, Dima*, who doubled as their interpreter. Dima was good at languages, less good at following orders. He'd wear a baseball cap on missions rather than a helmet, which wound Johnson up no end.

It had been a long tough day already, the OP in an exposed spot, everyone tetchy. A Russian drone was prowling overhead, fraying nerves further. A Ukrainian team who were supposed to be with them invented some excuse to pull out, much to Johnson's irritation. That left the three of them there alone, Dima demanding to know why they weren't withdrawing too.

'Why are we staying when those guys are going?' he asked Johnson.

'They are just being stupid, they're scared,' Johnson replied.

'Maybe it's you who are being stupid,' Dima said.

'What? What did you say?'

'I said maybe it's you who are being stupid. For staying here.'

'Right, I'm going to give you once chance to take that back, what you just said.'

'No, I think you're stupid.'

Something inside Johnson snapped. The next thing he knew, he'd leaped on Dima and grabbed him by the throat, pinning him to the ground, choking him out.

'I've had enough of you, you fucking little shit! Stop it or I will fucking end you!'

Dima was punching back, right-hooking as hard as he could. But Johnson was bigger than him, and had him pinned to the floor in a choke hold. He'd sized Dima up quickly beforehand, figured he could handle him. Careful battle planning as ever. Greg, his deputy, looked on, reluctant to take sides but rolling his eyes. Forward OPs weren't ideal places for punch-ups.

Johnson choked Dima until he was half-passing out, then let him go, sacking him when they got back to base. It wasn't exactly conduct becoming of an officer and gentleman, to assault one of his own soldiers. But he'd had enough. Not just of Dima, but of all the pressures of being in command with no back-up, of not a day going by without his authority being questioned, his advice being ignored. Wars weren't won by bloody committee.

He spent the new few days in Mykolaiv sporting a black eye, courtesy of one of the blows that Dima managed to land. Johnson later learned that he was a middleweight martial arts champion back in Poland. By rights, Johnson should probably have come off worst. Then again, his subordinate probably hadn't expected that a well-spoken ex-British officer would ever attack him. Plus his helmet had shielded him from the worst of it. If nothing else, Dima would perhaps now appreciate why it was important to wear one.

A few weeks later, Johnson decamped up to Kyiv, where he did some advisory work with the Legion's command. It was clear already, both to him and many others, that things needed to be better organised. Despite having been a magnet for cranks, delinquents and fools who wouldn't wear helmets, the Legion had also attracted some decent operators, whose efforts were being squandered. Rather than working as coordinated, effective units, they were scattering everywhere – some in Mykolaiv, others in Kharkiv or the Donbas – doing lots of little operations that made no strategic difference. Too much nibbling on the Russians, not enough chomping.

12

TRAUMA THERAPY

As they tried to make their way in a war that didn't always want them, most Legionnaires did find other consolations to life in Ukraine. While the battlefield was often hard to reach, time away from the frontlines revealed a land far pleasanter than many had expected.

For a start, they were at least welcome. For every Ukrainian commander who shunned their help, some passer-by would thank them for being there. In the streets, elderly *babusyas* would wander up, offering kisses and bags of home-cooked pancakes. In coffee shops, attempts to inquire 'How much?' in pidgin Ukrainian would meet with a dismissive wave of the hand. On patrols through villages, there'd be invites into cottages for snacks of *salo*, a Ukrainian dried pork delicacy, washed down with shots of moonshine vodka.

Ukraine's charms went beyond traditional hospitality. Most volunteers had come anticipating some grim, post-Soviet backwater, one that hadn't even made it to Eastern Europe's budget stag-do circuit. Instead, they found all the Western comforts they could want. Kyiv had bars and restaurants that wouldn't have looked out of place in Brooklyn or Hoxton. Even in provincial cities like Mykolaiv, it wasn't hard to find sourdough pizza and craft ale. Nor did the volunteers always dine alone.

Foreign fighters often drew attention from Ukrainian women – who, it was widely agreed, were the Slavic answer to the Swedes when it came to looks.

For veterans of Iraq or Afghanistan, where the local populations had turned against them, it was a different world. Rather than spend their time confined to heavily fortified bases, here they could wander the streets freely, not having to worry about being kidnapped or beheaded. The people they'd come to protect weren't tipping off insurgents about where to blow them up. Local kids weren't hurling rocks.

But it wasn't just the locals' gratitude that made the volunteers feel glad to be there. It was the simple moral righteousness of the war, which felt far clearer than the West's messy interventions in the Middle East. Not only had Iraq and Afghanistan been tough campaigns, but many veterans did not even have the consolation of feeling that they'd been doing the right thing. Defending Ukraine, by contrast, felt like standing up to the same naked, unprovoked aggression that saw Hitler invade Poland. For the first time in living memory – or since before Vietnam, anyway – they knew they were the good guys.

Among them was ex-US serviceman Alex Drueke, who'd served two tours of duty in Iraq. Like many other Americans, he'd signed up after 9/11, only to learn the long, slow and painful way that the War on Terror would prove no easier to win than the war in Vietnam. On his first tour of Iraq, he was 100 per cent behind it. By the second he was having his doubts. Ukraine was a chance to finally be on the right side of history.

For Drueke, though, it wasn't just about moral absolution. His time in Iraq had left him with crippling PTSD, which had helped wreck two marriages and left him unable to hold down a job. He'd come to Ukraine for a showdown with his demons, for better or for worse, to see if he could harness his jumpy, combat-flayed nerves for something useful. It wasn't exactly a textbook approach to therapy, more a final roll of the dice. After all, the last time he'd raised a gun in anger the weapon had been pointed at his own head.

*　　*　　*

Drueke was born in Alabama in America's Deep South, into a family that had been fighting for two and a half centuries. His forefathers had served in every major American conflict since the War of Independence. A grandfather who'd reached the rank of colonel had been Drueke's early role model in life. An uncle had fought in Desert Storm in 1991. Joining the military had also given the teenage Drueke the self-discipline he needed. In his last couple of years at high school he'd been getting into trouble, doing drugs and messing around. Nine-eleven had been a wake-up call, the moment he'd got his life together and signed up.

Drueke joined the US Army Reserve as a part-timer, reaching the rank of staff sergeant. In the first tour of Iraq, he helped guard US military supply convoys. In the second he was part of an elite VIP escort unit, guarding four-star generals and visiting dignitaries. Every convoy was a magnet for attack by al-Qaeda and Iran-backed insurgents, hoping to take out a high-ranking general or visiting secretary of state. As lead gunner, Drueke sat in the turret of an armoured Humvee at the front of the convoys, scanning the road ahead for trouble. Threats lurked round every corner: suicide bombers, snipers perched in buildings, carloads of insurgent ambush squads. Often, the top gunner wouldn't even see the threat coming. After one mission, Drueke returned to base to discover a dent from a sniper round in his turret shield. Three inches higher and it would have gone through his throat.

In his turret, he was armed with a 0.50 calibre machine gun, far more powerful than an M16 or a Kalashnikov. It could stop an oncoming car bomber in their tracks, or punch through a brick wall to kill a sniper. But it wasn't just people that he had to watch out for. The insurgents' favourite method of attack was roadside bombs, which could be buried in concrete, disguised as rubbish or even placed inside dead cats and dogs. As he scanned the route ahead, every pothole, every trash can, every piece of litter and roadkill represented a potential hazard.

He enjoyed it, but it was nine months of pure stress, on the road all day every day, his top half sticking out the vehicle, a target for snipers, grenades, everything. There was no choice but to make absolute peace with death, to live a good life while one could.

Upon his return to the US, that proved harder than expected. Drueke was now an adrenaline junkie, seeking constantly to recreate the intensity of his time in deployment. He'd drive down his local highway at 120 mph, sometimes drunk, just for the hell of it.

He blamed it on the state of hyper-vigilance he'd had to maintain in Iraq, where every single person, every car, every piece of trash could be a threat. Reflexes that had kept him alive out there, however, were a liability back home. Being out in public got difficult. If a car backfired, he thought he was being shot at. Once he had to leave a party when someone burst a balloon. Driving down a highway, he'd change lanes rather than drive over trash, even if it meant going into the oncoming lane.

He knew he probably had PTSD, but refused to acknowledge it. The America he'd grown up in was no longer the one depicted in movies like *The Deer Hunter*, where veterans' trauma went unrecognised. But a PTSD diagnosis could still hobble the prospects of any career-minded military man. So rather than seeking advice on techniques to deal with it, he relied on alcohol, as many veterans did. His marriage, already strained by his prolonged absences in Iraq, dissolved.

Drueke remained functional, holding down a day job while taking a bachelor's degree in leadership. Having commanded 40 other soldiers in Iraq, he was still keen to qualify as an officer. He dreamed of becoming a one-star general, outdoing his beloved grandpa colonel by one rank.

Yet by the time he applied for officer training in 2012, America had tired of fighting other people's wars. US forces were drawing down in Iraq and Afghanistan. Recruitment for future commanders was being scaled down. Seeking another job that might suit his skill set, he trained as a police officer, only to find it harder than expected. While the average Alabama felon wasn't as dangerous as an Iraqi insurgent, the rules of engagement were far stricter, and very triggering for his PTSD. You couldn't just point a 0.50 calibre at a drunk driver, knowing you could obliterate them if they didn't obey commands.

By now, his second marriage was failing too, as was what remained of his self-esteem. Not only had he lost out on his cherished army career but he couldn't even make it as a cop. During one particularly bad week, he found himself in despair each morning.

Do I want to put my uniform on and go to work? Or do I want to shoot myself?

One night, he went out into his backyard and put a gun to his head. His army career had ended. He couldn't fit back properly into the civilian world. He came very close to pulling the trigger, stopping only when he thought how devastated his mother would be.

Just like 9/11 nearly 20 years before, it made him realise he had to get his act together. No more sitting around moping, like a character from some downbeat country song. He contacted the Department of Veterans Affairs, where he was assessed as having serious PTSD and given a disability pension. That meant he never had to work again if he didn't want to. He started doing stretches of the Appalachian Trail, a 2,200-mile trek from Georgia to Maine that began near his home.

Made famous by the book *A Walk in the Woods*, the trail was already popular with people at a crossroads in life. Its valleys and ridgeways were packed with ex-soldiers, the divorced and bereaved, folk moving on from booze, drugs and broken homes. As someone who ticked many of those boxes, Drueke loved it. Eventually, he set his heart on doing the entire trail in one go, selling his house, car and belongings. In spring 2020, he set off on what he hoped would be an epic journey, one that would end with him back on the right path in life.

He'd done just over 200 miles when the Covid pandemic hit, halting him in his tracks. With no home to go back to, he ended up living alone at an old Drueke family farmhouse, adopting a rescue dog, Diesel, for company.

Then, in early 2022, he'd watched the Ukraine invasion on TV. Straightaway, he knew he wanted to go. Given his PTSD, many might have advised him to give the Appalachian Trail another try. But to Drueke, Ukraine seemed like the one place where his overwrought, hyper-vigilant instincts might serve him well. And if he volunteered to fight, it might save some young Ukrainian man who didn't have combat skills from risking his life.

* * *

By the time Drueke had put his affairs in order, the war was already six weeks in, and the Legion's bureaucracy overloaded. Volunteers sat idle in its recruitment bases, awaiting deployments that were constantly postponed.

Drueke wasn't too concerned. As a former platoon sergeant, he figured he'd be more useful as an instructor than on the frontline. When he got a slot to train some rookie Ukrainian forces, he felt a sense of purpose in life for the first time since leaving Iraq. There were 18-year-old kids on the parade ground, and a pensioner with his arm in a cast. They were keen to learn, and his knowledge was appreciated. The PTSD didn't bother him either, even when the town he was in was hit by Russian missiles. If anything, being back in a combat zone felt a little more normal.

However, after constant issues with paperwork, the training was discontinued. Seeking other work, Drueke and an ex-US marine named Andy Huynh ended up with Taskforce Baguette, a volunteer unit that included several Frenchmen. Baguette were attached to Ukraine's 92nd Mechanised Brigade based around Kharkiv, Ukraine's second-biggest city. It was up in the north-east, just 20 miles from the Russian border. As with Kyiv, the Russians had sought to capture Kharkiv during the first month of the invasion, only to be beaten back. But they still occupied much of the surrounding province, with battles raging around the border.

The newcomers arrived at Baguette's base in early June 2022, and were invited on a mission straightaway. A recon job was planned for the following morning near Izbytske, a village less than five miles from the Russian frontier. Drueke wasn't particularly keen, because their paperwork with the Ukrainian military hadn't been finalised yet. He sensed, though, that that if they turned the mission down, they'd be seen as pansies, not quite up for it. Plus it seemed a straightforward tasking – just setting up drones to look for Russian artillery, and passing the locations to the 92nd …

*   *   *

Izbytske was an hour and a half's drive from Kharkiv, in a belt of pine forests and lakes that flanked the Russian border. A team of eight Baguette volunteers set off the following morning, running late because of delays in securing equipment. By the time their three trucks neared the village, what had previously been a largely static frontline was no more. Previous intelligence had estimated just a few Russians in the area. Now the newcomers learned that an entire Russian mechanised battalion was advancing, with tanks, armoured personnel carriers and at least 100 troops. Artillery sounded around them, incoming and outgoing, getting louder and nearer.

They were told that the main Ukrainian unit in the area wanted to retreat, and that they were to cover their exit. They set up a perimeter, fanning out into the woodlands, some of the team already getting nervous. When word came that the larger Russian force was encroaching on three sides, one Baguette member suggested leaving before it was too late.

Soon Drueke glimpsed the Russians with his own eyes. Through a gap in the woods, he spied a Russian BMP fighting vehicle heading down a dirt track, slithering on caterpillar tracks like some giant reptile, a big white 'Z' daubed on its side. About 15 soldiers patrolling beside it, spread up and down the road.

It was time for Baguette to pull out. Then, as they prepared to up stakes, their team leader discovered that their sniper and their machine-gunner were missing. Neither were in the positions where he'd last seen them. A tense discussion ensued over whether to stay behind and look for them, or get out while they still could.

Some of the team wanted to leave straightaway. Drueke and Huynh, remembering their US military doctrine, felt they had no choice but to stay. Comrades were never left behind, no matter what. And if they drove off in the truck without the missing men, they'd be stuck on their own with no means to escape. They didn't want that on their conscience.

Eventually, the team split. Some drove back to Kharkiv. Drueke, Huynh and the team leader stayed put. They relocated to near a dirt track junction in the forest, with good vantage points. The team leader disappeared back into the woods to resume the manhunt, hollering the missing men's names. As he did so, Drueke heard an engine starting up. Not a car or lorry. Something much bigger. A low, loud rumble, plus a high-pitched turbine whine, like a jet plane.

The noise was coming from the direction of a nearby T-junction, where 40 tonnes of metal, driven by an 800 horse-power engine, was now grinding its way towards them. A Russian T72 tank.

As it neared them, Huynh readied an RPG. They'd been trained on them in the Legion. Basic, shoot-and-scoot devices, designed to be simple to use. From their vantage point in a dugout at the edge of the woods, they'd have a reasonable line of fire. Close enough to hit the tank as it went past. Far enough away to then scarper. But if they missed, the big beast would know where they were.

When the tank was about 80 metres away, Huynh took aim.

'Be cool, man,' Drueke whispered back. 'Be cool.'

As he spoke, Huynh fired. A deafening bang, a cloud of exhaust smoke engulfing them. But no explosion at the other end. The round missed the tank, disappearing into the woods. There was no time to reload.

They fled back into the woods, zigzagging to make themselves a harder target. Behind them, the tank fired twice, rounds crashing somewhere into the trees. They threw themselves in the first dugout they came across. Inside, they found themselves grinning at each other. The grins of men who, if nothing else, were still alive.

'Jesus, did we just get shot at by a tank?' Drueke whispered.

Huynh's grin didn't last. He looked at Drueke, suddenly serious.

'I've decided I want to live,' he said.

It wasn't quite clear what Huynh meant. No soldier wanted to die. But something in Huynh's tone suggested he was communicating something else. Like *Hey, Alex, I think you might be ready to fight, and I don't want to.*

There wasn't time to talk about it right now. Outside the dugout, the battle was getting louder, closer. Artillery, mortars, the odd burst of small arms fire shredding tree leaves. No telling who was firing what, or from where. Drueke guessed that the retreating Ukrainian force was probably trying to slow the Russian advance. At one point, there was a huge explosion on the road where they'd seen the tank. Later, they'd find out that it had driven over a Ukrainian land mine.

They stayed in the dugout for two hours, wondering what to do. Even if they could get back to one of the trucks, the roads were now too risky. No telling which ones the Russians now controlled. Staying put wasn't an option either. If the Russians secured the territory, they'd check every dugout in the area. Drueke's old staff sergeant's instincts were also coming out. He felt a duty of care to get Huynh out alive. The guy was younger than him, only 26. Had his whole life ahead. And nothing to

156

prove. It took guts to fire an RPG at a tank, whether you hit it or not.

The best plan, Drueke figured, was to trek back through the forest towards Kharkiv. This would not be like *A Walk in the Woods*. Kharkiv was 30 miles away as the crow flew. They had no maps, no idea of the route. Huynh's wristwatch had a GPS, but all it showed was a dot indicating Kharkiv, with a blank screen in between. No way to see roads and bridges, let alone contested territory. The only hope was that the forest would give them cover, and that sooner or later, they'd reach somewhere friendly. They set off, sneaking past abandoned fighting positions, watching for landmines and trip wires.

There were no paths to follow, and at times they ran into swampland and had to retrace their steps. Once they came to a den of a wild boar, whose angry patriarch chased them away. Sometimes, artillery fire landed close enough to scatter dirt over them. At one point they spotted a mortar team operating in the distance, but stayed away, unsure if they were friend or foe.

Late in the afternoon, and near-exhausted from an eight-hour walk, they reached a village that looked like one they'd stopped at on the way in. They paused at a trench on a hillock near a road junction, hoping to spot friendly forces. Then Drueke saw two groups of Russian soldiers. Eight of them on his side and six on Andy's side, no more than 20 feet away. Coming at them in a pincer movement.

The two Americans leaped into the trench. The Russians disappeared behind positions on the road. Drueke raised his gun to fire. He was going to die now anyway. Might as well take as many Russians with him as he could. Then, as he looked to check where Huynh was firing, he saw him putting his gun down.

What? Aw, come on, Andy! They'll kill us anyway!

No! He's told you he wants to live. If you shoot, you'll both die.

Drueke dropped his weapon too, the Russians watching. They gestured at them to come down off the hillock. *Hands up. Down on your knees.* He was blindfolded. Had his hands bound. Kicked. Punched. Kicked again.

A Russian platoon leader, who spoke English, barked questions, noting that Drueke was wearing US Army issue camouflage. Demanding to know what a pair of fucking foreigners were doing in Ukraine. Pressing a pistol to Drueke's head.

'How many Russians have you killed?

He could hear the pistol being cocked.

'HOW MANY RUSSIANS HAVE YOU KILLED? WHY DID YOU COME TO KILL RUSSIAN BABIES?'

Fuck me, I am about to die. Here on a dirt road, in some village north of Kharkiv in Ukraine. Here's where it all ended for me, Alex Drueke, of Alabama, after 39 years on this earth.

Go ahead then, shoot me. I love you, Diesel. I love you, Momma.

The shot never came. Instead, hands rifled through his jacket and trousers. The Russians helped themselves to the prisoners' watches, Huynh's boots and bits of Drueke's uniform. All better than Kremlin-issue gear. Then, after leaving them tied up for a while, they put them to work digging a trench. Technically, robbing PoWs and forcing them into labour was a breach of the Geneva Convention, Drueke remembered from his staff sergeant days. But as war crimes went, it was better than summary execution.

'While you're with me, you're safe,' said the platoon leader. 'But if you try to run, we'll shoot you.'

As they dug, the Russians came up to look at them, like they were exhibits in a zoo. There was the odd shove, poke and snarl. But they seemed to regard them as fellow soldiers, men who were just following orders, like they were. Occasionally, they'd offer a swig of water from a canteen, or a puff on a cigarette. Amid the hostility, there was curiosity.

'Biden? Biden good?

'Trump? Trump good?

'American women? Good?'

Cue standard international double-cupped hand-gesture, outlining a well-endowed female.

'Well, yeah, some of them,' Drueke replied.

The Russian platoon leader kept his eye on the prisoners, stopped anyone going to town on them with a rifle butt or a boot. Then, when some high-ranking commander turned up, the atmosphere changed.

A guy in his forties. Buzzcut, stripes on his lapels, an air of thuggish authority. The other soldiers looked scared of him. The Russian forces were said to be full of guys like this. Psychos with epaulettes, employed to terrify the rank and file.

Buzzcut hauled Drueke to his feet. Ordered him to strip to his underwear. A common Russian tactic, to see if prisoners had tattoos identifying them as Nazis or members of a particular military unit. Then he stood in front of Drueke almost nose-to-nose. Staring him out.

'Как тебя зовут?'*

'I'm sorry?

'Как тебя зовут?'

'I'm sorry, I don't speak Russian …'

'Как тебя зовут! Как тебя зовут!'

Buzzcut's eyeballs swivelled down, then up again. Then he fired his Kalashnikov right between Drueke's feet. By some miracle, the bullet didn't ricochet into his nether regions.

---

* 'What is your name?'

'Как тебя зовут!'

'Like I say, I don't speak Russian! Can you ask in English?'

Buzzcut replied with the butt of his Kalashnikov, smashing it over Drueke's head. Hard enough for him to see stars.

Drueke staggered, trying to keep his feet, looking for the platoon leader. Nowhere to be seen. He stared at the other Russian soldiers. Some of them, he knew, spoke English too.

'Please, can somebody translate for me? I will answer this commander's questions if I can.'

Silence. Not even eye contact. Drueke was blindfolded and put on his knees. Just as he was thinking about bidding farewell to his mum and Diesel again, the platoon leader returned.

He pulled Buzzcut aside for a long discussion. Judging by the number of times the platoon leader kept saying 'Ameriki', Drueke guessed that he was arguing that Drueke and Huynh were best kept alive.

The Kremlin, after all, would be delighted to get its hands on two captive Americans. Hugely valuable bargaining chips. And, from Putin's viewpoint, a propaganda coup. Living, breathing proof of his claim that Ukraine was just a US pawn. Kudos, too, for the soldiers on the ground who caught them. Promotions, maybe, for their commanders.

The next day, they were loaded on top of a Russian BMP, the metal scalding hot from the sun. They drove over dirt roads towards the Russian border, past a checkpoint with an abandoned duty free building. Next, they were stuck in a hot, airless tent. Plastic bags were wrapped over their heads. They were made to kneel, hands still tied behind their back. Soon they were nearly drowning in their own sweat, losing all feeling below the waist. When Huynh's legs buckled under him, keeling him over, a guard give him a kicking.

Several hours later, when they were loaded back in a truck,

Drueke savoured the tiny whisper of breeze that came through his plastic bag mask as they gathered speed. A few breaths later, a guard reached down and pulled the bag tight again. *No fresh air for you.*

They came to what seemed to be a makeshift prisoner of war camp. Rows of tents, separated by concertina wire fences. A separate one each for Drueke and Huynh. And their first taste of more considered, calculated, leisurely torture.

Drueke was made to stand blindfolded in one spot for the entire first night. He was beaten again, sometimes for shuffling his feet, sometimes apparently just for fun. After what felt like about 18 hours, someone punched him full force in the stomach. 'Welcome to Russia,' a voice said.

13

LORD OF THE FLIES

Black site prison, Donetsk People's Republic, June–July 2022

Drueke's cell was about two feet wide by six feet long. The size of a toilet cubicle, minus the creature comforts. No windows, no sink, and just a bucket to piss and shit in. Once a day, a guard would provide a loaf of mouldy bread and some cloudy water. There was nothing to do except stare at four walls all day. And much of the night too. The lights were on 24/7, making sleep nearly impossible.

He'd been there nearly a month. He knew every crack and smear on the walls and ceiling, and the daily routines of the cell's resident insects. Of the world outside the cell door, next to nothing. His best guess was that he was in some kind of Kremlin black site prison. Somewhere that didn't officially exist, where interrogators could feel free to express themselves.

He probably wasn't even in Russia. Captured PoWs, he knew, were usually taken to the Donetsk People's Republic, the separatist-controlled enclave in eastern Ukraine. That allowed the Kremlin to plausibly deny that they were on Russian soil. If he died in here, be it by torture, firing squad or neglect, the only people who'd know would be whoever disposed of his body. Plus, presumably, his interrogators – Moustache Man, Uniform Man, Fat Man and that fucker Dead Eyes.

He'd been driven here from the camp near the Russian border, freshly tenderised by his first really serious beating. After that night standing blindfold in one spot, someone had beaten him non-stop for an hour, aiming for his kidneys and ribcage. Hadn't even bothered asking any questions. Then, just as Drueke was trying to work out how many ribs he'd cracked – it felt like at least four – a translator's voice had cut in, all chummy.

'Alexander, would you like some breakfast?'

The bag that had been wrapped around his head was removed, revealing that he was already in a dining tent, with trestle tables and coffee urns. *Jesus*. What kind of brutes used their chow hall as a torture chamber?

While his rib cage was now one big bruise, they'd been careful not to touch his face. So when they'd later taken him into some office room and shoved him before a video camera, he looked completely unharmed. Some goon had ordered him to say he was being treated okay, and to say something to his family.

'Mom, I just want to let you know that I'm alive and that I hope to be back home as soon as I can be,' he'd said. 'Love for me. Love you.'

God only knew if she'd ever see the video. If she did though, she'd know he was still alive. As of then, anyway.

* * *

With hindsight, whoever had smashed his ribcage in was clearly just some enthusiastic amateur. The black site was where the professionals had taken over. Goons from Russia's FSB security service, the successor to the KGB. Graduates of a Kremlin school of torture that went back to Stalin's time and beyond, men trained in the art of inflicting exquisite pain.

His interrogators were clearly educated, judging by their fluent English. Yet they didn't seem very worldly-wise, judging by their lines of questioning, which seemed to be informed by Cold War airport novels. They were convinced he was a CIA agent, part of an elite cadre of undercover field operatives sent in to help Ukraine. Like he was some real-life Jason Bourne, rather than the real-life Alex Drueke.

Absurd as that was, he couldn't persuade them otherwise. Firstly, the Russians found it hard to believe that anyone would give up a comfortable life in America to fight for Ukraine of their own free will. Secondly, when they'd done some research on Drueke, they'd found out that he'd served in a CBRN (chemical, biological, radiological, nuclear) company while on his first deployment to Iraq.

All it meant was that his unit had been trained in how to identify weapons of mass destruction. No WMD 'smoking gun' had turned up in Iraq, and he'd never done much more than practise putting his hazmat suit on. But his captors reckoned he'd been teaching Ukrainian army units how to make improvised biological weapons. Perhaps they too knew it was nonsense. But if they could get him to say it, they could present him as a big propaganda catch to their superiors. Their very own WMD smoking gun.

Moustache Man, Fat Man and Uniform Man were his three main interrogators, summoning him from his cell every so often. He'd made careful mental notes of their appearances, in the hope that one day they might meet again across a war crimes court.

Moustache Man was in his forties, and wore jeans and tight tops, showing off a gym-honed physique. He always had a balaclava on, but sometimes a reddish-brown moustache could be glimpsed through the mouthpiece. Uniform Man was about the same age, and wore Russian military fatigues with no patches or insignia. Fat Man was in his fifties with a greying crew cut, always in civvies.

Their interrogations would usually involve beatings, followed by long hours in stress positions. Far worse, though, were the meetings with Dead Eyes, even though his torture sessions lasted just minutes. Dead Eyes first showed up during an interrogation session with Moustache Man. The moment Drueke saw him, he sensed he was in the presence of a man who enjoyed his work. He was ginger-haired, in his thirties, with pale blue eyes that stared vacantly. Like his soul had been switched off.

Moustache Man had ordered Drueke to lie on the floor on his front. He attached a crocodile clip to Drueke's left ear, another to his metal handcuffs. Drueke saw a wire trailing across the floor to his left, where Dead Eyes sat at a table. On it was a grey metal box the size of a car battery, with a dial on it. Dead Eyes grinned at Drueke and cranked the dial, sending a jolt of electricity through his limbs.

Drueke felt his entire body lock up, like every muscle and fibre was in rigor mortis. Normally, he never cried out during torture. It helped get him through it, knowing he wasn't giving them the satisfaction of hearing him cry and curse. This was different. He couldn't speak a word when the current was going through him, but when Dead Eye cut the power after about ten seconds, he let out a long, loud 'FUUUCK!'

He'd barely snatched breath when Dead Eye cranked the dial again. Once more, his whole body went rigid. His jaw was clenching so hard it felt it might break. A metallic taste in his mouth. Not the sweet, warm coppery flavour one got from a punch in the face, when the mouth filled with blood. More like a cold steel, like his tongue was a knife blade.

After the second jolt, they stuck him in a chair. Asked him yet again about some random guy he'd met a few months ago in

Poland, who they were convinced was his CIA handler. Said they didn't believe him. Then hooked him up to the wire again.

Fuck, this is how it's going to be from now on. They'll just keep doing this to me. It'll never end.

Okay. Try and go with it then. Don't fight it. Hell, try and fucking enjoy it. Look for the good parts. Fuck Dead Eyes. Make out like you don't give a fuck.

The fourth time the charge was turned on, he tried channelling his inner sadomasochist.

Okay, how does my body feel? Is there anything good about this? Might this make me orgasm or something? Aggh! Fuuuck!

Nope, nothing. Just his body locking up again. Not that many positives to torture by electrocution after all.

When they hauled him back to the cells, his body ached for hours, and he felt utterly exhausted, like he'd run several marathons. But they didn't do it again. Perhaps they were worried they'd kill him. Or maybe it was because they'd seen him looking at the metal box before that final blast, a kind of yearning expression on his face, wondering if it was ever going to do something good for him. Perhaps that made them think he was some kind of crazy, who got a kick out of being mistreated. The kind of crazy who came to Ukraine to fight.

* * *

Other modes of interrogation were easier to cope with. Their captors would play music at full volume in the cells during the day, hoping to drive the inmates mad. They seemed unaware that their choice of music – mainly Eminem, Slipknot and Rammstein, a German heavy metal group – were precisely the sounds that suburban Americans of Drueke's generation had grown up listening to. As if the prison DJ had asked for his personal Spotify selection. It was very loud, and numbingly repetitive – the same 80 songs on constant loop. But it helped him mark time, which was otherwise easy to lose track of in the cell's 24-hour light. If one assumed the average rock song was about three minutes long, then 20 songs marked an hour, and a full loop about four hours.

Another surprise came when he was taken to an admin building, where Moustache Man was waiting for him with a TV crew led by a pudgy, smooth-talking reporter with a British accent. The journalist introduced himself as Graham Phillips, a correspondent for the Kremlin-controlled Russia Today channel.* Phillips' spiel was that he was simply covering the war from the DPR's side, and that he was interested in getting Drueke's take on things too. His distinctly pro-Kremlin line of questioning, though, left Drueke with some questions of his own.

If you're British, why are you over here supporting a puppet state of Russia? And if you're a real journalist, would you really be interviewing me when my interrogator is in the room as well, plus a half a dozen armed men in balaclavas?

Otherwise, the worst problem was boredom. Exercise was banned, the guards once beating Drueke for doing push-ups against the wall. And with no books, TV or radio, time stretched endlessly. A minute felt like an hour, an hour like a day. Enforced idleness could feel as much of a punishment as hard labour. But while his muscles might waste away, he couldn't let that happen to his mind.

---

* A former civil servant, Phillips had worked in Ukraine and Russia for nearly a decade, and also had a pro-Kremlin YouTube channel. He was later sanctioned by Britain for acting as a cheerleader for Putin's invasion of Ukraine.

He replayed his favourite movies in his head, line by line, as if sitting at home watching Netflix. He built imaginary houses, drawing on his skills as an amateur carpenter. Drueke's Construction Ltd (Alabama and Donbas) specialised in traditional Southern wooden homesteads, handcrafted with loving attention to detail. Often, once he'd finished each house, he'd redo it after consultation with himself. He could be a pain in the ass as a client.

Sorry, but I think the lounge might be better this way. And how about putting the porch there?

Sure, we can redo that, sir. No, not at all, sir. Here at Drueke's Construction, we have all the time in the world.

He also used the spare hours to ruminate, just like he'd done on the Appalachian Trail. Mulling the life choices he'd made in the past. And the ones he'd make in the future if he ever got out of here, not that that seemed likely. His captors had told him that he was going to be tried and executed as a mercenary, and he had no reason to doubt their word. But that in itself gave him a unique, detached perspective on his own life. It was an opportunity for self-examination afforded to very few, whether they paid a $1,000-an-hour shrink, devoted themselves to Buddhist meditation or spent the rest of their lives walking the Appalachian Trail.

Okay, here's things I like about myself. Here's things I don't like. Here's things I could change. Here's things that will probably never change, but at least I'm aware of them.

It took his mind in unexpected directions. Had the new, improved Alex Drueke ever returned to the US, he discovered, he would have liked to work in a bookstore. A nice quiet one, the kind that had a coffee shop and a laid-back vibe. Terms and conditions applied. He only wanted to stock books on the shelves. Nothing customer-facing. No operating the tills, trying to sign folks up for the customer loyalty card. Just the odd bit of friendly small talk.

Yeah, sure, ma'am, the Mystery section's right over there.

He'd probably not earn much more than minimum wage. Definitely wouldn't be considered for the assistant manager scheme. But he'd be around people, doing stuff. That would be enough. Indeed, he missed being around people a lot. That was why jails back home tried not to keep prisoners in solitary too long. Because human beings were, essentially, social creatures, who needed the stimulus of others to remain psychologically functional. Without it, they went a bit mad. They'd start talking to themselves, or to the walls, or to flies and ants in their cells. Just as he was now doing.

Like his interrogators, he gave the flies nicknames. First there was High as Hell Harry. Real name Harold, actually, but he went by Harry. Always up round the ceiling. Then there was Enrique the Evasive, and Busy Betsy, who had a frantic flight pattern. In the end he had killed Betsy, as she was just too noisy. Felt bad afterwards.

As for the ants, they were good guys, really. Harmless little fellas, didn't bite, just roamed the cell. Some would sneak into his stash of stale bread to steal crumbs, and occasionally he'd eat one by mistake. But he took a lenient view of that. Extra protein, you could say. Where they crossed a red line, however, was if they came past the tiles towards his mattress.

Guys, I don't want to kill you. I'm about to die myself, I don't want that to happen to anyone else. But if you come past this line, you threaten my bed ...

Sorry, buddy, you were warned. So I am going to squish you real hard, to make it a quick death. No please, don't twitch like that. Okay, I am gonna squish you again, just to make sure. Because I don't want you to suffer like I'm suffering ...

*   *   *

With only insects to socialise with, even the interrogators became company of a sort. Any session with them routinely involved a beating. But at times, he actually thrived on the pressure they tried to bring. Because he was, if nothing else, a stubborn bastard. It was a character trait he'd had since boyhood. Probably accounted for some of his share of poor life choices and broken relationships. But here in the black site it was useful, driving him to seek out tiny victories that gave him a sense of control.

For example, he never went down on his knees when ordered to. He'd always wait until the guards forced him, even it meant a punch in the gut. During interrogations, he'd sometimes give a smart-ass reply – again, usually earning an extra beating, but still worth it. With Uniform Man, the most erudite of the interrogators, it sometimes felt like a chess match, both sides trying to outwit each other – and sometimes relishing the game.

Where Uniform and co. were not so clever was on how the US government worked. One day, Drueke was handed a phone and ordered to call 'Washington', to begin what they claimed would be negotiations for his release. They had no US diplomatic contacts, no spooks' hotline to their opposite numbers in the CIA. Instead, they had lists of US government departments downloaded off the internet.

Drueke rang various numbers in turn, with the speakerphone on so that his captors could listen in. He reached switchboards where nobody picked up, voicemail boxes that were already full and occasionally the odd baffled receptionist.

'Hi, my name is Alexander Drueke. I'm a US citizen from Alabama. I was captured on 9 June, north of Kharkiv, Ukraine, by Russian forces. I know this isn't your job, I know you can't help me, but ...'

The moment he introduced himself, most assumed he was a crank. After numerous fruitless calls, Uniform Man ordered Drueke to try a US number called 'Veterans Crisis Line'. It was not a government department at all, but a counselling hotline for US ex-military personnel. Drueke had called it himself a few times when his PTSD had been bad.

'No, that's not what you think it is,' he told Uniform. 'That's a mental health line. It's for veterans who are feeling suicidal, that kind of thing.'

Uniform looked baffled. Perhaps mental health and wellness treatment weren't big in the Russian security services.

'Yes, but you are a veteran,' he insisted, pointing at Drueke. 'And this is a crisis! So ring them!'

'Actually, do you know what, you're not wrong. Fuck it. Let's try it.'

Drueke rang them. One advantage with a 24-hour suicide counselling hotline was that, unlike government departments, they did at least answer the phone. Drueke launched into what was by now a familiar spiel.

'Hello, my name is Alex Drueke. Please listen to me. I am not drunk or high. I am not suicidal. I'm a former US serviceman, I've been fighting as a volunteer with the Ukrainian forces ...'

For the first time, the person at the end of the line appeared to believe him. She asked him several questions to verify who he was. Then she put him in touch with a man at the State Department, who said he was already in daily contact with Drueke's family. The guy said he couldn't go into detail, but that efforts were being made on his behalf.

A few days later, his captors made him call 'Mama Drueke'. His mother. He tried his best to keep it together when speaking to her. Didn't want to give the interrogators the pleasure of seeing him crying. First, his captors made him read her a statement saying he was being looked after okay. Then the two exchanged greetings, as if having a routine catch-up.

'How are you? ... I'm fine, thanks.'

The conversation was stilted, both participants aware that the other was probably being coached. The State Department guy, Drueke reckoned, might even have been in the room with his mom. That she was even capable of routine pleasantries was something. Despite the tension in her voice, she didn't break down once. One tough cookie, his mom. Said she was doing regular TV interviews to highlight his case. Diesel, his dog, had appeared in several, becoming an overnight media star.

Whether his mother had an inkling that he was being tortured, he had no idea. Years ago, when he'd gone to Iraq, he'd told her that if he was ever taken PoW and forced into making statements, the only thing she should ever take at face value was if he said, 'I love you, Mom.' He'd told her the same thing just before heading to Ukraine. Hopefully, despite everything he'd put her through, she still believed him.

PART III

ALL BUZZING ON THE EASTERN FRONT

Drones, learning on the job,
Kharkiv, Kherson

14

THE QUARTERMASTER

Ever since it first rolled off a Japanese production line in the late 1970s, the Mitsubishi L200 pickup has been one of the world's most popular all-terrain vehicles. Cheaper than a Land Rover but just as sturdy, it is ideal for the farmyard and building site, nippy enough for the school run and supermarket carpark. Not for nothing do Mitsubishi's sales brochures boast that it takes 'all off-road work in its stride'.

Even the most imaginative Mitsubishi marketing executive, however, might not have foreseen the new role that Ukrainians discovered for L200s. As well as being ideal for ferrying grain, sheep or the weekly shop, it was perfect for mounting a rocket launcher on. Hundreds were now in action on the frontline, peppering Russian troops with the kind of firepower previously only carried by armoured units. Had Russian intelligence drones been watching, they might also have noted that many of the Mitsubishi war wagons were from Britain, still bearing UK registration plates.

The cars had come to Ukraine courtesy not of some shadowy improvised warfare division of Britain's Ministry of Defence, but a parish councillor from the West Country. Freddie Ickenham* was an unlikely quartermaster for Ukraine's war effort. A retired civil servant in his seventies, he lived with his wife Emma*, a church warden, in a rambling manor house overlooking tracts of picture postcard English countryside. Freddie now roamed the length and breadth of that countryside, buying up old L200s from local farmers and driving them out to military units in Ukraine.

Often the grateful recipients would record video messages of thanks, together with footage of the vehicles in action. Numerous farmers now had a clip of their old truck on the frontlines in the Donbas or Kharkiv, blasting off rockets into the yonder.

As right-hand drive models, they took a little getting used to for their new Ukrainian owners. But on the battlefield, that had its advantages. A few weeks after his first L200 had reached the battlefield, Freddie had been sent a picture of it with one side of its windscreen frosted by a sniper's bullet.

'Got ambushed near Kherson,' read an accompanying message. 'A sniper tried to hit the driver. Don't worry, though, he missed. The Russians didn't realise it's a British right-hand drive!'

*   *   *

Freddie's entry into the war was through his son David*, who had spent the previous decade working in Ukraine and Russia as a freelance business consultant. David had studied Russian and Ukrainian, and was well-connected in both capitals. He first visited Kyiv in his mid-twenties, at the tail end of the anti-Kremlin Maidan Uprising, and like many visiting Westerners was impressed by the young activists he'd met. There was an infectious enthusiasm to their talk of independence and European values, the embrace all the keener for the knowledge that in this part of the world such things weren't taken for granted.

It contrasted with the talk at dinner tables and boardrooms in Russia, where many still seemed to regard Ukraine as Moscow's rightful imperial possession. It felt clear to him even then that the Kremlin would one day take drastic measures to get it back. He doubted the West would do much to stop it. In his early twenties, he'd been a reserve soldier with Britain's Territorial Army, where he'd been struck by how many Nato exercises were still geared around counter-insurgency in the Middle East. Why focus on the threat from a few insurgents far away, he wondered, when Russia, the superpower on Nato's doorstep, was once again becoming hostile? He'd helped plan wargames focusing on a Russian invasion of Ukraine, which proved prescient.

When the invasion had started in 2022, he'd expected Ukraine to capitulate, just like everyone else had. He knew the country well enough to be aware that not everyone was a flag-waving Europhile liberal. Besides, outside of the hardcore nationalists, many people would surely just be too scared to fight. He'd changed his mind in the war's opening hours, when he'd received a phone call from Irena, a Ukrainian activist friend, who was already busy helping Kyiv organise its defences. So too was her grandmother, who'd got her old military service revolver out of the attic. Both were also ethnic Russians, the very people Putin was expecting to switch sides the moment his tanks rolled in.

David reasoned that if even Ukraine's Russian-speaking *babushki* were taking up arms, then the best Moscow was ever going to get was a very bloody occupation. Eventually they'd be defeated, but it might take years, like the Soviet invasion of Afghanistan. It was in everyone's interests, therefore, to help bring defeat as soon as possible. On the second day of the war, he'd sent a round-robin message to friends.

'*Morning*

'As you are all well aware, Kyiv is more or less encircled, with Irena (many of whom you know) inside it. She's doing her best – as she did in 2014 – to provide food, medical assistance and support to the Ukrainian military in the city.

'Not only is this one of the clearest moral conflicts of our lifetimes, it is perhaps one of the most important. If Kyiv can stand, so can Ukraine. If Ukraine stands, change will likely follow in Russia and, more broadly, other powers will think twice about launching their own adventures (Taiwan). Any support we can gave Irena will be better spent than any other donation you give in your lives. Please give as generously as you possibly can!'

He'd expected to raise just a few hundred pounds. By the following day, £15,000 had been donated. He now had enough cash to start his own private humanitarian aid mission, as many others across Britain and Europe were already doing. But there seemed no point in just loading up with the usual staples, like food, clothes and medicine, which he knew would be flooding in. According to Irena, what Ukrainians really needed wasn't nappies and warm jumpers, but stuff to help them fight back.

At first, the main request was for drones. Not hi-tech military kit, just ordinary shop-bought commercial ones, the kind that kids flew in parks and amateur photographers used to film weddings. He bought ten, priced at less than £1,000 each, plus a mountain of gear sourced from army surplus shops: walkie-talkies, waterproof binoculars, boots and gloves. In mid-March he packed it all into a van and set off for Ukraine. As a chaperone, David took with him a former business client, a London-based Ukrainian who'd previously served in the military. Even for well-wishers bearing gifts, the Ukrainian border could be an unwelcoming place, with stories of aid consignments being confiscated by corrupt border guards. David's worries proved unfounded. When a big Polish border guard asked what the drones were for, David's Ukrainian companion barked: 'To kill Russians.'

'Excellent,' beamed the guard. 'In that case, you will need the Green Channel over there.'

*　　*　　*

The next few days in Ukraine were a study in how a people could rally to a cause. It had long struck David that if Britain was a nation of shopkeepers, Ukraine was a nation of volunteers. Everyone he'd ever met there seemed to have some moonlight role in civil society. Captains of industry would multi-task as anti-corruption campaigners. Bankers and lawyers would run medical charities, or fundraise for some volunteer militia in the Donbas. After decades of lousy, post-Soviet government, people had simply got used to doing things themselves.

Now, with the war on, that self-starter spirit was in overdrive. Cafés had become soup kitchens, fancy restaurants were dishing out free pizza, nightclubs were operating as aid depots. There were garage mechanics welding girders into tank traps, students setting up media hubs for visiting journalists. David couldn't help thinking of an old – and deeply racist – saying of some of his old Russian acquaintances. '*Where there is a Ukrainian, not even a Jew can find anything to do.*'

His local contact for dropping off the drones to was a case in point. Before the war, Yevhen Halych had been frontman of O. Torvald, a Ukrainian rock band who'd sung the country's entry in the 2017 Eurovision Song Contest. Now he used his vast Instagram following to front appeals for a volunteer drone reconnaissance network, headquartered in a cellar in Lviv. Halych connected David with another military contact in Kyiv, and put him and his drones on an intercity train. Despite the war, the rail services were still running, refusing to be cancelled by the risk of Russians-on-the-line. At Kyiv train station, a giant Ukrainian state security officer, all tattoos and beard, crammed David and his cargo into his wife's bright pink Mini Cooper.

They drove through snow and tank traps to a base, where half a dozen different Ukrainian units came in to collect David's drones. One was up in action 45 minutes later, directing artillery onto Russian troops near Hostomel airport. Satisfying as it was to see his donations in use, David felt a pang of shame. Why should people fighting for their lives have to be grateful for stuff that nine-year-old kids back home were getting as Christmas gifts?

He spent the night in Kyiv in a flat owned by a Scottish friend who'd been evacuated home. The keys had been delivered via an informal Ukrainian wartime courier network, a trans-European relay system of long-distance lorry drivers, with volunteers plugging the gaps. Glasgow to Kyiv in 28 hours flat, changing hands five times en route. Better than DHL.

Wars, David knew, weren't just won on the battlefield. Soldiers depended on good logistics lines, to keep them fed and armed through thick and thin. The volunteer networks were clearly doing that as best they could. All they needed was dedicated and willing suppliers at the other end. If he could help just a few of them, offering them their own private Amazon delivery service, that would be worthwhile. He didn't have much else to do right now anyway, as the war had scuppered most of his business work.

* * *

The donations continued to flow in. Ukraine's plight opened wallets in a way that other good causes didn't. Many donors liked giving to a private aid mission because it cut out intermediaries. The items they paid for weren't what some aid-agency HQ back in London thought important, but what the Ukrainians actually told David they needed. Besides, the likes of Save the Children were never going to send over drones for military use, even if it might help save children in the long term.

While David renewed his search for drones, his father began hunting for old SUVs. The Ukrainians had told David they would take any they could get their hands on, but the Mitsubishi L200 was their favourite. It was already in widespread use in Ukraine, so spare parts were widely available. Some enterprising mechanic had also designed a standardised template for a rocket launcher pad, tailored to an L200's measurements.

It wasn't the first time that civilian cars had been adapted for military service. In World War II, the prototype SAS had equipped Jeeps with mounted machine guns for hit-and-run attacks in North Africa. In Afghanistan, the Taliban's trademark battle wheels was a similarly modified Toyota Hilux. In post-Saddam Iraq, the Opel Vectra, a run-of-the-mill saloon car, had become the unlikely choice of anti-US insurgents, the electronic sunroof making a handy gun turret for drive-by assassinations.

With Mitsubishis, the same attributes that made them popular with farmers and builders made them ideal for the battlefield. Good manoeuvrability. Reliable mechanics. A chassis that could handle 1,000 kg of manure was robust enough to cope with having a rocket launcher or heavy machine gun mounted on it, plus stabilisers and optional armour plating. They were also great as general frontline runabouts, be it for drone operations or casualty extraction. Nearly every Ukrainian city now had some volunteer workshop adapting them for military service, along with other vehicles. Quad bikes were being customised for use by anti-tank snipers, minibuses into armoured ambulances, real-life versions of the improvised war wagons in the *Mad Max* films.

Luckily for Freddie, England had a glut of cheap second-hand L200s. Mitsubishi had recently ended its UK franchise, limiting their resale value on the second-hand market. Because they were right-hand drive, they couldn't be resold on the Continent either. Early models were available for as little as £3,000, well within the budget of Freddie's donors. Some local farms and traders had ancient ones with 150,000 miles on the clock, rusting in a garage or the corner of a field. They were happy to donate them to anyone willing to tow them away. A mechanic at Freddie's village garage volunteered to get them roadworthy again.

Freddie drove his first L200 to Ukraine in late April, packed again with drones and army surplus kit. He arrived in Lviv on a warm Saturday afternoon, just in time to see Angelina Jolie, the UN goodwill ambassador and Hollywood's roving conscience-at-large, being hustled by bodyguards into a bunker as an air raid siren went off. Nearby, a boy sat playing a game on a tablet, unaware that the actress who'd played Lara Croft in the *Tomb Raider* game franchise had just run past.

The next day, a middle-aged man, on hearing Freddie's English accent, hugged him in the street, thanking him for Prime Minister Boris Johnson's decision to send thousands of anti-tank missiles to Ukraine. *God bless Boris, God save the Queen.* Johnson might not be universally popular back home, but here there were streets being named in his honour. Freddie even saw Boris Johnson hotdogs on sale in a service station. Whatever your politics, it was nice to know that somewhere in the world, Britain was still appreciated, and was showing some balls for once.

He'd dropped the L200 and its cargo down near Odesa, returning with numerous messages of thanks.

'*Words fail to express the gratitude that we feel here in Ukraine for support from so far,*' wrote one soldier. '*Having a reliable vehicle like the one you provided usually means the difference between life and death.*'

Stuff like that would go down well with the donors. Although in terms of fulsome, unabashed praise, nothing beat the words of a soldier who'd received a pair of night vision goggles.

'*Wow, it's like I asked you for a Maserati, thinking you'd bring a Lada. Not only did you bring me a Maserati, but you also offered me a blowjob as well!*'

* * *

Over the coming months, Freddie and David delivered dozens more pickups to the frontline, gaining a detailed knowledge of which makes and models performed best. Land Rovers were good but not ideal because spare parts were pricey. Older L200s were better than newer ones, because they had less fancy gadgetry that could go wrong. Had *AutoTrader* magazine ever opened a subsidiary called *Combat Fleet Car*, Freddie and David would have qualified as product reviewers.

Soon friends and donors were coming on the aid runs too, travelling in convoy. Several were fellow septuagenarians, giving the mission the feel of a Saga holiday. On one convoy, Freddie's wife Emma joined them, somewhat to the alarm of an ex-diplomat friend, who felt that Ukraine was no place for female church wardens. She drove an L200 all the way to Kharkiv, arriving just in time for an incoming missile attack. The Ukrainian soldiers who were there to receive the car took her for a steak dinner, impressed at the unflappable *babushka* from England who hadn't panicked.

The episode would have made a good fundraising article for the Ickenhams' local West Country paper – *'Church warden's Ukraine missile drama'* – but they kept it quiet, as they had all their previous missions. Publicity might attract more donations and more volunteers. It would also bring bureaucracy and too many restrictions. Besides, some of the items David was now being asked for were best kept quiet.

Many of his Ukrainians' requests involved highly secret hacks and workarounds to improve their beg-and-borrowed battle-field kit. At one point, he was asked to source cheap circuit boards that could be used as signal scramblers for Chinese-made drones, Beijing having apparently told the Kremlin how to access where each drone was being operated from. The circuit board re-assigned the signal to a spot in the middle of the Black Sea.

Another time, he'd had a request from Andriy Pokrasa, a 15-year-old Ukrainian drone prodigy who'd helped Ukrainian artillery take out a column of Russian armour during the siege of Kyiv. Pokrasa wanted a special lightweight lithium-polymer battery, plentiful in model aircraft shops in England. David also become a regular visitor to Halfords, the motor parts chain, buying up a particular brand of car battery charger that worked very well as a charger on the anti-tank weapons that Boris Johnson had supplied. Another in-demand item was ball-bearings, used for packing into bombs as additional shrapnel.

Over time, the Ickenhams' house acquired a large collection of souvenirs given to them by their clients: signed flags and artillery shells, an array of shoulder patches bearing different units' insignia. In early September, a large portrait arrived of Freddie and Emma dressed as Ukrainian Cossacks, the nomadic warriors regarded as the country's founding creed. The painting was the work of two artists from a Cossack community in Ukraine, who'd previously done one of Boris Johnson in recognition of his military support for Kyiv. In gratitude to his parents for helping with the aid deliveries, David commissioned the artists to do one of his mother and father. Where Johnson's portrait had Parliament and the royal coat of arms in the background, the Ickenhams' portrait showed their manor house, with a drone flying overhead. Next to the house, where a Cossack's horse would normally have stood, a Mitsubishi L200 was parked. Normally, Freddie and Emma would have been embarrassed to have portraits of themselves on the wall. This picture enjoyed pride of place in the conservatory.

15

FIGURING IT OUT

Vernopillya, near Izyum, north-east
Ukraine, June 2022

The truck left in the pre-dawn, before too many Russian drones began prowling. A dozen volunteers wedged inside, not talking much, buzzing yet queasy. This was it, finally. Helmets and body armour on, guns locked and loaded. Their first day at the frontline.

They hadn't been told what they'd be doing, although the view from the truck offered a trail of clues. Bombed-out buildings everywhere. Fields scorched by shell marks, blackening the yellow wheat crops like giant cigarette burns. No longer the touchlines of the battlefield, but the pitch itself.

Like everyone else in the pickup, Douglas Cartner was trying to keep his anxiety at bay. Already he had a nagging feeling that somehow, he wasn't quite prepared. Like driving to the airport for a long journey, worrying that something vital had been left on the table at home.

Before they'd departed, their team leader, call-signed Ghost, had given them all one last chance to back out. Nothing to apologise for if they did, he said. Combat wasn't for everyone.

No hands went up. This was what they'd come to Ukraine for, to put their soldiering skills into practice, all those years of being run ragged in exercise drills and bawled at on parade grounds.

Or, in Cartner's case, to see if he could get away with a self-taught crash course in soldiering, much of it researched online. He'd always been good at winging it, at learning on the job. Back in Scotland, during his previous life fixing tractors, his working motto was: 'I'll figure it out.' Hopefully that could apply to combat too.

*   *   *

He'd come here from Scotland back in mid-March, not long after leaving the memory stick containing his will and testament in his bedroom at his parents' farmhouse. Since Kyiv's embassy in Edinburgh had told him his services wouldn't be required, he'd avoided trying to enlist with the Legion. With hindsight, that had probably been no bad thing.

While other volunteers had languished in the Legion's camps awaiting orders, Cartner had joined Task Force Yankee, a loose collection of foreigners that was one of scores of ad hoc human-itarian groups ferrying aid to the frontlines. Unlike big aid organisations, they didn't have HR departments demanding to see CVs and hostile environment training certificates. What was more important was to accept the risks and be a team player. A novice who was willing to muck in was more useful than an ex-Green Beret who wanted to run the show.

Through the Yankees, he'd met Ghost, a combat medic from Latvia who'd served with Nato forces in Iraq and Afghanistan. The pair got on well, and when Ghost had gone to Dnipro to help run some medical training, he'd taken Cartner and several others along with him. From there, they'd joined the Carpathian Sich 49th Infantry Battalion, a volunteer unit first formed to fight separatists in the Donbas in 2014.

By then, all Cartner had done by way of formal military

training was some basic first aid and a day or two on a firing range. He'd made a point of being honest about his lack of experience. With so many people going around pretending to be ex-SAS or Green Berets, other Legionnaires had at least appreciated his candour.

Soldiering wasn't a profession where one always had the chance to learn from one's mistakes. But wars, he told himself, had always involved amateur participants too. Millions of Ukrainians were having to learn from scratch, just like freedom fighters throughout history. Today's apprentice warriors could also consult General Google, which had everything short of a 'How to fight' Ted Talk. He'd downloaded a military field manual, watched videos on urban warfare techniques, consulted websites about close-quarters combat. Basic infantry tactics, after all, were simple, so as not to be forgotten in the heat of a firefight:

- If you come under fire, always seek cover. If the enemy attacks first, the chances are they did so because they had a clear shot at you. Don't help them further by staying put.
- Only leave cover to move to better cover. When doing so, get your comrades to provide covering fire, forcing the enemy into cover themselves. A shot or burst at random intervals every 1–3 seconds is usually enough.
- Moving targets are harder to hit. Sprint between cover as fast as you can, ideally in bursts of two seconds or less. Most enemy troops can't aim and fire that fast.
- Drill your skills until they're second nature. If you can't unjam your gun in practice, you'll never do it under fire.
- Act quickly and decisively. Even a bad call is usually better than dithering.

- Only psychopaths and liars don't feel scared in combat. The challenge is not to conquer fear, but to control it and stay functional.

The truck dropped them off at Vernopillya, a half-wrecked hamlet where the air tasted of dust, broken concrete and rotten garbage. An Alsatian, teeth spiking out of its lower jaw like Muttley from the *Wacky Races* cartoon, barked what was either a greeting or a warning. They could hear shells, not far away.

They ran from the van to their accommodation, a basement in a bombed-out school. The floor was damp and reeked of urine. A previous Legionnaire occupant had daubed graffiti in English on the wall, saying: 'I pissed here.'

Cartner laid out his gear and began brewing coffee. For much of his time in Ukraine, this had been his sole luxury, heated on his portable gas stove. The ritual of making it was part of the pleasure, as much as the cigarette that went with it. Just as he was about to take his first slurp, a Russian shell hit the school building above. The impact beat a cloud of dust from the ceiling, plus a small chunk of masonry that splash-landed directly into Cartner's freshly brewed coffee. Precision bombing indeed. Outwardly, he laughed with everyone else. Inwardly, he was fuming, like a child whose comfort blanket had been ripped up.

That's my coffee! IT'S FUCKED MY COFFEE!

They spent the next few hours trying to acclimatise to the noise, dust and piss. A Ukrainian soldier handed out some lung-searing army-issue cigarettes in camouflaged cartons. Another assault on the senses. As was the announcement that Russian tanks were now approaching Vernopillya.

'Tanks! Russian tanks!' shouted a Ukrainian commander, who suddenly appeared in the basement. 'Russian tanks attack!'

Fuck, here we go. This is it. No way out now. So what do we do?

'When you get the call, you go upstairs and fight,' said one of the commander's underlings.

Is that it? Is that all the instruction we get?

The newcomers checked their weapons and kit, exchanging uneasy glances. 'Go upstairs and fight' was not a proper battle plan. Some of them began taking photos of themselves. Not for the Instagram, look-at-me-on-the-frontline feed, but as proof that this was where they were last seen alive.

They sat chain-smoking, awaiting Russian tanks and, hopefully, more detailed instructions. In the end, neither came.

Rule one of life on the frontline: Never believe anything you're told until it happens. Not a rule they'd mentioned in Cartner's military field manual.

* * *

The next morning, eight of them were picked for a mission: setting up a forward position near some spot codenamed Edelweiss. Cartner would be coming as machine-gunner, manning his new weapon, a Soviet-made PKM belt-fed machine gun. Based on the same design as the Kalashnikov assault rifle, and regarded as its bigger, tougher brother. Capable of firing 600 rounds a minute, effective up to about a kilometre. A proven, reliable operator.

Unlike the man who would now be carrying one to Edelweiss. The night before, a Ukrainian officer had pulled a PKM from the armoury, and asked if anyone had used one before. Cartner had put his hand up, despite never having done so. *Fuck it, I'll figure it out.*

For a mechanic like him, it wasn't too complicated. Just an AK-firing mechanism turned upside down, really. And like all ex-Soviet kit designed for the simplest of simpletons, user-friendly to the humblest peasant warrior. He'd spent the previous night stripping it down and cleaning it, a good way to keep his mind occupied. By the morning, he was in love with the thing. He nicknamed it Sasha, after the massive machine gun used by that big Soviet dude in the *Team Fortress* video games.

The love affair cooled slightly when he realised how heavy Sasha was. The gun weighed nearly 10 kg, about twice the weight of a chainsaw. Plus he was going to have lug an ammo belt, several litres of water and all his other field essentials. Food, grenades, a trench spade, med kit, lung-searing Ukrainian fags.

They began walking to Edelweiss as soon as the route was declared drone-free. Their first steps into proper no-man's-land. Probably. Ukraine's frontlines, Cartner now realised, weren't the neat, well-organised worlds depicted in war movies, where friendly and enemy territory was neatly demarcated like a tennis court. Instead they snaked around like meandering rivers, surging forward here, receding there. Often they changed by the day or the hour, and patrols like theirs would be first to find out.

It was eerily quiet, just the rustle of the leaves under boots. Cartner had always kept himself fit, but soon he was struggling with the weight of the PKM, its sling strap rubbing his neck and shoulder raw. Up ahead, along a dirt road, was an abandoned fish farm, two big ponds side by side. A narrow, overgrown farm track ran between the ponds, bullrushes closing in on either side. Room for single file only. A textbook definition of what his field manual called a 'killing funnel'.

They headed in, bullrushes brushing their cheeks, the air suddenly humid. Sweat melting their camo face cream, like a cheap 'Nam movie. Pondering the many scenarios that might stop them exiting the bullrushes alive. A drone could be above them right now. Or some Russian artillery spotter on that ridge ahead, with the path's coordinates already dialled in.

Or landmines and booby traps. They scoured the path ahead for disturbed earth, but it was too rough and potholed to tell. Probing each step of the way with a trowel, as they'd been taught in landmine training, would take all afternoon, and this was no place to linger.

After what felt like an eternity, but was probably not much more than a minute, they exited the bullrushes and reached the position, a series of drainage ditches in some woods half a mile further away.

He and a German combat medic were told to hole up in one of the ditches, inside some woods overlooking a field. They sat there alone, like a pair of work experience kids, expecting some grown-up to arrive to tell them what to do, where to aim, what to expect. Nobody came.

Cartner aimed the PKM towards what he presumed was the Russian lines. Of all the military field craft he'd mugged up on, he'd at least expected to be told which direction to point his gun in. The hours went past. Just doing nothing was hard enough. They'd barely slept the night before. He lit a cigarette to stay awake. The sunlight began to dim under the tree canopy, playing tricks on his eyes. He'd see a branch sway in the wind and aim his weapon it.

Then, into his field of view, five soldiers appeared. Walking in from the left, moving purposefully, just outside the woods about 50 yards away. *Shit*. Friends or foe? From his position under the trees, all he could see was their silhouettes. Couldn't tell if they were Russian or Ukrainian uniforms.

The five silhouettes stopped, peering into the woods. They started moving in Cartner's direction. *Who the hell were they?* He cocked the PKM. Finger on the trigger.

Fuck. Fuck. You might just have try to try to kill these people. Right here. Right now.

The silhouettes were about five feet apart. Cartner lined up the middle guy in his sights. Even with a belt-fed machine gun, he'd be unlikely to hit them all. At best, he might take out three or four. At worst, he'd clip one and send the rest scattering for cover, giving away his position in the process.

Do I do it? Do I not? DO I DO IT? DO I NOT?

Fuck, now they were splitting up. Two moved out of sight, the other three were still heading his way. Weaving in and out the trees, sometimes falling back. Any second now they'd spot him.

Come on! It's either them, or it's you and your mates. Remember, a bad decision is better than none at all.

Okay. Okay. Set a dead point. If they come past it, and you still can't ID them, fire a warning shot. Put a three-round burst over their heads, and shout something.

Like what? 'Stop?' 'Halt?' 'Who goes there?' They probably don't speak English!

His heart was bouncing, trigger hand shaking.

Fuck! Fuck! Do I shout or not shout? Fire a burst or not?

Then, just a few feet short of the dead point, the lead soldier raised a hand, and shouted something. As they came under a break in the trees, Cartner saw they were wearing Ukrainian uniforms. The lead guy was waving at him, speaking pidgin English.

'Hi. Ghost? Ghost here?'

'Er, no. No. Ghost not here.'

'Ah. Okay.'

'Sure. No problem.'

Jesus Christ. What was the Ukrainian for 'I nearly shot you all, by the way'?

He unpeeled a sweating palm from the PKM's trigger grip. So many ways that could have ended in disaster. Even if he'd just fired a burst over their heads, they might not have understood whatever he'd shouted by way of warning. Like him, they might have confused friend with foe. Unlike him, they might not have hesitated. If their battle instincts were well-honed, he'd have been dead before anyone knew better. He could see the headlines now.

'A British military volunteer has been killed on his first day at the front in Ukraine. Douglas Cartner, who had no previous soldiering experience, was shot after mysteriously opening fire on his own side.'

Unable to tell his side of the story. Unable to point out that if things were better organised round here, there wouldn't have been friendlies sauntering into his line of fire in the first place. The field manuals prized decisiveness over dithering. On this occasion, dithering had probably saved everyone's lives.

Later that day, when Ghost reappeared, Cartner told him how he'd nearly wiped out five Ukrainians on his first day at the front. Or, as it had turned out, four Ukrainians and a fellow British volunteer, James Chadwick. Chadwick was one of the two silhouettes who'd peeled off just as Cartner was levelling the PKM at them. He was Cartner's age, and his best mate in the team. A nice bonus that would have been, to have shot him too. Ghost didn't seem too surprised. Friendly fire was a hazard on any frontlines. But especially here in Ukraine, where forces were often bigger on fighting spirit than field discipline.

The next 24 hours brought more friend-or-foe quandary. As Cartner and Chadwick dossed down that night in a trench, they heard a gentle crunch of feet on leaves, creeping towards them in the dark. They readied their rifles, wishing they had night vision goggles. The footsteps stopped, then resumed, circling the trench, closer and closer. Then, just as they began to feel like the doomed campers in the *Blair Witch Project*, the mysterious intruder hove into view. A fox on the prowl. Wondering, perhaps, why these human fools were digging dens on its turf.

They readied their guns yet again the following day, when they spotted a figure sneaking his way towards them, his helmet camouflaged with branches and twigs. By the time he pulled up behind a nearby tree, their fingers were taking up the slack of their triggers. Then they noticed a tiny Union Jack on the man's shoulder patch.

Fuck, hold on. Is this guy British?

The man stepped forward.

'Were you about to shoot me?' he inquired, in a heavy Ukrainian accent.

'Er, yes we were.'

The man they'd nearly shot introduced himself as 'Britansk'. He was actually Ukrainian, not British, but had worked in Britain as a builder. He was also, it turned out, their overall commander. And highly amused that they'd nearly shot him. They couldn't have asked for a better introduction.

* * *

Like many volunteers, Cartner was a restless soul, prone to questioning who he was supposed to be in life. Partners had come and gone, so too had jobs: fine for a while, then routine began to bite. By that same criteria, he should have found front-line life unbearable. Most of it was stag duty, staring out for hours over the same patch of turf. The trenches combined the stresses of war with the privations of a particularly uncomfortable camping trip. No washing facilities, lousy food, insects for company, constant mud when it rained. After a few weeks,

Cartner developed trench foot, the soles of his feet slowly rotting. On the rare occasions that he took his boots off, the smell reminded him of a particularly pungent rugby changing room.

Despite the spartan conditions, he couldn't have been happier. On the frontlines, the focus was on the essentials, not the petty rules that consumed so much of civilian life. And the long, empty hours on stag offered plenty of time to get to know the other volunteers. When you didn't know how many more hours you might have left in life, no subject of discussion was off-limits.

He and Chadwick ranged far and wide. Work. Food. Sex. Future plans. Past plans. Best shags, worst shags. Fittest girlfriends. Not-so-fittest girlfriends. Relationships that had gone well, relationships they'd fucked up. Favourite films, from *Forrest Gump* to *Black Hawk Down*. Why *Rick and Morty* was one of the best cartoons ever. And, of course, why the hell they'd both ended up here in a trench in Ukraine, rather than leading normal, conventional lives. It was proper, serious conversation, the kind of stuff lads normally only chatted about late at night after a lot to drink. With the added advantage that the next day they could actually remember what they'd said.

While others preferred to sleep in abandoned cottages or farm buildings, Cartner was happy to sleep rough in the trenches, where he could watch the stars at night. Because of the night-time blackouts across Ukraine, there was little light pollution, and the galaxies would sparkle on the frontline like trails of broken glass. He'd sip coffee and smoke, trying to work out what was a shooting star, and what was maybe a Russian drone.

Cartner's team were one of three units in the 49th – one that spoke English, a Spanish-speaking unit that included volunteers from Latin America and a parent unit of Ukrainians. With fighters from Europe, the Americas and Ukraine all together in the trenches, they embodied the spirit of the Legion as much as anyone. Many knew each other only by call-signs – Moth, Pykey, Santa, Toasty, Valkyrie, Messi (named after the Argentinian footballer) – and had only a vague familiarity with each other's back stories, yet the conversation never ran short.

They swapped stories of close scrapes, whatever-you-dos and whatever-you-don'ts, fuck-ups by other people and fuck-ups of their own. They counselled, therapised, gossiped and tried to decipher the rumours that buzzed constantly along the front like drones. Any news on those two casualties that were casevac'ed down the road yesterday? Was it true the Russians were bringing in a new artillery unit that could actually shoot straight?

First-hand accounts of battles got particular attention, the newcomers wondering how they'd fare when their turn came. Most willed that day on, figuring that the more one became acquainted with real fear, the easier it got to control. Cartner felt scared most of the time anyway, even when things were quiet. The only way to cope was to keep busy, even if it was just checking in on comrades and making sure they were okay.

When he'd first come to Ukraine, he'd thought it would be all about defending the country and its people. The longer he spent on the frontlines, the more it became about defending his comrades, the people from all over the globe with whom he shared the trenches. It was natural, when Russian artillery came calling, to want to run away. But if doing so would endanger people he cared about, it wasn't an option. Especially if he knew they'd do the same for him. War, he realised, was about protecting friends as much as fighting enemies.

16

REDEMPTION

By the summer of 2022, visitors to Kyiv could be forgiven for wondering if the war was still going on. Bars and restaurants had reopened, the parks were full of sunbathers, and the city's arts scene was back, with everything from live jazz to the Kyiv National Opera. On a typical Friday night, the capital was full of carousing hipsters, sometimes earning dirty looks from those on R&R from the frontlines, who'd grumble that the western half of Ukraine had forgotten about the eastern half.

Even the long-range Russian missile attacks, which still hit Kyiv every few days, had lost their power to terrify. Most were shot down by Ukraine's air defences, and when they did get through, the casualties could often be counted on the fingers of a single hand. A regular roll call of one dead here, two injured there was nobody's idea of normal life. But for those who remembered the stranglehold of the siege days, it was a 'lightning strikes' risk, acceptable odds in a city that still housed a million people. When air sirens sounded now, the only people who'd pay heed were visiting politicians and celebrities, for whom it looked good to be filmed diving for cover.

Yet should any passing VIPs have needed a potent symbol of how Ukraine was still bleeding, they didn't have to go far. In Kyiv's Independence Square, where the revolution had taken place in 2014, a patch of neatly manicured lawn had been become a makeshift memorial garden for the nation's war dead. Whenever someone perished in battle, their comrades or family would plant a small Ukrainian flag there, the kind normally sold to tourists in nearby souvenir shops. The flags had quickly covered the whole lawn, thickening like newly grown grass. In their midst, a black plaque bore an angry inscription:

'*These flags each represent an innocent life stolen by a single madman, Vladimir Putin. It was decided here in this sacred square that Ukraine wished to be free and independent, and no greedy tyrant can take that away (why is he still alive?).*'

With President Zelensky's government sticking to its policy of keeping military casualty figures secret, the memorial garden was a rare public snapshot of the war's death toll. By a rough count, there were at least 1,000 flags in there by mid-June 2022. And they represented only those whose loved ones had had the chance to honour them at Independence Square. Most estimates put the total number of Ukrainian military casualties during the war's first three months at around 10,000. That was less than the Russians, who were thought to have lost twice that, but already more than the 7,000 Western troops who died during two decades in Iraq and Afghanistan.

Nor had the successful defence of Kyiv meant the worst was over. The atrocities at Bucha and Irpin had blunted Ukraine's interest in a peace deal, and if anything, the fighting was intensifying. In June, Oleksiy Arestovych, an advisor to Zelensky, said that up to 100 Ukrainian troops were dying in the east every day, as the Russians tried to seize the Donbas city of Severodonetsk. For every soldier who came home in a body bag, two or three times that many suffered life-changing injuries: missing limbs, burns, torsos so full of shrapnel it could never all be removed.

It was grown-up, industrialised warfare, and among the Legionnaires nobody could rule out the possibility that a flag in their own memory might one day appear in the memorial garden in Independence Square. Already there were at least a dozen Legionnaires commemorated there: Union Jacks, Stars and Stripes and European tricolours sprouting like flowers amid the field of yellow and blue.

Many Legionnaires gave it little thought. Morbid rumination was dangerous on the frontline. A good soldier focused their mind on killing others, not being killed themselves. If ever there was a profession where a positive attitude wasn't just HR bullshit, it was combat. The question of what happened if they died was something to be addressed in a will before leaving home, folded away in an envelope and thought of no more.

Some, though, were more sanguine about dying than others. For those escaping difficult pasts, coming back in a coffin would at least absolve them of further troubles, be it broken relationships, dead-end jobs, addiction or run-ins with the law.

One such Legionnaire was 30-year-old James Durose, another member of the British contingent alongside Douglas Cartner in the 49th. Like Cartner, he had never served in the military before. Unlike Cartner, he hadn't agonised much over whether to come, as there'd been little prospects for him back home in Britain. If his lack of experience got him killed, as everyone kept telling him it would, so be it. It would still be a happier story than the last time he'd got mixed up with guns.

* * *

Durose was from Middlesbrough in Teesside, a former steel town in north-east England that shared many of the problems of Ukraine's Donbas rustbelt zones. The steel and shipbuilding industries it had been built to serve had shut down half a century ago, consigning generations to the dole queue and leaving some with only a nodding acquaintance with work. Once the blacksmith of Britain, producing a third of the country's iron, today it was better known for grim headlines about social deprivation. The highest unemployment in Britain. Record levels of opiate and crack use. Regularly voted one of Britain's worst places to live. Even asylum seekers, for whom it was used as a dumping ground, would often move elsewhere if they could.

At times, the only people who seemed to talk the place up were visiting politicians, trying to prove they still cared about England's rustbelt corners. It was the kind of town they would tour to show they hadn't forgotten about the old white working class, although most turned up too late. In 2016, Middlesbrough voted overwhelmingly in favour of Brexit – a gesture widely seen as a despairing two-fingers to the political establishment.

If Middlesbrough was a showground for broken Britain, Durose could once have been its poster child. His father had left home when he was young, and his mother had proved unable to look after him, leaving him to be raised by his grandmother. He'd doted on her, then gone off the rails in his late teens when she'd died of cancer. He'd had constant run-ins with the law, arrests for fighting, drunkenness and anti-social behaviour. His personal life had been rocky too. Bouts of depression and anxiety; a relationship that petered out, leaving a young son he didn't see.

In his twenties, he'd graduated to more serious crime, working for a drug gang that operated across the north of England. He'd courier packages from A to B, not knowing what was in them, only to keep his mouth shut if he got caught. It was decent money, although he'd never really seen himself as a real gangster, just a lad who had to hustle to get by. After all, no serious villain would have a sideline, as he did, as a TV pundit for his local football team. He was a regular match day presenter on Boro Fan TV, where he and fellow fans would dissect the performance of their beloved Middlesbrough FC, whose fortunes, like those of the town itself, had waxed and waned.

Then, in 2019, his career as an amateur Gary Lineker was rudely interrupted by an underworld assignment. The drug gang called by one day and told him to drive a car to Liverpool. Unusually, they'd told him what was in the boot, not that he'd wanted to know. Not drugs, this time, but a gun. A Kalashnikov. He'd known straightaway that he was in too deep, but assignments like this weren't take-it-or-leave-it.

He'd barely left Middlesbrough with the cargo when a police car had appeared in his rear-view mirror, trying to pull him over. He'd panicked and put his foot down, leading them on a 120 mph chase before being stopped. The judge in his case told him he would have done seven years had the AK47 not turned out to be a replica. He gave Durose 18 months, and a not-so-friendly warning to take care about who he hung around with in the future.

* * *

Prison gave Durose time to mull over the judge's words. He wanted to go straight, if only to escape the clutches of the gang. He feared they'd blame him for losing their weapon, and knew they'd have no trouble tracking him down if they wanted to. They had eyes and ears everywhere. While he was inside, they knew when he was getting moved from one prison to another. Even if they didn't blame him, he didn't want any more offers of couriering jobs.

After getting out, he'd got a job as a welder, and his own place. Family encouraged him, hoping it meant the return of the stabler, happier James from the days before Gran had died. But just as he was trying to shed his old reputation, others were now revelling in it, trading on it. For a certain sort of person, there was status to be had in saying you were a mate of James Durose. *Aye, proper hard case, that lad, works for a serious firm. Got caught with a machine gun, did 18 months behind the door. Kept his mouth shut, mind.* It was a cartoon version of the man he used to be, made for bragging about in pubs or on street corners.

Then the Ukraine invasion happened, bringing scenes of tank battles and missiles onto his TV screen and mobile phone. He watched it obsessively, rediscovering an interest he'd had in soldiering since he was a kid when he'd read World War II magazines, done Airfix kits and listened to an old neighbour's war stories. Lots of lads from Middlesbrough joined the army, and he'd thought about it himself, doing cadets at school. He'd liked the discipline, the rules, had sometimes wondered if life would have worked out better if he'd stuck with it.

When Zelensky had issued his call for foreign fighters, he'd decided straightaway to go. The Ukrainian embassy had turned down his application, but by the time he'd received their email he'd already booked a flight to Poland. He sent photos of his tattoos to an auntie up in Edinburgh, who'd replaced his gran as his mentor, telling her they could be used to ID him if he got blown up. If anyone found a left forearm with a Boro FC tattoo, that'd probably be him.

In truth, he didn't really expect to come back alive. Warzones held particular dangers for people like him, who weren't always the best judge of their own welfare. If it came to a choice between proving himself in some daft venture on the frontlines, or doing the sensible thing and bottling out, he knew which he'd take. So what. This was a chance to atone for his past wrongs, to fight for the good guys for once. And was there really much to lose by leaving Middlesbrough? Much as life was now going okay, it could all turn to shit tomorrow, as it had in the past. No telling when he might get another text message from the gang, another job offer he couldn't refuse.

He wouldn't be the first person to seek redemption on the battlefield. Some of the Britons who'd gone to fight for Islamic State in Syria had been ex-convicts, seeking to cleanse their souls. In Ukraine, though, he'd be taking up arms in support of a democratic nation, not some terrorist death cult. And if he came home dead, at least he'd have proved that he wasn't the guy some people thought he was. At his funeral, they'd hopefully remember the James Durose who took up a weapon in a decent cause. Not the James Durose who had one stashed in the back of his car.

* * *

With his criminal record and lack of military experience, Durose was just the kind of person many volunteers had in mind when they said the Legion needed to tighten its vetting procedures. At the recruiting base in Yavoriv, other recruits cast wary glances at the skulls tattooed on his neck and his broken front tooth, punched out during a brawl back home. Word went round that he was some kind of ex-mercenary, in Ukraine to keep his battlefield skills sharp.

Yet while plenty of Screamers had hoodwinked their way in, Durose had no wish to be one of them. He'd come to Ukraine for a fresh start, to do things by the book. In his formal interview with the Legion recruiting staff, he'd admitted his lack of credentials. If he bullshitted his way into some frontline unit, he'd put not just his own life at risk, but other people's. No more fucking things up.

Honesty hadn't paid off. The Legion had said all they could offer was jobs around their bases, driving other recruits around. Other units turned him down flat. He was on the point of giving up, when he'd stumbled across a recruitment advert on the Facebook page of the 49th. It was encouragingly vague.

'We're looking for new recruits. If you have ever fired a gun before, get in touch.'

Technically, he met that criteria, if firing a gun included firing 0.22 target rifles at cadets. He dropped the 49th a line, expecting never to hear back. Ten minutes later, a Ukrainian recruiter rang him. Either they were desperate for people, or they appreciated his honesty.

'No, sir, no need for combat experience, we'll give you a month's training, then send you to the frontline. Are you okay with that?'

'Aye, that's what I'm here to do.'

* * *

Seven weeks later, Durose arrived at the 49th's base at the old school in Vernopillya, newly trained in anti-tank weapons, landmine awareness and infantry tactics. None of which prepared him for the frontline induction session that the Russians laid on that afternoon. Five Russian tanks began rolling their way towards them, preceded by a salvo of Grad missiles. In the school's basement bunker, Durose could hear the Grads getting nearer, like giant's footsteps, engulfing the bunker with dust. As medics were scrambled to treat two casualties, he found himself wishing he'd never left Middlesbrough.

What the fuck have you got yourself into, are you fucking crazy, what have you done?

Pull yourself together, man. You've spent all this time training, you're not going home now.

Twenty minutes after the Grad salvo, orders came through to get out 'on position'. Durose had no idea what that even meant. He followed a German soldier out through a tunnel from the bunker. Most of what remained of Vernopillya seemed to be on fire. They crawled up behind a mud mound, overlooking a field. He'd had plenty of fights back home over the years, and some nasty moments in jail, but this was fear of a different league. A tank round landed nearby, showering him with earth and leaves.

Fuck, I am going to die, right here, right now.

Wasn't that what you were expecting?

No please, not today, a bit more time.

Somewhere further down the line, he could hear a gunfight. Word came in that one of the Russian tanks had been destroyed. And another. Then, as suddenly as it had begun, the battle was over. His comrades wandered back to the school base to eat, as if nothing much had happened. He'd seen more excitement when Boro got a nil-all draw.

Maybe they were used to it. He wasn't, though. And that night, when the fear had subsided, he felt a euphoria coursing through him. Better than any drug he'd ever taken. Better than all those courier runs he'd done, even when good money was in his pocket, because he just worried about the next job coming up. Better than Boro winning the FA Cup.

So James, your match-day report?

Er, that was just fucking crazy. Very close, with that tank round, but do you know what? I sort of liked the feeling afterwards.

He'd lain on his bed smiling to himself, unable to sleep but feeling contented for the first time in years. At 3 a.m., he finally dozed off.

17

BLOOD ON THE CLAW

*'Battle is the most significant competition in which
a man can indulge. It brings out all that is best
and it removes all that is base.'*

General George Patton, 1944

After two months with the 49th, both Douglas Cartner and James Durose both felt like old hands. Artillery no longer bothered them much unless they were very close. At night, bombardments became like a snoring neighbour: irritating, but not worth getting out of bed for unless it got really heavy.

Both also knew that what they'd seen so far was nothing. Word had it that a big Ukrainian operation was planned. Something called Operation Claw. A proper, full-on assault – not just holding ground, as they'd been doing until now, but seizing it, taking the fight to the enemy. As Cartner's military field manual pointed out, assaults carried a much higher risk of casualties. They'd be entering hostile turf, where the Russians would be dug-in, waiting for them. Assaults were what real warfare was all about.

Operation Claw got its name from the shape of a Russian-held treeline, which resembled a lobster claw outstretched on the map. Within it were up to 250 Russians, who used it as a command-and-control HQ. The assault was planned for Ukrainian Independence Day on 24 August, which also marked six months since the start of the invasion. Independence Day was normally an occasion for big military parades nationwide, but this year all public gatherings were banned for fear of attracting Russian missiles. Instead, Kyiv's military chiefs were planning a rather more practical demonstration of their fire-power. Operation Claw would be a curtain-raiser for a much bigger autumn counter-offensive all along the north-east Ukrainian front around Kharkiv. The Russian lines were increasingly demoralised, underequipped and disorganised. With a decent shove, they might collapse altogether.

The 49th's troops got no specific details in advance, only that something big was coming up, and that they might want to tell their families. Durose rang his ever-patient auntie in Edinburgh, testing her composure to the limits.

'I think I am going on an operation, a serious one,' he told her. 'I might not make it back.'

'Well, try to take care of yourself and make sure you do make it back. You're no good to anyone as a dead soldier, are you?'

His tone was melodramatic. But on the day when word finally came down for the operation to start, his commander, an ex-US soldier call-signed Jesus, made no attempt to correct the record. At midday, he lined Durose's squad up outside a farmhouse in Vernopillya, delivering a pep talk over the baa-ing of goats and the clucking of chickens.

'If any of you don't want to go on this operation, put your hand up now,' he said. 'Doesn't make any of you any less of a man.'

No takers.

'Okay, everyone, look at your comrades to the right. Then look at your comrades to the left. Look at their faces, cherish the memories of them. Because I have got to be honest, on this operation, not everyone is going to be coming back.'

The English-speaking contingent of the 49th was divided into groups of ten, Durose in one group, Cartner in another. A few hours later, the orders to came to go.

* * *

Durose's squad moved forward treeline by treeline, trench by trench. Watching for mines underfoot, drones above, Russians to the front and sides and wherever else they might pop out from. Take one step, then another. Then look around. In the distance, they could hear engagements, but the first enemy positions they reached were empty.

They pressed on, Durose taking a turn as point man, hoping against hope. Nobody in their right mind wanted to get in a firefight with a squad of well-prepared Russians. Equally, nobody wanted *not* to get in a firefight with a squad of well-prepared Russians. Having got all revved up for this important fixture, it would be unsporting for the other team to do a no-show.

Then, popping up just 50 metres ahead, he saw the enemy for the first time. Five of them. No guns blazing, but clambering from a trench, hands above their heads. Two who looked like teenagers. Two who looked like pensioners. One who looked like a street drinker from back home, his nose a splatter of burst blood vessels.

He should have felt sorry for them. He didn't. Thanks to Russians like them, one of his comrades, a very good lad called Trevor, had ended up with shrapnel in his brain a few weeks ago. His first proper friend on the frontlines, now in intensive care somewhere.

Don't play the fucking innocents with me, boys, with your hands up. I know your fucking game. And now you want to surrender, like let's all be friends, eh?

They got the prisoners prone, emptied their pockets and zip-tied their hands. What were they going to do with them now? They were supposed to be in the middle of an assault. They couldn't be dragging five PoWs around with them.

Britansk, the Ukrainian commander, was quizzing the prisoners in Russian. Durose went over to him. In the heat of the moment, the old James was coming back. The bad lad, who acted in haste and repented at leisure.

'Let's just fucking kill 'em. Fuck 'em.'

'No, James, no.'

'Come on! We're in enemy lines. Not time to take prisoners! Just get rid of them and push on.'

'No, James, no. *Calm down!*'

One Russian kept putting his head up, looking around. Durose slammed the Russian's head down on the ground, glowering at him. The temptation to stick a bullet in his skull was frightening.

But Britansk was right. He wasn't in Ukraine to become a war criminal. Instead, he leant down and whispered in the Russian's ear. A message, on behalf of the Legion, and the world, delivered via a foot soldier from Middlesbrough.

'We are English. American. German. French. We are all here to fight you. *Yous are all fucked.*'

* * *

214

James Cartner tried to pack for every contingency that Operation Claw might throw at him, turning his daysack into a miniature armoury. Nearly 200 rounds of spare ammunition, in addition to the seven magazines on his belt. Plus three dozen under-barrel grenade launcher rounds, which fired out of a tube clipped to the front of a Kalashnikov. Capable of tossing a grenade into a trench 400 metres away.

Like Durose, Cartner got the sense that up close the Russian army wasn't quite the formidable force it was supposed to be. Some dead Russians they came across had only a rifle and two magazines each. During a break on day two of the operation, he saw a captured BMP fighting vehicle that looked more like a museum piece. Ever the curious engineer, Cartner nosed around inside. The dashboard instruments were like those an old Austin Morris. Old glass fuses, the kind most vehicles stopped using in the 1980s. Like something you'd find at an auction of old farming equipment back home in Dumfries. He took a spanner, engraved 'USSR', as a souvenir, and crawled underneath the BMP for a nap. Thirteen tons of reinforced steel was good artillery cover, no matter how old it was. He slept like a child, oblivious to the sounds of battle, until a Russian shell landed barely ten metres away.

The sound wave deflected off the metal floor of the BMP, leaving him deafened. All he could hear was a strange, watery sound and a high-pitched whine. His rucksack, which he'd dumped by his side as he'd slept, took some shrapnel that would otherwise have embedded in his face.

Further down the line, another position was under fire. Cartner's comrade, a man call-signed Toasty, crept forward to observe, and spotted Russians coming down a treeline about 400 metres away. Toasty put down a burst with his Kalashnikov, then grabbed his sniper rifle, watching the Russians through his telescopic sights. With Toasty's guidance, Cartner started firing the under-barrel grenade launcher. The first grenade exploded 20 metres wide of the Russians. The second a little closer. The third dropped right on their position.

Cartner put down as many grenades as he could, Toasty correcting his aim through the telescopic sights. After a dozen rounds, he re-stocked and fired five more from another spot. Through his scope, Toasty could see Russians lying injured or dead. Other Russians appeared, dragging the casualties into the treeline. The woods were soon ablaze, smoke obscuring the Russians from view.

The grenades were his first shots fired in anger. There was no way of telling how many Russians had been killed. But amid the smell of smoke was an acrid, barbecue scent, like burgers mixed with burning rubber. With it came the realisation that some injured Russian might be stuck in the blaze, unable to get out. And with that, there vanished any sense of satisfaction that he might have had about striking a blow.

Fuck, I hope those grenades kill them straightaway. Burning alive, that's no way to go.

* * *

Durose's squad offloaded the Russian PoWs onto another Ukrainian unit. He pressed on towards the Claw, thankful that Britansk had stopped him delivering any on-the-spot justice. He'd spent enough of his life looking over his shoulder already, didn't need The Hague coming after him too.

Ahead was a Russian armoured vehicle, parked up in trees. Armed with a 0.50 calibre machine gun. No sign of anyone manning it. Durose, carrying a PKM, pushed up close, Britansk just behind him.

'Quiet, quiet,' hissed Britansk. 'They're coming from the left.'

Britansk raised his Kalashnikov, a modern one with an infra-red sight. Directly in front, no more than 25 metres away, was a Russian walking past a treeline. Britansk fired a single shot, as calm as if he was at the practice range. The Russian dropped.

Behind the first Russian, three others loomed into view, none with body armour on. Clearly not expecting trouble. Durose fired three five-round bursts with the PKM. Not quite the surgical precision of Britansk's sharpshooting, but another of the Russians crumpled to the ground. The other two vanished, as other guns joined in. Then things went quiet.

There was no time to contemplate what he'd just done, in taking another man's life. The eyes had to stay front, the hand on the trigger, the mind on the job. Even Russians who'd been caught napping would have mates who'd seek payback. Sure enough, ten minutes later, there were more exchanges of gunfire and some shellfire. A sharp blow to his ribs, like being kicked with a steel toe-capped boot. He saw a jagged hole in his flesh, just above the hip.

'Fuck, I've been shot!' he shouted. 'I've been shot!'

He got back on the PKM and started returning fire. *Go down fighting, take a few more Russians with him.*

Jesus, the American commander, arrived to deliver first aid. A brave man indeed, running his way here with bullets flying overhead to save a dying comrade. He checked the hole in Durose's side, and pulled out a piece of shrapnel the size of a currant.

'Quit being a bitch,' Jesus said. 'Just a flesh wound.'

* * *

The Russians seemed in disarray. In some of the trenches, they'd left not just food behind but weapons: PKMs, grenade launchers, crates of ammo. Things they'd normally have lugged away if staging a tactical retreat. While some had fled, others were still holding the line, apparently unaware that it was crumbling around them.

Not far from where they'd shot the first two Russians, Durose saw another emerging from a treeline. A big fat guy this time, yet another elite Moscow operative. Perhaps trying to investigate what had happened to his two dead comrades. And, in the process, making himself an easy target. Another few bursts on the PKM, and he went down.

By early evening, their commanders called the advance to a halt. Jed Danahay, an Australian volunteer, began digging a forward observation trench for them to bed down in for the night. Durose kept watch, looking out now for friends as well as enemies. Another Ukrainian unit was also pushing through somewhere. There was as much chance of them suddenly traipsing through the woods as Russians.

Suddenly, at the edge of some trees ahead of the trench, Durose saw a single soldier. Dressed in black, carrying a gun but not pointing it. Their eyes met. Durose raised his weapon. Behind him he could hear Britansk shouting: 'Make sure he's not a friendly ...'

The man in black looked surprised, as if he'd knocked on a friend's door and found it answered by a stranger. Then his face changed, the penny dropping a thousand miles.

'Get your fucking gun down!', Durose shouted. *'Get your fucking gun down!'*

The soldier charged forward, then dropped prone, firing a burst. Durose fired one back. He thought the rounds hit. But then the Russian raised his weapon and fired again. Durose shot at him another five times. This time his body started going into spasm. His eyes met Durose's again as the life drained out of him, a glassy, accusing stare.

Between the Russian and the trench, Durose could see a second body. Jed's. As the Russian had charged, Durose had seen Jed leap from the trench, apparently trying to get a clean shot at him. Instead, it seemed, he'd strayed into the Russian's last burst.

'Jed's down! Jed's down!,' he shouted.

Then, behind Durose, someone else's voice.

'Craig is dead! Craig is dead!'

Word came back that Craig Mackintosh, about 15 metres behind the trench, had also been hit. Probably, again, by that Russian's last burst of fire. Either the guy had got lucky, or he'd not been quite as clueless as he'd first looked when he'd strayed into their position.*

Durose stared down the barrel of his gun, tears rolling down his cheeks. They held the trench for a further ten minutes while some of the squad put Mackintosh's body onto a stretcher. Then came orders to pull back. There was no telling how many other Russian soldiers might be lurking further forward, now alerted to their presence. Danahay's body, lying out beyond the trench, had to be left where it was.

* * *

---

* Some accounts from other fighters say it was not clear who fired the shots that killed Danahay and Mackintosh, and that the Russian killed by Durose had several comrades nearby who were also shooting.

Neither Durose nor Cartner had known their two dead comrades well, beyond odd snatches of conversation in the trenches. The paths that brought them to Ukraine in the first place, though, had been similar to their own.

Mackintosh was in his forties, a father-of-four from Norfolk, who'd quit a job as a landscape gardener to volunteer in Ukraine. Danahay, 27, was from Queensland in Australia, a restless soul who'd spent his twenties backpacking, working as everything from a dog sledder in Sweden to a house restorer in Britain. Both had hoped of joining the army when they were young, but had been turned down on medical grounds.

Like Cartner and Durose, both had then achieved that ambition in the open arms of the 49th, where being among fellow novices created a bond all of its own. Cartner had once spent an afternoon in a bunker with Mackintosh, just long enough to look forward to meeting him again. He was another friendly face from home, another comrade to protect and be protected by, another buddy to drink victory toasts with some day, perhaps, when all this was over. Now that friendship would consist of one last gesture – to act as Mackintosh's battlefield undertaker, to ensure his body and Danahay's body got home to their families. Danahay was still lying up in no-man's-land, beyond the trench they'd pulled back from. If the Russians had spotted it, they might well have the area under watch, knowing that the deceased's comrades might attempt to retrieve him.

Nobody, though, wanted Danahay left where he was. Too much risk of some Russian unit picking him up and posting trophy pictures online, boasting about the foreign mercenary they'd killed. When volunteers were requested for a six-strong stretcher team to pick him up the following day, no hand went unraised.

Cartner was among those picked. En route, they willed the Russians to show themselves. Woe betide anyone who got between them and their dead comrade. They found Danahay lying just beyond the trench, looking like he was asleep. One leg crooked, one arm over his face, as if shielding his eyes from the light. Cartner half-expected him to suddenly sit up, do his usual Aussie joker thing. *'Hah, what the fuck are you all doing here? I was just having a nap!'*

As they stretchered Danahay back, whatever sympathies Cartner had felt for those Russians who'd died in his grenade inferno vanished. Now that they'd spilled blood from his own ranks, he felt a hatred for them, the kind he'd sensed in some Ukrainians. If he'd come across an injured Russian, begging for help, he was no longer sure what he'd do. First aid, as per the Geneva Convention? Or a final bullet? Hmm. Now he realised why the Ukrainians kept fighting. Not just for honour and camaraderie, but revenge. Revenge for a war that could wipe out two people you knew within seconds of each other.

Both he and Durose often wondered how they'd feel at this moment, when a peer got killed. Might it suddenly jolt them to their senses? Might it make them want to scuttle back home, where the naysayers would shake their heads wisely, and point out that they'd been right all along, that war was for professionals, not enthusiastic amateurs?

Mind that laddie Cartner? Went to fight in Ukraine? In a right mess now ...

See that James Durose? Aye, used to think he was hard. Ukraine's gone and fucked him up though ...

Maybe the trauma would come later. But if anything, the idea of quitting now seemed out of the question. Home, for all its safety and comforts, would offer little satisfaction as long as the task was unfinished.

* * *

After Operation Claw was over, Cartner was treated in hospital for concussion from the shell that had landed while he was sleeping under the Russian armoured vehicle. He rang his family, wanting them to know about the deaths of his fellow volunteers before they heard it on the news. He'd planned to play it as the cool, calm warrior, simply telling it like it was, only to break down in tears. A splurge of raw emotion, the kind of thing a soldier was supposed to keep to himself and his comrades. His parents suggested it was time to come home, to which he'd agreed. Or had he? His mind was still a concussed mush, didn't know what was going on. A week later, he was back at the base.

The Russians started shelling one day, and they piled into a dugout to wait it out. Cartner shuffled through a new Spotify list on his headphones. Up came Britney Spears, singing 'Hit Me Baby One More Time'.

As if one cue, a shell hit the dugout. A massive flash, blowing him to the floor. Deafness again, dust as thick as a smoke grenade. And this time, blood everywhere. On his face. Over his trousers.

He patted himself down, but could feel no pain. When the dust settled, he saw the blood was coming from Messi, the Argentinian, whose kneecap was missing. A volunteer called Watchman had shrapnel to the face and several broken bones. Watchman was screaming loudly, but it was Messi that Cartner went to first. Rule one of battlefield first aid: always prioritise the quiet ones. Those still capable of screaming could usually wait.

Messi was at risk of bleeding out. Cartner put a tourniquet on his leg and elevated it, allowing gravity to reduce the blood flow to the wound. Then, somehow, a gas canister from Cartner's coffee stove ignited, setting the dugout ablaze. As Cartner was trying to secure the tourniquet, flames ripped up his trouser leg and up the walls. *Fuck, what next?* Now was not the time for 'Ring of Fire' by Johnny Cash. Messi, ignoring his pain, grabbed a bottle of water and emptied it over the floor, trying to extinguish the blaze. Some medics arrived, hauling Cartner out the bunker. More tank rounds came in. For the first time ever in his life, he prayed.

Please God, if you can make this stop, and let me and my guys get out, I promise I am done here. Honest.

The salvo duly did end, after which he was treated again for concussion. But Cartner didn't keep his promise. God could look after himself, his comrades back at the 49th couldn't. Yet again, he returned to the front. The 49th were transferring to fight in a Donbas town named Bakhmut, which already had a bad reputation. They were warned to prepare themselves mentally and physically. A medic took one look at Cartner, and declared him unfit on both counts.

It wasn't a difficult diagnosis. By then, Cartner was struggling to remember the names of his comrades, and even everyday objects. Like that drink he enjoyed … *What was it? Oh yes, coffee.* His brain was struggling to process anything, like his bandwidth had shrunk. He'd pull out a cigarette, stick it behind his ear while rummaging for his lighter, then take another from the pack and smoke that.

Once again, there was a sign from Spotify. This time, not the White Stripes with their 'Seven Nation Army', but a playlist called 'Bakhmut'. He couldn't even remember making it. Probably some attempt to create an inspirational soundtrack for the battleground ahead. Composed entirely of dire heavy metal covers of perfectly decent songs.

What the fuck is this shit, when did I find the time to put it together, and where ON EARTH did I find such shit songs?

Now, it was finally time to return to Scotland. A few days later, he was on his way back to his parents' farm in Dumfries and Galloway.

*　　*　　*

Durose, like Cartner, carried on longer than he should have done. A few days after the tank round that injured Cartner's comrade Messi, Durose went on a further push into the Claw. It now all seemed oddly normal, just another day at the front. Perhaps this was what it felt like to be a real soldier. Or perhaps he'd just lost all judgement. While manning his PKM in a tiny, exposed trench, he heard a drone overhead. Seconds after, a tank round hit just ten yards away. The blast left him gasping for breath, temporarily deaf and convinced at first that he'd lost his left hand. From then on, he began strapping a tourniquet onto every limb, ready in case it was severed. Two days later, a medic took one look at his glazed eyes, and ordered him off the battlefield. 'If you take another tank round like that, you'll end up with brain damage,' the medic said. A few days later, he left Ukraine and flew home to his long-suffering auntie in Edinburgh.

18

HOMECOMING

Winding their way past dense birch forests and the odd baronial castle, the highways of Dumfries and Galloway usually reminded Douglas Cartner that he was back home. But as he and friends drove down a dark country lane one night, the sight of dense woodland zipping past put him back to the road to Vernopillya. The road where, any second, a tank round could land.

He knew it was just a flashback, his mind inadvertently sign-posted down an unwelcome memory lane. But a blanket of anxiety still descended, a full-on panic attack, all the worse for knowing what it was, yet being unable to stop it. Might as well have tried to think his way out of a broken leg.

He told his friends to pull over, threw a bag of his belongings on the ground and started pulling everything out, instinctively preparing for battle. Only this time there were just clothes inside – no gun, no grenades, no first aid kit. And, as he had to admit to his baffled friends, no real explanation for what he was doing. The military field manuals that had kept him alive in Ukraine covered how to survive on the battlefield. They didn't have much to say about how to cope back home.

Even if they had, little of it would have applied to a Legionnaire returning from Ukraine. For them, a homecoming was very different to that of regular soldiers. There was no ticker tape parades, no cheering crowds. No warm words of congratulations from their country's leaders. No barracks full of comrades who knew the score, who could nod sympathetically about why a country road might bring bad vibes. And no official channels to turn to if it all got too much. No Armed Forces welfare service, no dedicated Help for Heroes or Walking Wounded charity. The nearest most Legionnaires got to an official welcome was a quick meet-and-greet from the police, waiting for them as they arrived at the airport.

Douglas James Cartner? Could you step this way, sir? Just a few questions about your time in Ukraine.

This time, at least, they weren't hauling volunteers off to the cells and charging them with terrorism, as they'd done with YPG fighters in Syria. Instead, the cops seemed to be trying to use them as intelligence assets. Were they aware of any weapons smuggling in Ukraine? Had they seen the Russians using Western kit that they weren't supposed to have? Any other fancy new Russian weaponry that should give HMG cause for concern?

Most of the time, the cops appeared to know far less than the Legionnaires. But the tone was still frosty, the conversation strictly one-way. For all that it was keen to pick their brains, the government's official line remained that Britons should not fight in Ukraine. The Foreign Office still warned that anyone who did 'could be prosecuted' on their return to the UK. It was a standard government fudge, with a whiff of hypocrisy. Britain's leaders might talk big about the war being a fight for democracy, but if any of their own citizens fancied taking part, they were on their own.

While the government gave volunteers warnings rather than campaign medals, the news headlines about Ukraine told a different story. The north-east counter-offensive had been Ukraine's most significant victory since the defence of Kyiv. Ukrainian forces had recaptured nearly 1,000 square miles of land, including the towns of Izium, Lyman and Kupiansk. It was the most serious Russian battlefield defeat since World War II, the Russian lines completely collapsing in many places.

Back in Britain, though, interest in the conflict was already waning. If Cartner and Durose mentioned the counter-offensive to people back home, it often drew blank looks. A few didn't even know if the war in Ukraine was still going on.

Sometimes, the lack of curiosity was a blessing. Cartner and Durose might once have imagined themselves holding court at their local pub, reliving their exploits. In reality, talking about Ukraine could be irksome. It was too intense, too personal, too raw, for casual conversation. Even with close friends and family, the fear and emotions were hard to do justice to.

Durose got fed up with people casually asking whether he'd killed anyone. If he replied that yes, he had, they'd sometime ask for selfies with him. Once again, folk trying to trade off his name. Cartner honed a stock response to being asked what it was like, designed to be polite but discourage further questions. 'It was great,' he'd say. 'And it was shit.'

The 'shit' bits Cartner dealt with through the company of two close friends, whose house he'd visit for beers, chat and a good cry. He'd have a few drinks, then download, almost on auto-pilot, about the tank rounds, Mackintosh and Danahay, Operation Claw, the smell of burning Russians. The next morn-ing, he'd wake up with no recollection of what he'd said. It was good therapy, cathartic. But it didn't stop life back in peacetime Scotland feeling somewhat weird.

The family farm, where he'd gone back to live, was a quiet place at the best of times, and hard to get used to after the din of the frontline. There was something of an uncomfortable silence, too, with his parents. They'd never really come to terms with his decision to join the Legion, and had spent the last six months trying to block it from their minds. His mother would turn the TV off if Ukraine came on the news.

It was only when he got back that he appreciated how hard it had been for them, how they'd lived in constant expectation of a phone call with bad news. He'd been the one risking life and limb, but they'd had to be heroes too. He realised, belatedly, that he'd often gone for weeks without contacting them, when even a quick text would have sufficed.

Glad as his parents were to have him back alive, they saw changes in him that worried them. The old Douglas didn't jump out his skin at any loud bangs. The old Douglas didn't run for cover when RAF jets did their low-flight drills near the farm, as they'd done for years. The old Douglas had his life in order, even if being a tractor engineer didn't exactly fill him with joy. Now he only seemed interested in the war, scrolling and WhatsApping on his phone constantly, with no obvious plan to settle again. What he saw as a new-found sense of perspective, to take life as it came and simply appreciate being alive, they feared was a loss of focus.

*　　*　　*

Whatever the difficulties in re-adjusting to normal life, Cartner and Durose were proud of what they'd done. Against all the odds, against all those who'd doubted and scoffed, against the fearful voices in their own heads, they'd prevailed, put themselves to the test and somehow passed.

Not only that but they'd played a part in one of Ukraine's most successful campaigns so far. Operation Claw had been merely an opening salvo in the north-east counter-offensive, but it had pushed the Russians back far enough for many Ukrainians to feel safe to return to their homes. They had fond memories of seeing families going back to their houses, some even thanking the foreign fighters directly.

They now also realised that fighting in a war wasn't like some bucket-list goal, a case of box-ticked and itch-scratched. Instead, scratching the itch had just made it worse. They missed the camaraderie and the buzz, and they felt bad for leaving comrades who were still fighting. With Mackintosh and Danahay's deaths, the 49th's foreign contingent was already two men down.

Durose, in particular, felt restless. Every morning, he'd wake up, frustrated that he wasn't going back into battle. He'd finally found something he was good at, where aggression could keep you alive, not land you behind bars. Out in Ukraine, he'd had a fresh start, felt like a contender once again. No longer was he James Durose, the ex-jailbird. He was James Durose, the Legionnaire, one of the guys who'd come to help. Rather than crossing the road to avoid him, people would see his uniform and buy him coffee.

Cartner's parents made it clear they expected him to go back to a normal life. He was lucky to be alive at all, said his dad. It would be suicide to return. Besides, even demobbed freedom fighters had to earn their keep, so soon he was back repairing tractors again. But his big kitbag, the one he'd taken to Ukraine, still sat his room, as if ready for re-deployment. He couldn't quite bring himself to unpack it.

19

DROPPING IN ON
THE ORCS

By the autumn of 2022, many Ukrainians no longer referred to the invaders as 'Russians', opting for a rich array of insults instead. On the frontlines, the enemy was routinely referred to as the *Pidory*, or faggots. Putin himself was *Khuylo*, or 'dickhead'. Cheerleaders for his imperialist mission were *Rascists* – a pithy portmanteau of 'Russian', 'racist' and 'fascist'. Most popular of all, and used by everyone from President Zelensky to Ukrainian schoolchildren, was 'Orcs', a name borrowed from Tolkien's novel *The Lord of the Rings*. The Orcs were a race of dim-witted marauding goblins, in thrall to a malign Dark Lord, for whom they would slaughter other races without compunction. It fitted Ukrainians' view of the average Russian soldier perfectly.

The term made uncomfortable listening for some of Ukraine's Western allies, who even after the horrors at Bucha and Irpin, preferred the language of war to stick to diplomatese. In liberal European circles, some fretted that Ukrainians were 'dehumanising' their enemies. That, though, was the point. For those on the frontlines, tasked with killing the enemy, it wasn't always helpful to be reminded that Russians were living, breathing people. Especially when one was hovering a drone over them in their trenches, close enough to watch them brewing tea or taking a smoke. For that was when the like of Henry Stevens, volunteer turned drone pilot, would press a button on his joystick, dropping a grenade that would plummet from the sky. And, hopefully, blow those fucking Orcs to kingdom come.

*   *   *

Drones had been buzzing around the frontlines ever since the invasion had begun, and were fast becoming as vital on the battle-field as tanks or machine guns. They could direct artillery fire and monitor enemy movements in a way that no amount of recon units could do. Before, if the Ukrainians wanted to know about the presence of high-ranking Russian commanders, they needed a spy behind enemy lines. Now, if a drone spotted a posh-looking car driving about, or saw some soldiers saluting someone, the Ukrainian radio chatter would immediately pipe up. *'Some important faggot is in town. Some big Orc has just turned up.'*

The real game-changer, though, was the use of drones as mini-bombers. The Ukrainians began fitting commercial drones with sets of drop-rigs, made on 3D printers, which could carry grenades. All a drone pilot had to do was hover directly over a target, press a button to activate the drop-rig, and gravity would do the rest. The drones' zoom cameras, which provided magni-fication up to 16 times, allowed for precision bombing. A skilled operator could drop a grenade down a tank's open hatch, a level of accuracy comparable to a guided missile.

Kyiv's forces had the upper hand in drone innovation, thanks partly to their ranks having many soldiers whose day jobs had been as tech workers and software designers. It was a huge boost for an army that didn't enjoy conventional air superiority, and soon nearly every Ukrainian battalion had its own dedi-cated drone units. The foreigners began getting in on the act too

– sensing, as ever, a chance to make themselves useful to an army that otherwise seemed lukewarm to them.

One of the first was Stevens – who, on arrival in Ukraine from his home in Germany, had spent weeks languishing at a military base. He could understand the Ukrainians' reluctance to deploy the volunteers, given how many at his base seemed to have substance abuse problems or mental health issues. One fellow recruit had committed suicide in a nearby tent one night, close enough for him to hear the gunshot. But having invested time and money to come here, Stevens was reluctant to simply give up and go home.

Eventually, he'd headed north to Kharkiv to join Taskforce Baguette, serving alongside Alex Drueke and Andy Huynh, the two fellow Americans who'd ended up being captured on their first mission. Stevens had avoided the same fate by little more than chance. On the day of their mission, he hadn't yet been issued with a helmet, and so had stayed behind at base. He'd listened, horrified, as reports had come in of Drueke and Huynh going missing in action. Later, he'd had to break the news of Drueke and Huynh's capture to their respective families.

The incident had let to recriminations within Taskforce Baguette, amid claims that Drueke and Huynh had been abandoned to their fate. Whatever the rights or wrongs, it reminded Stevens of the perils of frontline infantry missions, and to be careful about who he worked with. He'd ended up joining forces with a German ex-paratrooper, call-signed Boxer, to form a drone unit. Less risk of ending up dead or captured. And a chance, also, to put their own particular skill sets to good use.

Stevens, as an IT expert, was at home with the technology. And Boxer was trained in improvised warfare and explosives – skills taught to every German paratrooper since the Cold War, in anticipation that Russia might once again march on Berlin.

Stevens and Boxer had met during their very first days in Ukraine, and bonded as fellow German speakers, a rarity among the volunteers. While Stevens had never been in a warzone before, Boxer had served in Afghanistan and been wounded in combat. He was just the kind of foreigner Ukraine needed, but as he spoke only German was at a disadvantage among foreigners whose lingua franca was English. It made sense for him and Stevens to combine forces, and the two soon became 'battle buddies' – partners in combat who'd fight together, and watch each other's backs. Each also took custody of a sealed envelope containing a letter to the other's next of kin, to be delivered in the event of their deaths.

*　*　*

The pair's early operations were on the frontlines east of Kharkiv, where Stevens got a crash-course in Russia's blunderbuss artillery tactics. While a bullet might have one's name on it, the Russian artillery shells seemed to be simply marked 'to whom it may concern'. When they landed close, Stevens felt as if at the mercy of some mythical force from Tolkien's realm. A 120 mm mortar shell was like being swatted by the hand of a giant. A 152 mm artillery shell, its bigger cousin, felt like being swatted by the hand of God himself. He'd half-expected to end up a traumatised wreck, as a few other newcomers did. But there'd been no shakes, no inner voice screaming: *'Holy shit, why I am I here?'* He put it down partly to Boxer having primed him on what to expect. *It'll be loud, chaotic, just try to keep your wits about you. Nothing you can do but sit it out.*

Compared with a Russian artillery shell, which could kill and wound within a 100-metre radius, their bomber drones didn't pack much punch. They were fitted with old Soviet grenades, designed for nothing more than clearing a trench or a room. But they could drop them exactly where they wanted them, and if the drone flew at sufficient height – 100 metres or more – the Russians often couldn't see or hear it as it moved in for the kill. Stevens and Boxer practised for several hours in a football field in Kharkiv, dropping cans of tinned meat onto a plastic bag on the pitch.

Their first operation was on a soldier who did supply runs to some Russian lines east of Kharkiv, driving daily between a big private house and a set of known mortar positions. They were too high to see him clearly, but every time he left the house, he loaded boxes into the car. Theoretically, he could have just been a local civilian delivering food, which would have ruled him out as a target. But every time he got into his car, he made a distinctive shrugging motion that they themselves knew well – that of a soldier unslinging his rifle, loading what looked from above like a long stick into the car. That was enough to seal his fate.

Early one morning, Stevens and Boxer primed two attack drones and lay in wait for the driver to make his first supply run, normally around 8 a.m. Timing was important, as the drones had a battery life of less than an hour. Stevens followed the car down the road, planning to wait until the driver reached the mortar positions. Then he began to worry that the drone's battery would run flat. Instead, he flew 20 metres ahead of the vehicle, then released the first of the drone's two grenades. It landed three metres to one side, but still sent the car careering into a ditch. He dropped a second grenade directly onto the bonnet, engulfing it in flames. He hovered above for a few minutes, peering down on the burning wreckage from 200 metres up. The driver did not emerge.

There was a certain satisfaction in inflicting a blow on the Russian war machine, with all its brute artillery power, using just a shop-bought drone and an old Soviet grenade. At their house in Kharkiv, Stevens and Boxer would while away hours building new improvised drone armaments, aided by how-to video from a Ukrainian volunteer, who whistled breezily as if he was on a YouTube DIY channel. Their kitchen table, where they supped on borsch and played cards by night, resembled a scene from *The Anarchists' Cookbook*, covered with grenades, bricklets of Russian TNT and ordinary household items that could boost the munitions' effectiveness.

Nails bought from local hardware stores could be taped around a grenade as extra shrapnel. A grenade's power could be increased by sticking it in a Coke can packed with TNT. Like a successful contestant in the TV show *Bake Off*, homemade munitions required a deft command of weights, temperatures and timings. The Russian TNT was as hard as old chocolate, but by heating it up – very carefully – in a double boiler, it would melt at 92 degrees centigrade. It could then be poured into a Coke can and mixed with shrapnel, like some infernal cake mixture. Ball-bearings were more expensive, but could pierce armour. Nuts and bolts tore messy, ragged holes, more effective on humans.

Stevens and Boxer worked out how to time their grenade drops so that they would explode in the air rather than when they hit the ground, which otherwise absorbed too much of the shrapnel. The average Soviet grenade had a fuse of just over four seconds, so if dropped from around 80 metres, would airburst ten metres above the ground. That way, targets who might otherwise have got away with just light injuries would be killed outright.

It was a steep and sometimes perilous learning curve. Drones were the only warfare in Ukraine that did resemble something from *Call of Duty*: it helped to have a basic mastery of a computer joystick and handset. But beginners could easily make mistakes, such as despatching a drone with a live grenade on it, failing to find a target and then returning to land it back at base having forgotten that the grenade was primed to explode. Several Ukrainian teams learned that mistake the hard way.

* * *

Stevens and Boxer got plenty of time to field-test their designs. In August and September of 2022, they took part in the Kharkiv counter-offensive, forming their own two-man drone unit that operated on a quadbike. They'd move forwards just behind the advancing armour, providing forward drone recon. It was an intimidating place to be, zipping amid the tanks and APCs like a mouse amid the big jungle beasts, but they got a drone's eye view of the enemy in full retreat, and were there when Ukrainian forces retook the town of Kupiansk. They recovered a Russian flag, which they used to clean their boots.

Sometimes they attached a small speaker to their drones, from which they would broadcast the Russian national anthem over enemy bunkers. When the occupants emerged, curious to identify the mystery patriot, the drone would drop its bombs. Then the Ukrainian anthem would play, and sometimes a voice recording crowing: *'Fuck off, Russian sons of bitches.'* Some of their munitions had flight stabiliser fins, produced on a 3D printer by well-wishers in Latvia, who inscribed them with messages written in Russian. *'Fuck off, it's not your country. Or stay here and die.'*

The impact of drone warfare on enemy morale was immense. Previously, soldiers in the trenches could assume they were relatively safe as long as they weren't under direct artillery fire or within sniper range. Now, anytime they left a bunker to take a smoke or a piss, a near-invisible foe could be stalking them from above. Nor could the Russians hide their positions with camouflage, even in the dense woodlands outside Kharkiv. Like trackers hunting prey, Stevens and Boxer soon learned to spot signs of their presence. Brushwood that was cut down and placed over foxholes only stayed green for a few days, before turning a tell-tale brown. Vehicle tracks stood out, as did other interruptions of nature's patterns – anything too square, shiny, or neat. On a cold night, a soldier who'd gone for a piss outside would leave a patch that glowed for 20 minutes under a drone camera equipped with thermal imaging.

Stevens and Boxer lost no sleep over those they killed and maimed. Had they been in a Nato army, some shrink would probably be fretting about the impact on their own psyches as much as the enemy's. Most soldiers never even glimpsed the enemy, and if they did get in a firefight, seldom had any idea who'd they killed. Stevens and Boxer would observe their targets in their last moments alive, watching them blown apart by bombs that they themselves had designed. The only other soldiers so intimately acquainted with death were snipers, who'd watch people crumple in their magnified crosshairs. Military lore often considered snipers a breed apart, for whom a certain sociopathy was practically a job requirement, because their kill counts were so high: the best snipers in Iraq claimed more than a hundred; the best in World War II five times that.

Stevens kept no such tally. It was often hard to tell who was dead or who was just injured, and he had no interest in knowing anyway. But between autumn 2022 and spring 2023, he flew more than 500 missions, most of which ended with a bomb being dropped. He also experienced the terror he was inflicting on others, when the Russians began copying the Ukrainian drone techniques. One Russian bomber drone chased his unit's vehicle down the road. It ran out of battery and crashed to the ground, just as they were reaching for a shotgun in a desperate bid to shoot it down.

He didn't enjoy killing. He'd been raised in a religious household, where taking any life was considered wrong. But those who preached about turning the other cheek hadn't met Ukrainians in places like Kupiansk, and heard what life was like under Russian occupation. They hadn't lost comrades. They hadn't known units of decent Ukrainians who were alive and joking one day, half-wiped out the next. If they had, they too might feel comfortable with killing. And they too might come to see the Russians as just 'Orcs'.

For that was how he too now saw them – inhuman, unworthy of sympathy. They had invaded a peaceful, democratic country, raping, pillaging and enslaving, kidnapping children, killing grandmothers, shooting dogs and cats for fun. *Fuck 'em, let them burn.*

20

AT PUTIN'S PLEASURE

'He wasted, and became slowly weaker and worse,
day by day, from the day when the prison
door closed upon him.'

'Life in Newgate Prison', from
Great Expectations by Charles Dickens

Compared to Moustache Man, Dead Eyes and all the other thugs that Alex Drueke had met during his time in Russian captivity, Artyom wasn't that bad. He was a prison trusty in the jail Drueke had been transferred to from the black site interrogation centre. And if one overlooked his cadaverous face, faded Nazi tattoos and rotten, curiously misshapen teeth, there were positive qualities to be found. He was the prison handyman, not an interrogator, so when he came into your cell with a set of tools, it was to repair a lightbulb or the CCTV, not use them as torture implements. Unlike many of the other prison staff, he also resisted the temptation to mete out a few kicks or punches for fun.

This was a jail in the DPR, however, not *The Shawshank Redemption*. Artyom wasn't there to create a warm vibe about humanity prevailing in darkness. He spoke no English, so had no way of telling the foreign inmates what he'd done to end up in jail. But the guards were happy to speak on his behalf.

'Many years ago, when he was just 19, he murdered three people and then ate them,' a guard gleefully explained one day, as Drueke stood with two other inmates in the exercise yard together. 'He has been in this prison ever since.'

Artyom nodded, apparently proud of his status as the jail's own Hannibal Lecter. Warming to his theme, the guard also said that Artyom was keen to try some foreign dishes one day, should any PoW end up dying in custody. He then pointed at Drueke and his two cellmates. 'Artyom, which of these three would you prefer to eat?' he asked.

Artyom cast his eye up and down the menu options. Stood alongside Drueke were Andy Huynh, the Vietnamese-American US Marine whom he'd been captured with, and Patrick*, an African businessman who'd been working in the DPR and accused of pro-Ukrainian activism. Artyom pointed at Alex, flashing a long, nasty grin. Anthony Hopkins, who won an Oscar for his portrayal of Lecter in *The Silence of the Lambs*, couldn't have done better.

Hey, why me, thought Drueke. He wouldn't have made much of a meal. He'd already lost two-fifths of his body weight thanks to the prison diet. And after months in his windowless cell, his skin was lily-white, like some human veal. Ah, maybe that was it.

Yeah, I get it, of course you want the white meat. Cos you're a fucking Nazi racist. No ethnic food for you, eh?

Drueke looked at Artyom's teeth, imagining them snacking on one of his arms or legs. Unless his mind was playing tricks on him, it looked like two of Artyom's incisor teeth had been filed into points, Dracula-style. Or perhaps they'd just rotted in that fashion.

Still, aside from the thought that he might want to eat you, there were worse people to have paying a visit to your cell than Artyom. Sometimes, if he was in a good mood, he'd even give Drueke the cigarette butts from the guards' communal ashtray. Pulled apart and re-rolled with scraps of Russian newspaper, they produced a serviceable smoke. Then again, if your idea of a triumph in life involved scrounging old cigarette ends from a convicted cannibal covered in swastika tattoos, it did suggest things could be better.

* * *

Drueke was now one of hundreds of PoWs languishing at Vladimir Putin's pleasure in jails across Ukraine's separatist-held republics. Among them were large numbers of regular Ukrainian troops, plus at least a dozen Legionnaires. Most of the foreigners, like Drueke, had spent several weeks being tortured in solitary in black site interrogation centres, before being corralled together in a regular jail in the DPR.

Compared to the black sites, day-to-day life in the regular jail was more bearable. No more psychos like Dead Eyes, no more conversations held with the aid of high-voltage electric current. The guards mostly treated the foreigners as regular prisoners, and didn't single them out for punishment. The foreign fighters had their own wing, held three to a cell in a row of cinder box pens.

It was one of the biggest multi-national gatherings of PoWs since World War II, with Americans, British and Europeans under one roof. Drueke was in a cell with Huynh, whom he'd been captured with outside Kharkiv, and the British fighter John Harding, who'd served with Azov in the siege of Mariupol and then been forced to surrender. Elsewhere in the foreigners' wing

243

were Andrew Hill from Plymouth, who'd been wounded and captured outside Mykolaiv, and another British soldier, Sean Pinner, captured outside Mariupol.

The war movie buffs among them were reminded of the PoW camp in *The Great Escape*, Hollywood's retelling of the Allied PoW breakout from Stalag Luft III. Nobody thought, however, of trying to emulate the plot. The security around their prison was formidable, with CCTV cameras watching them in the cells. There'd be no Charles Bronson digging a tunnel, no Steve McQueen riding away on a motorbike. Nor, though, did they think they could simply sit the war out until it ended.

The Kremlin had made it clear that foreign 'mercenary' fighters would face no mercy. Pinner had already been sentenced to death by a DPR court, the verdict announced the very day Drueke had been captured back in June. Theoretically, there was the possibility of a prisoner exchange with Kyiv. But with the West getting ever more embroiled in the war, providing tanks and missile systems, it seemed likely Putin would prefer his pound of flesh.

At best, they might be spared execution and – like Artyom – spent the next few decades in jail here. Not that they'd probably last that long. The conditions were dire: the food a meagre bowl of *kacha* porridge each day, the water filthy, the mattresses full of lice. Even if the body held up, mind and soul were another matter. In a tiny wall cavity above his bunker, Drueke had hidden a metal nail that he'd pulled from his rickety bed frame. *In extremis*, it could be used to stab a guard, should circumstances require it. But it was also there in case he needed to slash his own throat one day.

As in combat, all that kept them going at times was each other's company. It was one thing to lose all hope for oneself. It was harder to watch a cellmate do the same, to see them disappearing down a rabbit hole of despair. They'd coax each other out of dark moments, play word games, tell jokes, pep-talk each other like a boxing coach with a punch-drunk fighter. And if nothing else, they could remind themselves that at least it was better than being held alone in the black site interrogation centres, from where everyone had emerged with a long personal horror story. Each with its own particular twist that made anyone else who heard it think they'd got off lightly.

* * *

The first thing the Russians had done to Andrew Hill after capturing him was to save his life. His bullet-wounded arm had refused to stop bleeding, so he'd been taken to a field hospital for emergency surgery. He'd been put under general anaesthetic, unsure if he'd wake up again. When he'd come to, they'd also put a bandage over his eyes so that he couldn't see. Blinded and groggy from the anaesthetic, he'd panicked, thinking at first that he was dead.

Two hours later, the bandage had been removed. At the foot of his hospital bed was a video camera. An interrogator had ordered him to speak into it, saying who he was and why he'd come to Ukraine. Or, rather, why the Kremlin thought he'd come to Ukraine. A coached statement.

'I was duped, I thought this was a good cause, but this war is a private matter between Russia and Ukraine. My advice to other foreigners is to stay away. If you do come here, you probably won't come back alive.'

It was nonsense, humiliating drivel. If broadcast, though, at least his family would know he was still alive. He also made a point of asking the interrogator if he was going to be safe, to which they'd replied: 'Yes, don't worry, no harm will come to you.' Not that he believed them, but at least it was there on tape. If he didn't come back alive, maybe his captors might have to one day explain to The Hague why they'd broken their promise.

He'd spent a couple of days in the field hospital, wired to a drip, surrounded by wounded Russian soldiers. A minder was posted to his bedside to stop the other patients attacking him.

Then he'd been driven to the DPR. Two days in a truck, stopping en route outside Mariupol, where he could hear artillery from the closing stages of the Russian siege. By then his anaesthetic and medication had worn off, allowing the scale of his predicament to hit home. What had he been thinking of, coming to fight in this war? Should have stayed at home, scaffolding. For all the bullshit he'd had to talk in that statement on camera, the bit about staying well away from Ukraine suddenly seemed very sensible.

He'd arrived in Donetsk to a reception committee of local separatist fighters at an old military camp. A bunch of old salts. Long hair and beards, ragged uniforms, wild-eyed and crazy from months in combat. While his previous interrogators had been careful to always wear masks, this lot didn't give a shit. Staring at him with eager, excited faces, all anticipating their first bit of fun in ages.

They'd started with a welcome tour of the facility, showing him all the kit in their torture cupboard. A big radio antennae that they used as a whip. An old-fashioned army field telephone with a dial on it, used to deliver electric shocks. A 'phone call to Putin', it was called, apparently.

They'd noticed that he had his nose pierced. Fashionable back in Britain. Less so in the DPR. Another sign of how the West was corrupting Ukraine's moral fibre.

Are you gay, my friend? We are going to pull that fucking ring out. Slap, slap. Thump, thump. Hey, you see this cell here? This is where we execute faggots like you.

That was the warm-up, the foreplay. The next day it was a bag over the head, batons hitting the back of his legs. Tied to a chair, towel in the mouth, face taped over. The field telephone wired up, first to his hip and left foot, then to one of his fingers. His body spasming so wildly from the electric shocks that he'd broken free of the chair. They'd been about to clip the wires to his injured arm when some other interrogator had stepped in, dragged him off to make another statement on camera.

Professionals again this time, in balaclavas. Showing him a news article about his comrade Scott Sibley, the fellow Brit from his unit killed near Mykolaiv. Pointing to a picture of some missing volunteer he'd never met, demanding to know who he was. *Tell us the truth, or something bad is going to happen to you.* Like nothing bad was happening already. Then another scripted statement.

'*I was forced against my will to take part in combat. I personally witnessed Russian prisoners of war being executed by Ukrainian forces. I warn people again, do not come to Ukraine to fight.*'

He kept the tone of his voice monotonous, and stuck to the exact script, full of clunky phrases in semi-pidgin English. The weirder he sounded, he figured, the more likely people back home would realise these weren't his own words.

At times, his captors seemed to think they could genuinely win him over to their point of view. One man, driving him from one black site holding facility in the DPR to another, had taken the opportunity to act as an ambassador to the region. He'd stopped at a petrol station, bought Hill sandwiches, drinks and chocolate. He'd let him stretch his legs, shared cigarettes, told him all about the area's history.

Did Hill know that the Donbas's steel industry was founded by a British man, John Hughes, a metallurgist from Wales who came over in the nineteenth century? That Donetsk, the DPR's capital, had once been called Hughesovka in his honour? Why yes, of course, the British were still well-regarded by the Donbas people. But no, nobody here wanted foreigners interfering in this local fight with Ukraine. It was a private dispute, a messy domestic, hard for outsiders to understand. Best not get involved, it would only make things worse.

The guy had continued in tour guide mode when they'd got back in the vehicle, proudly pointing out steelworks, mines, places of interest. Everything short of stopping at a local bar for a few vodkas. Indeed, a week or two later, there had been drinks all round. Ninth of May was Victory Day, the commemoration of the Soviet Union's defeat of the Nazis, an occasion still widely celebrated in Putin's Russia. Late at night, Hill had been dragged from his cell and taken to his interrogators' room, expecting more torture. Instead, there'd been bottles of whisky and vodka on the table, small plastic cups filled to the brim, a discussion on history.

So who won World War II, eh, Andrew?

Well, we all did, defeated Hitler together, the Soviets, the British and the Americans.

You're wrong, it was just us Soviets, wasn't it?

No, my grandfather was a Spitfire pilot. He took part in the Battle of Britain, flew over France and Belgium.

Really? Is that so? Well in that case, let's have a drink to celebrate.

The last thing he'd wanted was alcohol. He'd been fed nothing but scraps of bread for the last few days, leaving his stomach empty. But it was made clear that not joining in the toast would be very disrespectful.

He'd downed two small cups, then passed out completely. Either he was more of a lightweight than he thought, or they'd spiked him with some drug to rob him of his senses. Perhaps now, on some video camera somewhere, there was footage of him drunkenly toasting Moscow.

* * *

As a foreigner fighting with the Azov Brigade, John Harding had felt like a condemned man twice over. Not only was he a mercenary in the Kremlin's eyes, but he was a mercenary on the payroll of Ukraine's premiere Nazi outfit. Before surrendering at Mariupol, his commanders had told him to pretend he was serving with Ukraine's 36th Marines, who'd also been fighting there. But it wouldn't take a particularly wily interrogator to find gaps in his story. He didn't even know who the 36th's commander was. He'd told his first interrogator that he'd suffered amnesia because of all the bombing.

'If we break your chest, will it cure that amnesia?' the interrogator asked.

After that, there hadn't even been any more questions. Just several successive bunches of goons beating the shit out of him. One goon had stood on Harding's pelvis and jumped up and down as hard as he could. Harding tried to wind the goons up, telling them that they 'hit like his sister'. They seemed intent on beating him to death anyway, so best get it over quick.

He'd been left with a fractured sternum, several broken ribs, several missing teeth, damage to his coccyx, and blood in his piss. Later, during a visit to the Donetsk prosecutor's office, it turned out they'd known all along that he was Azov. A DPR official had produced his entire pay records, which the regiment had forgotten to destroy. *Fair cop*, thought Harding.

* * *

Despite beating them to within an inch of their lives, their captors maintained the pretence that due process was being followed. Each PoW was occasionally taken to the local Donetsk prosecutors' office for updates on their pending 'trial', not that anyone there seemed eager to mull over guilt or innocence.

'We are going to kill you,' one female official warned Drueke. 'We are going to give you the death penalty.' The official, he was told, was his defence lawyer.

On one Kafkaesque occasion, he was taken for assessment by a DPR psychiatrist, to check whether he was 'mentally fit' to be sentenced to death. After a few cursory questions, the shrink spent most of the session haranguing him.

Do you realise that America has started every war ever?

And that the Soviet Union always wins them?

How many Russian babies have you killed?

The psychiatrist showed no more interest in Drueke's inner feelings than Dead Eyes had. And it was clear that he thought only deranged psychopaths would volunteer to fight in Ukraine. Despite this, he pronounced Drueke to be of sound mind and judgement.

* * *

Like the black site prison, the jail offered few concessions to welfare. No TVs, no radios, no newspapers, no mobile phones. The International Red Cross, which would normally provide PoWs with welfare packages, had not been allowed access to the

DPR's jails. While the PoWs did have their cellmates' companionship – an improvement on life in solitary – they had to settle for a generous definition of what passed as entertainment.

Drueke and Huynh made a chess set, each piece denoted by a scrap of paper placed inside a bottle top. Andrew Hill walked endless laps of his cell, pretending he was strolling around the village where he'd grown up in Cornwall, and endlessly browsed some Russian travel magazines that the guards gave him. Should he ever wish to holiday in Siberia, he'd know everything there was to do on a wet afternoon in Novosibirsk.

Drueke read through what was probably the world's smallest prison library, consisting of three random books brought in by the guards. There was a tattered copy of *The Great Gatsby* by F. Scott Fitzgerald, a well-thumbed *Harry Potter and the Philosopher's Stone* and a dog-eared *Great Expectations* by Charles Dickens. With its grim depictions of Newgate Prison, where convicts in Victorian London awaited the hangman's noose, *Great Expectations* felt almost biographical. After ploughing through its 400 pages three times, Drueke came away with a question rarely asked by Dickens' modern readers: *why couldn't it be a bit longer?* It was the one time in his life when he could have handled a 1,000-page Dickens doorstopper, like *David Copperfield* or *Bleak House*. Come to think of it, why could none of the guards lay their hands on a copy of Tolstoy's *War and Peace*?

Often, the best way to while away the hours was simply by talking light-hearted twaddle. A favourite pastime of Drueke and Huynh's was 'Celebrity Beer or Fight', in which contestants debated whether prominent figures from showbiz, politics and sport should be bought a drink or punched in the mouth. Ideally, both sides would produce compelling arguments for and against – as in the case, for example, of Danny DeVito.

Drueke: Good guy, funny. Definitely a beer.
Huynh: Nah. Fight.
Drueke: Huh? He's cool …
Huynh: Sure, but he's small, so I could kick his ass …

Their repartee might not have earned them a slot on *Saturday Night Live*, but it kept them entertained for hours, taking in everyone from Morgan Freeman to Sir Ian McKellen. So too did another version, 'Celebrity Fight or Fuck'. It extracted the bombshell confession from Huynh that if he had to – like, his life depended on it – he'd 'go gay' for *Deadpool* star Ryan Reynolds. That news brightened up an entire afternoon. By the 100th round or so, the game began to drag. But when they couldn't think of any more names, they missed it greatly.

Another favourite word game, which they played when John Harding joined them as a cellmate, was 'Twenty Questions', although the choices of animal, mineral or vegetable tended to take a morbid turn.

Drueke: Is it animal, vegetable or mineral?
Harding: Mineral.
Drueke: Is it a metal?
Harding: Yes.
Drueke: Is it a bullet?
Harding: Yes.
Drueke: Is it a bullet to the head by firing squad?
Harding: Yes!

It was graveyard humour. Or to be precise, on-death-row-in-a-Kremlin-prison-while-accused-of-being-a-mercenary humour, which was even darker. But that made it all the more precious. There was plenty of time to feel utter despair. Anything that lifted the mood for a while was welcome.

The longer their time inside, the slower it went. They ran out of word games to play. In desperation, they tried 'I Spy with My

Little Eye', the first time they'd played it since childhood. It might have worked in the back of Mum and Dad's car, looking out the window. It didn't work in a tiny prison cell, surrounded by four walls painted a shitty institutional brown, where the only feature of note was the CCTV camera in the ceiling, the real-life 'little eye' that spied on them all day.

I spy with my little eye, something beginning with 'T'.

Is it red?

Yes.

Right, well, it's your toothbrush then, because that's the only red thing in the fucking room …

Drueke sensed his mind was slowly softening, like a fruit turning to mush. He found it harder to keep mentally stimulated, or even to daydream. He no longer thought about a new career in an indie bookstore, or about doing home improvements. Drueke's Construction Ltd (Alabama and Donbas) had ceased trading. He would sit, staring into space, not a single thought passing through his head. Devotees of Buddhism strived their entire lives to reach that state, of complete emptiness of the brain. But it was one thing to achieve it voluntarily, another to have it forced upon you.

Collectively, they tried to stay positive, even when it felt like an act of blind faith. They introduced the '49/51 rule', which meant that no matter how bad the day got, they had to stay 51 per cent positive. If someone tipped to 49 per cent, it was their job to let the others know, so their cellmates could crack a morbid joke, start a game of bottletop chess, or rack their mushy brains for some B-lister that hadn't yet been Fought or Fucked. Something, anything, to haul them back to 51 per cent.

Staying positive did not mean ignoring the negative. At times they debated how it would be best to be executed. A firing squad seemed preferable to the gallows. Although as Harding pointed out, the poor marksmanship of the average DPR soldier could still make it a long, lingering death. Suicide was also discussed. Huynh, a practising Christian, ruled it out. Drueke didn't. When he'd come to Ukraine, he'd been agnostic, but his time in prison had turned him into an atheist. No loving, caring God could ever allow people to be treated this way. So there was no shame in taking fate into his own hands.

He'd give it another year in jail, he reckoned, and consider his options then. He could use that rusty nail he'd hidden away. Or maybe hang himself from the bunk with a few knotted sheets, assuming the shitty nylon material was strong enough to take his weight. Huynh wasn't impressed.

'Oh great, so you're gonna kill yourself, and I'm going to be stuck in here alone with your rotting corpse for company. Thanks.'

That got a laugh.

* * *

As much as they could, the prisoners swapped tips and tactics on how to survive. In their days as regular soldiers, Drueke, Huynh, Harding and Hill had all done conduct-under-capture courses on how to cope with life in enemy hands. Try to be the 'Grey Man', neither passive nor aggressive. Befriend the guards where possible, see them as a source of extra food and favours, even if was just persuading Artyom the Cannibal to part with his cigarette butts. Tiny victories like that allowed a sense of control.

Some of the jail's inmates, however, found it harder than others. One who struggled was the British detainee Paul Urey, who was not a soldier but a volunteer aid worker. The 45-year-old, from Warrington in Cheshire, had arrived in Ukraine in

April, and had been captured after straying into Russian-occupied territory near the southern city of Zaporizhzhia. The Kremlin had accused him of being a mercenary, a claim that nobody who'd met Urey could take seriously.

He was substantially overweight and a type-1 diabetic, requiring daily injections of insulin to stay alive. No army would have considered him for combat duty – not even the Legion, which had turned him down. He'd come to Ukraine after several years jobless, joining a loose fraternity of freelance volunteer aid workers, many no more qualified for the frontlines than some of the Legionnaires. The mainstream aid agencies wouldn't employ them, but they could tout their services as drivers ferrying evacuees from towns caught up in fighting. It was perilous work, especially for foreigners who neither spoke the language nor knew the locale. Urey had been detained after running into a DPR-run checkpoint on one of his very first missions. His captors had at first assumed he was a spy, given his lack of any paperwork identifying him with any organisation.

The other prisoners had realised Urey was way out of his depth, and had advised him to follow their own survival techniques. But he was poor at looking after himself, and at times showed a child-like naivety, forgetting to show the guards enough respect. He'd neglect to stand up when they entered his cell, risking a beating for everyone inside. He'd demand food and cigarettes, seemingly unaware that in a DPR jail these were privileges, not rights. Had the local psychiatrist's office assessed him properly, they'd have realised he was a vulnerable adult who should never have been in Ukraine in the first place. Nor was he robust enough to handle physical punishment.

On a visit to the prosecutor's office one day, he and several other inmates were forced to spend hours on their knees in a stress position. Hill, who was among them, could hear Urey moaning and complaining. It irritated the guards, who beat Urey up severely. He was beaten again on the bus back to the prison, to the point where he vomited, and yet again upon getting off the bus. He spent the next two days in his cell, coughing, rasping and refusing to come out for the daily exercise hour. Two days later, he was found dead.

For once, the guards seemed worried. While the beating had happened outside the jail, and technically not on their watch, the British government knew Urey was being held there. The jail's governor could face sanctions. So might his superiors in the Kremlin. That could spell trouble for everyone down the line.

As news of Urey's death became public, DPR officials put out a statement saying that he'd died from his pre-existing medical problems. They did not explain why, given his poor health, they'd allowed him to be put in prolonged stress positions and then viciously beaten. The British government bought none of it, summoning the Russian ambassador in London for a dressing down. Downing Street said Moscow bore 'full responsibility' for Urey's death.

In the coming days, word went round that FSB officials were nosing around the jail, asking questions. Conditions suddenly improved. Casual beatings stopped altogether. A prison nurse was deployed to examine the PoWs every time they went to and from the prosecutor's office. Urey's old cellmates were even given a TV, as if that would make them forget about it. They could now watch pro-Russian films, the Women's European Football Championship and local DPR news reports. Of Urey's death there was no mention.

21

REPUTATION MANAGEMENT

In late September, the guards told the foreign PoWs to pack their belongings. They were taken to a holding compound, ten of them in the same room for the first time. Some had never seen each other before, matching faces to what had previously just been voices from neighbouring cells. *Hey, I thought you'd be taller ... wow, you don't match your voice.* The banter hid a profound unease. Were they just moving prisons? Were they off to be executed? Or, dare they hope it, might they be on their way to freedom? There'd been rumours of a prisoner exchange buzzing around the cells, but nothing concrete, only vague speculation from the guards. If this was it, surely they'd have had some visit first from the Red Cross, or a phone call from the UN?

The guards said they had no idea. Then again, if they were about to face a firing squad, the prison staff would probably pretend otherwise, if only to make it easier to corral them all together. The guards were also being unusually generous with cigarettes, giving them out to anyone who asked. Drueke stood smoking one, wondering if it was some final gesture of sympathy. Then the guards handcuffed the PoWs and put plastic bags over their heads. Thick masking tape was wrapped on top of the bags around their eyes, so tight it made Drueke's head throb.

They were marched to a flatbed lorry and made to sit in a row on the floor, one wedged tight behind the other. Each prisoner had his handcuffed arms looped around the waist of the man in front of him, binding them all together. The arrangement left each man sat half on top of the man behind, squashing legs, feet and groins.

By the time the truck left the prison, there were already moans of pain. The guards adopted a brutish, not-to-be-messed-with mood. Hill heard the crackle of a taser on someone who wouldn't shut up. As the hours went by, some limbs went completely numb, others hurt ever more. Existing injuries – Hill's bullet-shattered arm, Harding's fractured sternum – made it even worse.

The truck rumbled through the night, heading for what everyone guessed was Russia. Nowhere in the DPR would take that long. Occasionally the guards stopped to refuel, refusing to let the prisoners budge. Anyone who felt the call of nature had to urinate in their pants, soaking the men in front and behind them. Drueke could feel his head swelling either side of the binding, cutting off the blood circulation around his face. Under the plastic bag, he felt the vision in his eyes blacking out. Even after months of enduring stress positions, this was discomfort of a different league.

It's worse than the fucking electricity. Please just kill me now.

For the first time in captivity, he began praying for death. If God was out there – yeah, sure, the guy he said he no longer believed in – could he please just end it all now? Never mind if they were on their way to a prisoner swap. He'd swap the rest of his life as a free man just to be dead, rid of this fucking pain.

They stopped only as dawn was breaking. When they were finally untied, it was ten minutes before Drueke could get to his feet. They were led, still blindfolded, into a building. A smooth marble floor squeaking underfoot. The whirr of automatic doors opening and shutting. Not the typical sounds of a military base or a prison.

When the blindfolds were removed, they found themselves in an empty airport terminal. A blank departure board, deserted check-in desks. A sign said they were in Rostov-on-Don, a city near Russia's border with south-east Ukraine, one of main rearward operating bases for the invasion. That much made sense. What didn't was the group of Arab men sat at a table in one corner, conferring with the guards.

Who the hell were they? They could, theoretically, have been UN representatives from a third country, despatched in secret. Or might they be Syrians? Here to whisk them off to the tender mercies of Bashar al-Assad, Putin's good mate and fellow war criminal?

Drueke was summoned forward. The Arab men asked for his next of kin details, and took his blood pressure. The paperwork on which they wrote everything down bore a letterheading saying: 'Government of Saudi Arabia.' *Saudi Arabia?* What had they got to do with all this? His thoughts ran riot. Months in captivity had not inclined him to give strangers the benefit of the doubt.

Why do you need to know if I've got high blood pressure if you're going to shoot me in the face? And what do you need Mom's details for? So you can ring her afterwards and say: 'Hey, we shot your son in the face?'

Bottles of water were dished out. Bathroom visits laid on. There was the occasional sharp word between the Arabs and the Russians. Some of the Russian guards were taking their masks off, Harding noted anxiously. That meant they no longer cared if the prisoners recognised them. Surely that could only mean one thing.

The PoWs were loaded onto a bus, made to kneel on the floor and told not to look out the windows. The bus drove down a runway, stopping next to a lone jet. Arabic writing on the fuselage. One by one, the prisoners walked up the aircraft stairs.

Inside they were greeted by a Saudi guy in a Savile Row suit with a pistol bulge. He patted them down, then ushered them into the smartest airliner any of them had ever seen. Whatever the next class up from first class was. An entire lounge, with Ottoman settees. The smell of expensive leather. Fit for a head of state. A wealthy one.

Beyond the lounge was another section, with giant La-Z-Boy recliners. The PoWs sat down. This was *weird*. Was this Putin's way of really messing with their heads? Presumably, Drueke figured, there was a bomb on board somewhere, ready to detonate once they were airborne, thinking they were finally free. Blown to pieces in this well-upholstered execution chamber, along with their unsuspecting Arab hosts. The Kremlin spin machine would do the rest.

Foreign prisoners killed in mystery plane crash over Russia.

PoWs had been released as part of goodwill gesture, says Putin.

Initial inquiries point to 'mechanical failure'.

They took off. Stewards bustled back and forth. Harding, too, was convinced that it was all too good to be true. Sooner or later those well-tailored Saudis would make their move.

'Would you like a drink, sir?

'Eh? Me?

'Yes. Coffee, sir? Tea? Water?

'Er, coffee, please.

'How would you like it, sir?'

How would he like it? *How would he like it?* At that point, something clicked. People who were going to kill you wouldn't think of little details like that. Assassins, even slick professional ones, didn't do milk and sugar.

Another of the Savile Row Saudis appeared, one of the guys who'd been in the airport terminal.

'Gentlemen, welcome aboard. You have been part of a prisoner exchange. We are flying to Riyadh, capital of Saudi Arabia. Members of your embassy will be there to meet you.'

A cheer broke out.

*　　*　　*

The flight to Riyadh would take around four hours, the Saudis said. Cigarettes were distributed. Decent ones, not Ukrainian lung-scrapers or roll-ups from a cannibal's castoffs. *Yes sir, you can smoke on this plane, it's a private jet.* From PoWs to rock stars, in just a few hours.

The stewards served shawarmas, took steak orders, gave each PoW a duffle bag containing toiletries and clean clothes. Someone, clearly, had known they'd look and smell like street bums. Who, though? Who had brokered this deal?

A clue came in the form of another well-dressed man, who appeared occasionally from the plane's lounge, an aide in tow. In his fifties, maybe. Grey hair and cropped beard, boyish face. Not Saudi, a European. A dead ringer, Harding and Hill thought, for Roman Abramovic, that Russian oligarch who owned Chelsea FC.

The well-dressed European roamed the aisle, making small talk. He spoke good English. As he chatted to Harding, another PoW, Sean Pinner, couldn't help himself.

'Do you know, by the way, that you look just like Roman Abramovic?'

261

The European man smiled. 'That is because I am Roman Abramovic.'

Could this get any weirder? First the release, then the luxury jet. Now one of the world's richest men, a billionaire many times over, with them on the plane. Abramovic had helped broker the deal to get them freed, his aide said. He couldn't reveal further details right now, but he was happy to have helped out.

Had they not been incarcerated for the last few months, the prisoners might have known that Roman Abramovic was the Chelsea boss no more. Following Russia's invasion of Ukraine, he'd been among seven Russian oligarchs who'd had UK sanctions slapped on them. His assets had been frozen. Chelsea FC, the club whose fortunes he'd transformed, had been put into trusteeship and then sold.

The British government had said that Abramovic's business empire had benefited from ties to the Kremlin. Abramovic had insisted he was being unfairly scapegoated. Since then, he'd acted as an unofficial peacemaker, popping up at talks between Russia and Ukraine in Istanbul, apparently trying to redeem himself in the West's eyes. Hence his presence on the plane, acting as a go-between in a prisoner swap deal, ridding the West of a big diplomatic headache.

A clue about the other key player in the deal came in the prisoner's duffel bags. Inside each was a brand-new iPhone to call their loved ones on when they reached Riyadh. A personal gift, the Saudis said, from His Royal Highness Mohammed bin Salman, the ruler of Saudi Arabia, an absolute monarch. And, like Abramovic, another rich man who wanted to repair his image in the West.

In 2018, he'd been accused of ordering the murder of a prominent Saudi journalist, Jamal Khashoggi, a *Washington Post* columnist. Khashoggi had been killed by a Saudi hit squad in their consulate in Turkey, his corpse dismembered and disposed of. The grisly killing had caused international outrage, casting Bin Salman into the diplomatic wilderness. Couriering the prisoners out of Russia might help rehabilitate him.

At the time, the prisoners knew nothing of this. But Hill did notice that everything they did on the plane – scoffing shawarmas, smoking cigarettes, doing selfies on their new iPhones – was being photographed by the Saudis. Someone clearly had a PR opportunity in mind. Better this, though, than more propaganda videos for the Kremlin.

* * *

After landing at Riyadh, the passengers were photographed again by local Saudi press and met by ambassadors from their respective embassies. It was only then, shaking hands with diplomats from their own countries, that many convinced themselves it wasn't just some elaborate hoax. A high-ranking Ukrainian official was also there. He'd planned to get Zelensky on the phone to speak to them in person, but couldn't get through.

They were bussed to hospital for medical checks, quickly debriefed by embassy officials, then taken to a hotel. The Saudis said they could stay as long as they wanted, as His Majesty's personal guests. But most were keen to get home. There were family and loved ones waiting for them, many of whom had campaigned for their release. Who were now owed hugs, kisses, thanks and, in some cases, explanations.

Harding and Hill opted for the next available flight home, and were escorted to Riyadh airport by Saudi security. They didn't have passports, and were told they couldn't get on the plane. There were advantages, however, to being the guest of His Highness.

'We are from the Prince's Office,' one of the escorts told the desk staff. 'These men are getting on the plane. Otherwise it's not taking off.'

They embarked to curious looks from the other passengers. They were all now wearing the clothes from their duffle bags, which were largely the same. Who were these strange, skinny men? A team of footballers who'd done a particularly gruelling tour? A stag party that had strayed off-course? During the flight, one passenger sitting near Harding took a guess.

'Have you been fighting in Ukraine?' he asked.

'Aye, yes.'

'Can I buy you a drink?'

The VIP treatment continued at Heathrow. The pilot asked the other passengers to remain seated while the 'special guests' disembarked first. Outside the plane, two armed police officers were waiting.

Harding's heart sank. He'd already been questioned a few times coming back from Syria in his YPG days. Was his past about to catch up with him, and his present too? Swapping one jail cell in the DPR for another in Britain?

'Welcome home, gentlemen,' said one officer. 'We know you haven't got passports, so we're going to escort you out. Then we'll take you to a hotel near here, where your families are waiting.'

Harding was greeted by his sister and cousin, family he hadn't seen since leaving Ukraine to join Azov four years before. Hill was greeted by his mother, aunt and grandparents, who could barely recognise him. The strapping 15-stone scaffolder who'd left Plymouth was now just nine stone. His bullet-wounded arm was still healing, barely usable.

He felt bad even letting them see him in this state, but right now there was just smiles, tears and hugs. *You daft bastard. Don't do it again. Well done though.* Even his grandad, who'd warned him not to go, seemed proud.

*　　*　　*

By the time Drueke had landed in Saudi Arabia, he could no longer see. The tape bound around his head during the lorry trip had left him with huge welts above the eyes, and as the swelling had subsided, fluid had slowly drained back down through his face, forcing his eyelids shut like drawdown blinds. When he'd disembarked, he had to use Andy Huynh like a guide dog, putting his hands on his shoulders and following him down the steps to the runway.

He'd been taken to a Saudi hospital for observation overnight, worried he might lose his sight for good. The doctors assured him the blindness was only temporary, although they clearly hadn't been told the full story. 'So when did you discover you were allergic to plastic?' asked one medic, who seemed to think that Drueke had been engaged in some sadomasochistic practice.

Like all the PoWs' families, Drueke's hadn't been told in advance of the prisoner swap. All that his mother, Lois, had got was a cryptic hint from a US State Department official, saying she might get a phone call from an unexpected location.

Even then, she struggled to comprehend when it came through.

'Hi, Mom, it's me, Alex. I'm in Saudi Arabia.'

'What do you mean? What are you doing in Saudi Arabia?'

'Well, I'm free …'

'You're what?'

'Free! *I'm free!*'

Drueke and Huynh flew home to the US together. At the final security checkpoint before getting on the plane, they dithered like sheep. It was the first time in three months that someone hadn't been there escorting them, telling them what to do.

At the airport in New York, an FBI team were waiting. The last thing Drueke wanted was yet more burly men ushering him into a room for questioning, but he stuck with it. They wanted to photograph his injuries while they were still fresh. Who knew, maybe the photos would one day be presented at The Hague, with Dead Eyes sat in the dock.

The FBI drove them to a hotel, where Drueke's mother and Huynh's fiancée, Joy Black, were on their way to meet them. When Drueke turned on the TV in his room, he saw his own face staring out on a CNN broadcast about the prisoner swap. Along with the 10 foreign PoWs, 205 Ukrainian soldiers had been released, including the Azov commanders who'd led the last stand at Mariupol.

In exchange, the Ukrainians had freed 55 prisoners, including Viktor Medvedchuk, a Ukrainian oligarch who'd led a pro-Russian party. Putin had lined him up as the man to take over from Zelensky once Kyiv fell. Another part of his invasion plan that hadn't worked out. Zelensky was talking on CNN right now about the prisoner swap, how it showed Ukraine didn't forget its defenders, be they Ukrainians or Legionnaires.

'This is clearly a victory for our country, for our entire society,' he said. 'And the main thing is that 215 families can see their loved ones safe and at home.'

A few hours later, Drueke's mother and Huynh's fiancée arrived at the hotel. The two Legionnaires hid in the lobby, jumping out at them. An ambush, just like that one up near Kharkiv back in June. Only this time it was them, not the Russians, who had surprise on their side.

22

PIPE DREAMS

The terms of the deal that freed the foreign PoWs remained shrouded in mystery. The Kremlin would have regarded them as valuable bargaining chips, and would not have given them up lightly. There was speculation that beyond the basic prisoner exchange, whatever deal had spared the PoWs from the gallows might have taken extra greasing.

Had Roman Abramovic pulled some favours in Moscow? Had the Crown Prince written a few cheques in Riyadh? Or had London or Washington made some secret concessions? If they had, they weren't saying. The only comment from Downing Street was a tweet from Liz Truss, then in her brief tenure as Prime Minister:

'Hugely welcome news that the British nationals held by Russian-backed proxies in eastern Ukraine are being safely returned. I thank @ZelenskyyUa for his efforts to secure the release of detainees, and Saudi Arabia for their assistance.'

Anyone reading the statement got the impression that the swap was all down to Zelensky, and that Kyiv was clearly prepared to go to special lengths for its foreign volunteers. Yet on the ground, the Legion continued to fall somewhat short of the ideal that Zelensky had first sold the world. For from being Ukraine's answer to Spain's International Brigade, it remained a shambles – beset by low morale, and losing what few decent soldiers came its way.

At the start of the invasion, few had been surprised by the Legion's shortcomings. Ukraine had been plunged into war overnight, the president and his retinue huddled in an underground bunker. Six months in, however, many felt things should have improved. Among them were three Legion officials, who compiled a secret internal report, based partly on their own concerns and partly on those raised by disgruntled volunteers.* They sent it to Zelensky's office several months into the war, warning that many Legionnaires now felt betrayed:

'When President Zelensky announced the creation of the International Legion, his speech gave the impression that this would be a well-structured institution that would welcome foreign fighters … The reality has proven quite different. Many of our brothers-in-arms feel that the Ukrainian army has let them down and sold them a pipe dream.'

The report ran to 80 pages. It warned that the Legion was 'a PR disaster waiting to happen', and cited plenty of examples to back up its claims. For a start, the Legion didn't officially exist. No law or presidential decree had ever been signed to create it. Nor was there a proper paperwork trail. Many Legionnaires had never even been issued proper contracts, meaning they had no official protection under the Geneva Convention.

Volunteers, the report complained, had been accepted 'regardless of experience', allowing undesirables to tarnish the Legion's reputation. Equally bad were some of the Ukrainian commanders put in charge of the Legion. Several were incompetents who had risked volunteers' lives unnecessarily. At least one had links to organised crime.

---

* Copy of report seen by author.

The picture painted was of an administrative mess, created with little forethought about the practicalities. Which, as far as the Legion staffers understood, was exactly what had happened. When Zelensky had issued his appeal for volunteers on the war's third day, rumour had it that he'd done so without notifying anyone else in his government. He'd apparently blindsided his own army chiefs, who had no capacity to train large numbers of foreigners unfamiliar with their language or military customs. Nor did they have any real need for them, given the hundreds of thousands of Ukrainian volunteers queueing at their own recruitment offices.

By then it was already too late. Zelensky's appeal had been broadcast worldwide, with thousands of volunteers already streaming in over the border. To start off with, just one single government official was put in charge of receiving and hosting the Legionnaires – hence the chaos and lack of vetting at training centres like Yavoriv. In the early days, some training camps hadn't even had toilet paper or food, the report said. Legionnaires had used toothbrushes to clean their weapons.

A small cadre of the more experienced foreigners had been deployed straight into battle during the siege of Kyiv, where some had played a useful role. But others had been made subordinate to Ukrainian commanders who were at best incompetent, at worst a danger to themselves and others. The report singled out one Ukrainian commander, Vasyl*, whom a number of Legionnaires had described as 'mentally unhinged'. It included a sworn statement from one of the foreign officers in his command, who had eventually refused to work with him.

'It soon became clear to me that Bogdan was without any kind of organisational skills. Planning seems to be disregarded as "not important because there is a war on" … and being proof

of me and the other foreign officers lacking an understanding of the realities of war.'

Tensions had been exacerbated by Vasyl's poor punctuality, the officer claimed, saying that he kept his soldiers waiting while he took footbaths. When the officer himself once turned up late for a meeting, Vasyl had then fired him, leading to a near-mutiny among other Legionnaires. That in turn had led to the officer being hauled before a 'Stalinist-styled people's court' and accused of espionage.

'Vasyl had prepared a judge (his chief of staff), a jury (his second-in-command) and witnesses (a couple of disgruntled drunk soldiers). He was clearly trying to convince the other foreign officers that I was indeed a Russian spy, who was trying to get them all killed.

'The only thing that saved me was the utter incompetence of the Ukrainian command and their inability to form a logical argument and the fact that the foreign officers were not buying any of it.'

Another foreign officer – a 'highly regarded former company commander' – said that he and 20 other Legionnaires had eventually left Vasyl's command because they felt their lives were in danger.

'Please, for the love of God, replace him with anyone before good people get hurt or die. Do everything in your power to end the insanity, it will be a massive PR fiasco. People are telling their families to blame him, not the enemy, in case they die.'

Many Legionnaires were not attached to the regular Ukrainian army, but to the HUR, Ukraine's shadowy military intelligence wing, which used them for recon missions. The war had already made a legend of the HUR's boss, Kyrylo Budanov, whose campaigns behind Russian lines had seen US officials hail him as 'George Smiley meets Jason Bourne'. Less impressive were some of the underlings that the HUR had put in charge of the Legionnaires.

One underling was a commander known as 'Colonel Eugene Kuchynsky', whom the *Kyiv Independent*, an investigative newspaper, later alleged was a Polish gangster operating under a pseudonym. According to a dossier of sworn statements sent to the president's office,* Kuchysnky ordered a group of Legionnaires to loot a supermarket in the Donbas in the summer of 2022. Among them was a Canadian ex-police officer.

'During our operations in Severodonetsk, Eugene Kuchynsky ordered me to go the mall to collect certain items on his behalf, as I understood including furniture, jewellery, electronics, etc. I directly heard Kuchynsky's order to the soldiers of my unit to break into the shopping centre, collect the furniture as soon as possible, and collect all possible valuables along the way. I know that during the above illegal actions ordered by Kuchynsky, we found residents on the streets of the city who, seeing this, shouted that you were "no better than the Russians".'

The report also said the Legion's bureaucracy was in a mess, with many volunteers missing out on their $600 monthly stipend. Nor did they get any official recognition or thanks when leaving.

'Foreigners who came to this country, leaving behind their homes, families, jobs and businesses, risking their life in often very challenging conditions … leave the army and the country without any recognition from the state. No pay, no thank you, no medals or recognition.'

The poor bookkeeping also meant the Legion had patchy next-of-kin records, making it difficult to notify family when they'd been killed. In the first two months of the war there had

---

* Copies of statements seen by the author.

also been no proper system for repatriating those killed in action, sometimes forcing relatives to pay for repatriation themselves. In the case of Scott Sibley, the first British Legionnaire to be killed, his body had got stuck for weeks in an overcrowded morgue in Mykolaiv, where some of the dead were being stored in shipping containers. Eventually some of his comrades had taken matters into their own hands.

One day they had turned up at the morgue in their uniforms, bluffed their way in by saying they were there to collect Sibley's body, then loaded it into a waiting van. They drove the corpse 500 miles to Lviv for collection by embassy officials, where further delays took place because of the lack of a death certificate. Sibley's comrades had feared that his corpse wasn't being looked after properly, or might simply go missing, especially if Mykolaiv fell back again under Russian control. But Ukrainian officials had not been pleased at what they saw as an act of bodysnatching. Warrants had been issued for the Legionnaires' arrests, later dropped.

It was yet another example of how things could go wrong when volunteers were left to fend for themselves. Had they all been enlisted into large, self-contained battalions from the outset, there'd have been far fewer opportunities for getting into trouble. Instead, they'd had to tout their services haphazardly around the frontlines, making as many enemies as friends. While some volunteers had impressed the Ukrainians, others were seen as a law unto themselves, part-timers who could quit when they wanted, more familiar with Kyiv's bars and brothels than the battlefield. Many Ukrainian commanders felt the Legion was a waste of time, the report warned.

'*Resources are being spent on food, salaries and weapons (for the Legion) that could be going to Ukrainian units, and on the field of battle the results have been disappointing. The brass seems to have formed an opinion of our Legionnaires being deserters, cowards and rookies in the field of battle.*

'But it can hardly be surprising that the Legions' results have yet to impress, considering the piecemeal approach that has been adopted to the Legion's setup.'

The report's authors said they feared that speaking out could lose them their jobs, but that their own bosses had ignored their concerns. Their superiors had dismissed the volunteers as lazy cowards 'who desert the battlefield at the first opportunity, and therefore nothing they report can be trusted or relied upon'.

As well as the president's office, the report was sent to the General Staff of Ukraine's Armed Forces, along with a warning to keep it private for fear of jeopardising Western support to Ukraine. Perhaps its authors thought that, as a consummate showman himself, Zelensky would be acutely sensitive to the Legion generating bad headlines. But by the time the president gave his speech congratulating the PoWs on their release, they'd still had no response.

23

NOWHERE TO RUN TO

Kherson, autumn 2022–spring 2023

Ever since its capture in the first week of the invasion, Russian-occupied Kherson had served as a warning to the rest of Ukraine not to succumb to the same fate. Anti-Kremlin protests in the city's Freedom Square had been met with tear gas and gunfire. Anyone suspected of pro-Ukrainian sympathies was arrested and tortured. More than two-thirds of Kherson's 300,000 people fled, while those who remained felt like they were back in Soviet times. Shops and businesses shut, collapsing the economy to the level of a car boot sale. Food was sold was on street corners, at black market prices. Many residents spent nearly all their time indoors, avoiding the eyes of Russian security forces and the ears of neighbours who might be collaborators.

The Kremlin tried a charm offensive, hoping to make Kherson a showcase for Mother Russia's embrace. Newly installed commissars re-erected Soviet monuments and introduced pro-Russian cultural programmes in schools. The rouble was introduced as the currency, locals offered Russian passports.

It didn't work. By summer 2022, a well-organised resistance movement was underway. Hit squads of partisans targeted the commissars, planting bombs in their cars, gunning them down in cafés. Activists scrawled anti-Putin graffiti on street corners, alongside 'Wanted' posters of alleged collaborators. On the frontlines outside Kherson, Ukrainian forces and their Legionnaire allies, including groups like Daniel Burke's Dark Angels, continued to skirmish with Russian forces.

The real game-changer, however, came from far behind the frontlines, in the form of new US-supplied High Mobility Artillery Rocket Systems. The Himars, as it was better known, could plant 100 kg of explosive onto a dinner table-sized target from 50 miles away. The Ukrainians used them to pulverize Russian supply depots, bridges and command HQs around Kherson, making the city ever harder to defend.

As the autumn drew near, talk grew of a major Ukrainian push to recapture Kherson, building on the momentum of the north-east counter-offensive. The Dark Angels were hoping to take part, although Burke knew that even with 'General Himars' behind them it would be a tough fight. By then, he had a new team, with Jack Knight as his second-in-command, and several new volunteers who hadn't seen combat before. During training sessions, he warned that as they pushed towards Kherson casualties would be inevitable.

'This isn't Iraq or Afghanistan, where you can work around problems to avoid casualties,' he told them. 'There will be days when a Russian position has to be taken, where you know you'll get multiple casualties, because you can only approach through a few treelines that are vulnerable to Russian automatic gunfire.'

Nobody pulled out. This promised to be the most important battle since the defence of Kyiv. A chance to liberate not just a few hundred square miles of fields, or a few bomb-wrecked towns, but an entire city and its people, now living in misery. They'd be taking part in history.

Then, in typically unsporting fashion, the Russians spoilt it all. On 9 November, Russia's top commander in Ukraine,

General Sergey Surovikin, announced that the 40,000 troops in Kherson were withdrawing. He blamed Ukrainian forces, whom he said were 'firing indiscriminately at the city', putting civilian lives in danger.

Given Surovikin's hardman reputation – he was nicknamed 'General Armageddon' for his scorched-earth campaign in Syria – it seemed unlikely that humanitarian concerns were really his priority. Yet, sure enough, Russian convoys promptly left Kherson and pulled back across the bridges that led east over the River Dnieper, dynamiting them in their wake. In the following days, Ukrainian troops swept back into the city. Freedom Square filled with cheering crowds, popping champagne corks and tearing down pro-Russian posters.

It was a great moment for Ukraine, less so for the Legionnaires. The Dark Angels weren't invited to take part in securing the city, and only learned of the Russian pull-out on the TV news. A few drove down there out of curiosity, by which time the party was already in full swing. Jack Knight stood in Freedom Square, exchanging handshakes and hugs from locals, who spotted the small Union Jack on his uniform.

He was probably the only person in the crowds who felt a slight tinge of disappointment. Nice as it was to be hailed as a conquering hero, he hadn't really had to fight. He'd come to Ukraine to follow in the footsteps of his great-grandad, William Young, the one who'd won the VC at the Somme. If his ancestor was looking down on him now, he'd be telling him to find some other frontline to prove himself on.

* * *

The euphoria in Kherson was short-lived. Having retreated to the far side of the Dnieper, Russian forces simply began shelling the city from afar. Random mortar fire landed round the clock, slaughtering dozens of civilians. Soon the streets were even emptier than they were during the occupation. Meanwhile, fighting intensified for the islands of the Dnieper delta south of Kherson, where the river emptied into the Black Sea. Whoever controlled them controlled access to Ukraine's main waterway, which wound back 800 miles to Kyiv and connected half the country's big cities.

Among those now fighting on the islands were a Legionnaire unit called Vidmak. The name meant 'Warlock' in Ukrainian, and on top of other volunteer units like the Dark Angels, Wolverines and Spartans made the Legion sound like the billing for a heavy metal festival. In common with many rock groups, most units had ever-changing line-ups, brought about by casualties, personality clashes and irreconcilable combat differences.

Within Vidmak, for example, were a couple of ex-Dark Angels, and Christopher Perryman, who'd gone home in April 2022 after running out of money. He'd vowed to come back if he could find a good unit to fight with, and felt he'd done so with Vidmak. Even though life on the islands was about as far from a typical battleground as one could imagine.

Most of the islands were patches of grassland no more than a mile or two wide, separated from each other by channels, swamps and lakes. They were full of holiday chalets and shutterboard retirement shacks, where pensioners would tend vegetable patches and brew moonshine. Compared to the grimy Donbas, with its steel factories, trenches and tank battles, it felt quite literally like a backwater. Yet it had perils all of its own.

The only way in was via speedboat from the Ukrainian-held side of the Dnipro – a high-speed dash through the ice floes, with no hiding from Russian drones and artillery. They'd then be left on the island for a week at a time, aware that if things went wrong, there was no way off. Many islands were split between Ukrainian and Russian control, so the task was largely just to man OPs, holding the ground. The problem was finding firm ground to hold. It was too marshy to dig trenches, and the shutterboard retirement shacks offered no protection against artillery. The only proper cover was in the islands' few brick buildings, which the Russians shelled pre-emptively.

The artillery was relentless, as were the drones, which buzzed their way over the marshes like giant mosquitoes. Some would even hover outside windows, peering in. That prevented the soldiers having lights on at night, or even brewing tea for fear that a stove light might be spotted. The windows couldn't be closed in case they needed to open fire, and at night temperatures could drop to minus 10 degrees centigrade. Watch duty was limited to an hour at a time to stop the risk of hypothermia.

There was little to do except take turns in the observation point and sit out the bombardments. On Perryman's third mission, a shell directly hit the house he was sleeping in, destroying two walls. He woke up covered in bricks, bits of cupboard and garden soil. His grab bag by his side was shredded by shrapnel, while his flak jacket resembled a dartboard. Stuck in it were dozens of 'flechettes', pieces of arrow-shaped shrapnel designed to tear human flesh. Why he wasn't dead, he had no idea.

They were sitting ducks, unable to swim away. But what some might have found an unrewarding soldiering experience, Perryman saw as a challenge. It was a marathon of mental stamina – an endless stake-out with no escape route, where just one flechette could kill if it hit an artery. Not that anyone dwelt on it. To do that was to invite a breakdown. The only thing was to focus on the task, waiting to see if the Russians might finally try a big push. Then, finally, there'd be a chance to fight back.

* * *

While life on the islands might not have suited the average Instagram warrior, it didn't stop the Vidmak Group becoming social media heroes. Like many volunteers, they had big Twitter followings, from policy wonks and keyboard warriors to well-wishers round the world. They took their role as frontline 'influencers' seriously, giving running commentaries on the war, and appealing for donations of funds and equipment.

Perryman alone had more than 20,000 Twitter followers, some of whom seemed to regard him as a personal friend. He'd get dozens of messages a day, and would often spend hours drafting personalised replies, especially if people had been generous. The last thing he thought he'd need in Ukraine was his own PR man. It was a change from life in the Fusiliers, where the only fan mail was the odd letter from the Duke of Kent, its honorary colonel-in-chief.

Not all the Legionnaires' followers were well-wishers. Some were pro-Kremlin trolls, denouncing the volunteers as knaves and losers, whose main reason for coming to Ukraine were the opportunities for gay sex in the trenches. They'd warn that the only way home was in a body bag, and would post gloating comments whenever that happened.

Some of Vidmak's members gave as good as they got, waging trolling duels with pro-Russian accounts, including some belonging to soldiers fighting on the Dnieper delta islands. Or so it seemed anyway. The posts could just as easily have been coming from a Russian troll factory in Moscow.

* * *

One evening in March 2023, Perryman was manning an OP at a place nicknamed 'Faggot Island', in honour of the Russian troops who occupied parts of it. The OP was in a stone-built, two-storey summer house, an open-plan diner-kitchen below, an upstairs room with a balcony that offered a decent watch position.

Perryman was with four others: an American call-signed Tuc, an Aussie named Matt, an Albanian named Tony and a Ukrainian named Igor, who doubled as translator. They were already tired and on edge. The night before, they'd been on an operation to take a few hundred metres of new ground, during which a Ukrainian unit who'd pushed ahead had got into a fire-fight. The Ukrainians had radioed for help, but could not give an accurate location of where they were. Without that, the volunteers would have been wandering into a gunbattle in the pitch dark, so they'd stayed put. It was the right call, although it hadn't pleased the Ukrainian unit's commander, who felt he'd been abandoned. It had been a tiring, stressful 24 hours, and everyone was now praying for a quiet night.

With Tuc upstairs on watch duty, Perryman had clambered into his sleeping bag on the kitchen-diner floor. It was only early evening, but he'd barely slept the night before, and he was on guard duty later. He'd been woken up later by something crashing onto the floor. Ten feet away, under one of the diner benches, was a cylinder the size of a toilet roll, pumping out smoke.

What the fuck? Fucking smoke grenade …?

He felt his way in the dark towards the stairs, the taste of smoke already in his throat. No time to grab his body armour, or his sniper rifle. If someone was close enough to chuck in a smoke grenade from outside, the next thing they'd probably do was fire a burst through a window. As he reached the top of the stairs, he saw Matt carrying the PKM.

'What the fuck is going on?' Perryman asked.

'There's Russians outside, they're trying to get in!'

'I know! They've just put a smoke grenade into the fucking living room!'

Perryman went through to the watch position, where Tuc, Igor and Tony were. He could now also smell tear gas.

'Russians have just walked down the garden speaking English,' Tuc said. 'They've told us to come out, they want us to surrender.'

Perryman got on his hands and knees, trying to find his other weapon. His sniper rifle, which was big and heavy, wasn't best in close-quarters stuff, so he kept an assault rifle as a back-up. He'd left it here upstairs, next to the watch position. Where the fuck was it?

As he searched, he could hear more grenades downstairs. The tear gas was getting stronger. The others were running around, trying to take positions. He could hear voices outside. Matt, at the top of the stairs with the PKM, fired several bursts down the stairs.

The smoke and gas got thicker. Perryman started to choke. He opened a balcony door to let in air. A volley of fire smashed a window, forcing him to the floor. Igor was screaming down the radio for help. He told command that if another unit could get near, they could just spray the lower half of the house with gunfire. None of the Legionnaires were downstairs now, but some of the Russians might be.

There were several Ukrainian teams nearby, one in a house just a few hundred yards away. None radioed to say they were coming to help. *Why the fuck weren't they doing anything?*, Perryman wondered. Not that he was being much help himself.

With no weapon and no body armour, he was no use to anyone, a bloody civvy again.

Rounds kept coming in, plus more CS gas and stun grenades downstairs. Confusion took hold, everyone groping around in the pitch dark. Something hit Perryman's right hand, half-severing a finger. Some shrapnel shattered Tony's weapon, leaving him unarmed too. He pulled out a combat knife and stood at the top of the stairs, ready to plunge it into anyone who clambered up. The attackers were shouting at them in a mixture of English and Russian, telling them to surrender.

Hey, Suka (bitch). Come down! Come down!

Perryman saw no other option. They had no back-up, and he had no weapon to fight a last stand with. If they surrendered now, hopefully all they'd get would be a kicking and some rough stuff in jail. Besides, it seemed the Russians knew they were foreigners, in which case they'd want them alive.

'Igor, tell them we fucking surrender,' he said.

'No way,' Igor replied.

A rocket-propelled grenade hit the house, sending everyone sprawling. When the dust cleared, half the roof was caved in, beams and tiles everywhere. Then silence.

'Anyone dead?' Perryman shouted.

No answer.

'Anyone dead? Anyone hit?'

No answer.

Fuck, were they all dead? Perryman crawled to the balcony, now half-destroyed, Better to be out here and risk getting shot, than stay inside and choke to death. Outside he could hear people shouting, crying in pain. Earlier, Igor had thrown a couple of grenades. Perhaps the Russians had taken casualties.

Parts of the house were now on fire. He looked down from the balcony. A long drop. Twenty feet perhaps. But outside, the darkness would be his friend. A chance, maybe, to get away unseen.

Fuck it. It's that or stay here and die.

He clambered over the handrail, lowering himself down as much as he could. Then he let go, feeling like he was on the field obstacle course at training back in Harrogate. Only this drop was onto solid concrete, not a sandpit.

His legs buckled under him as he hit the ground, pitching him forward and smashing his head into the wall of the house. He was dizzy as he got up, one ankle feeling like it might be broken. But he could still move. He staggered to a woodshed nearby, breathing his first fresh air in half an hour. He could hear Russian voices in the garden. Getting closer.

He rummaged amidst the shed's woodpiles for a weapon. No point in trying to surrender now. If the Russians had taken casualties, they wouldn't be merciful. He found a metal bar, couldn't hold it properly because of his injured finger, so grabbed a brick. Anyone coming through the shed door would get it in their face. He ripped his sniper badges off his uniform. Too many stories of snipers being singled out for torture because they'd shot some Russian's buddy.

Okay. Give yourself a few minutes. Get your breath back. Calm down. Then think about how to get out.

There was a fence around the garden, seven feet high. If he could clamber over that, despite his messed-up ankle and hand, maybe he could get to one of the nearby houses with Ukrainian troops in. They hadn't done a fucking thing to help so far, but he could at least scrounge a weapon off them.

He hobbled out of the shed and leaped blindly at the fence, adrenalin somehow carrying him over. The nearest Ukrainian position was a house about 500 metres back. He crawled and staggered towards it, stifling coughs from the CS gas soaked into his clothes.

At the house, he banged on the door. No answer. He could hear someone approaching. He hid in some bushes, close to the muster point where the speedboats came in. The figure drew nearer. To Perryman's astonishment, it was Matt. He'd thought Matt was dead with the others in the house.

Matt helped him to a Ukrainian position for first aid. A message came on the radio that three people had been pulled out from the house. *Fuck. Half the mission team killed.*

Perryman sat exhausted, projectile vomiting from the CS gas. A speedboat arrived to take them back to Kherson. As he got near the boat, Perryman thought he heard a familiar voice. Was that Tuc talking? No, Tuc was dead. He must be in shock.

They boarded the boat to find Tuc, Igor and Tony all already on board. All bandaged up from injuries, but all still alive. In the chaos of the assault, with grenades, gas and smoke engulfing them in the pitch dark, everyone had somehow made their way out separately, convinced the rest were dead.

* * *

They spent the next few days in hospital, while Ukrainian command launched an investigation. The Legionnaires were asked for formal written statements, and told not to contact the Ukrainians in the battalion. Something had gone very wrong. How had the Russians known there were foreigners in there? And why had no Ukrainian units come to their aid?

At first, Perryman wondered if they'd been set up by their own side. Perhaps it was because of bad blood with that commander, the one who'd asked for help during that firefight the night before. Tempting as it was to believe, though, would it really be that easy for anyone to tip the Russians off in a fit of pique? They couldn't just ring up the Kremlin. They'd need a trusted contact on the other side, who'd know it wasn't just an attempt to lure them into a trap.

The whole thing was a blur for all involved – a gunfight in the pitch dark, with smoke, CS and grenades everywhere. But it might have been cock-up rather than conspiracy. The Russians had approached the house without firing at first, suggesting they were unaware it was even occupied, or thought it was one of their own OPs. Two had even knocked on the door, at which point someone upstairs had shouted for a password. That could have alerted them to the foreigners' presence.

As to why no Ukrainians had come to their aid, one senior officer confided that he thought the troops had simply frozen. Not their finest hour, he admitted. Although as the Legionnaires themselves knew, getting involved in someone's else's firefight in the dark was not something to be done lightly.

There were recriminations within Vidmak itself, as they pieced together the night's events. The others were unimpressed that Perryman had been without his weapon during the battle and therefore combat ineffective. Perryman said it been upstairs on the watch point where he'd left it, and that one of the others had grabbed it during the assault. His comrades said he should never have let it leave his side in the first place.

In truth, they'd all done well to get out alive. Somewhere during the fight – either thanks to Matt's PKM bursts or Igor's grenades – they'd caused at least a couple of Russian casualties, forcing the attackers to pull back. That they'd fought their way out, though, made the others resentful of Perryman's advice to surrender. To him, it had seemed like the right call at the time. To them, it was the actions of a man caught on the hop without his weapon.

They tried to keep it cordial. Everyone made mistakes, just like they did in civilian jobs back home. The difference was that a bad day at work here could get everyone killed. And the arguments over the night's events also laid bare wider tensions. Much as the others considered Perryman a good soldier, there were disadvantages to having a seen-it-all old hand on the team. They felt he could be set in his ways, not keen to be told when he was wrong.

Perryman had his own gripes about Vidmak. He didn't like how a couple of them would smoke weed while on mission. It wasn't unknown for soldiers on Ukraine's frontlines to have a quiet puff while on stag duty, but in Perryman's British Army-trained mind it broke every rule in the book.

So too, in his opinion, did Vidmak's social media troll battles with Russian units. It was one thing to do some PR for the unit on Twitter. It was another to goad some bunch who might be right on the opposite side of the river. He couldn't help thinking that that was why they'd been tracked down in the house. Vidmak's other members told him that was nonsense, that they never posted pictures of where they were.

The plan was to treat the whole incident as a 'lessons learned' episode. But a few days later, while feelings were still running high, things nearly came to blows between Perryman and another team member during a meal in a restaurant. The rest of Vidmak told Perryman they wanted him to leave.

He wasn't bothered. Some of them he'd remained on good terms with. Others he felt had ganged up on him, and no longer wanted to be with anyway. Besides, he'd already had an offer from a new unit, one that might offer better roles for a sniper. Meanwhile, more importantly, he was off for some much-overdue R&R, to see his son back home. The lad didn't know what he was up to out in Ukraine, so no need to talk about events on Faggot Island. He'd think of some excuse for that injured finger.

24

BACK ON THE HORSE

Plymouth, Devon, summer 2023

The weekly 'Man Down' meetings in Plymouth were a new self-help group trying to get men to open up about their problems. Aimed at those more used to just having to 'man up', it was tailored to a clientele wary of showing their sensitive side. Nothing too touchy-feely, no New Age therapy speak. Just blokes in a room talking about their problems. No topic off-limits, be it sex, depression, drink and drugs or mid-life crises. Even so, there was something of an awkward silence when a new face one night took his turn to share.

'Hello, my name is Andrew Hill. I don't know if you're aware of who I am, but I am ex-military. I went to Ukraine to fight, and was shot and captured. After that I was held as a prisoner of war. I was tortured and beaten, and told I would be executed.'

It was the shortened, one-minute version of his five-month ordeal, minus all the gory details. But he could still see jaws dropping. The others had all been talking about stress in their personal lives: difficulties with the wife and kids, not wanting to go to work, problems with divorce settlements, benefits payments. This was stress of a different league. Then, after the silence, the questions started.

Why did you go over there?
What was it like fighting there?

What did they do to you?

It was supposed to be a free-ranging 90-minute session, everyone chipping in about their issues. In the end, they spent most of it just talking about him. Perhaps it put their own lives into perspective a bit. Or perhaps it was just more interesting than hearing yet more domestic woes.

Hill had been referred to Man Down by an ex-army pal, who said it was good, no-bullshit stuff. But he quit after two sessions. It was tailored to civilian life, civilian problems. What he'd been through was something only fellow soldiers would identify with, and even then, not many. No ex-British Army people had spent time in PoW camps since the Korean War, let alone been tortured by Kremlin thugs.

It all added to a sense of loneliness that had been stalking him since he'd got back, through which booze was becoming his only companion. The euphoria of his release had been wonderful, like being born again. But when he'd got back to his family in Plymouth, he'd been reminded that their lives had had to grind on as normal while his had hung in the balance.

His nan had coped by keeping mementoes of him around the house – a pair of his gloves, his beanie hat – telling herself that they needed to stay where they were because Andrew would soon be back to get them. His grandad had done the same, spending long hours working on Andrew's motorbike. His youngest kid had looked almost scared when Daddy had first turned up, barely recognising the pencil-thin figure waving hello with his one good arm.

Others in the suburb where he lived recognised him all too easily. No longer was he Andrew Hill, private citizen, who could mind his own business, nip out for a quiet pint undisturbed. He was now Andrew Hill, the Guy Who'd Been in the News, who'd fought in Ukraine. A local hero, whether he liked it or not. Every time he went out, be it to walk the dog, buy fags from the newsagent or go to the pub, he'd get people coming up to him, staring at his injured arm and asking him how he was.

Most were supportive. Some had even prayed for him at his local church, where the reverend had asked him to be remembered every Sunday. Yet for a quiet suburb of Plymouth, a surprising number seemed to take the Kremlin line, claiming the British media was lying about the war, and that Hill shouldn't have fought for Ukraine. One guy in the pub was borderline aggressive, insisting there was no Legion, that it was all Western propaganda, that Hill had never actually been to Ukraine. Not even the Russian interrogators had tried to claim that. It was a tense encounter, made all the worse by Hill feeling that if it had come to blows, he'd have had only one arm to fight with.

Celebrity, he realised, did not agree with him. It was one thing to recount a few war stories over beers with mates. It was another to have random people coming up to interrogate him, including lunatics who'd been reading Kremlin propaganda online. Plus he was tired of being asked questions about it. When he'd first been released, the Counter Terrorism Branch at Scotland Yard had debriefed him intensively, showing him mugshots of various Russian spooks, asking him to describe every room in the black site prison in minute detail. It had taken nearly three weeks.

He felt a sense of drift, of struggling to re-adjust. If he'd been on an army deployment to Iraq or Afghanistan, they'd have been given decompression time before coming home. A few days on a base in Cyprus, drinking beer, relaxing on the beach. With the prisoner swap, they'd been in prison one day, back in Britain the next. Suddenly back with people he'd never expected to see again. Everything felt far too normal, and at the same time not normal at all. He struggled to sleep at night, and would jump at the slightest noise. The only thing that took the edge off things was booze – at first in the pub, and when that got irksome because of the unwanted attention, in the living room at home.

While self-medicating, he would also self-diagnose. Part of it, he sensed, was survivors' guilt, beating such long odds when so many others in Ukraine hadn't. Since he'd got back, he'd learned that several other Legionnaires he'd fought with had died or been seriously injured. It was hard to simply move on in life, knowing that the war was not yet won, that his comrades were still fighting. Everyone out there was telling him that he'd done his bit, that he'd suffered quite enough. But it wasn't as simple as that.

Being a soldier was part of his identity, the more so since his time doing proper combat in Ukraine. He wanted to know if he was still that person, the one who could stay calm under fire, who didn't flinch at artillery. Just like a horse-rider getting back in the saddle after a fall, or a surfer going back to the waves after a bad wipe-out, the only way forward was to face his dangers again. The thought of it scared him, even more so than last time. If he got taken PoW again, he'd surely get no mercy. But if he didn't go, he'd feel weak, cowardly, unsure who he really was anymore. It was, yes, very much the 'Man Up' school of thought, not the 'Man Down'. But he was a soldier, not a civilian. This would be his way of seeking closure.

* * *

Candice, Hill's partner, was aghast at the idea of him returning to Ukraine. He'd put everyone through hell once already, and what, now he wanted to go and do it again? It might represent closure for him, but for the rest of his family, it would re-open wounds that were still very fresh.

Every household who had a loved one taken PoW in Ukraine had had a difficult time, but Hill's had endured particular horrors. When he'd first been captured down near Mykolaiv, the police had visited to tell them he'd gone missing. The following day, however, Candice had received a call from a Legion official, saying he'd been killed in action. It was yet another case of the Legion's bureaucratic ineptitude, but the family took the official at their word. They'd spent the rest of the day in mourning.

Then, just as they were beginning to wonder about how to get his body back, a relative had chanced to look at Hill's Facebook page. A video had just been uploaded on it, showing him bandaged and undergoing an interrogation. His captors had hacked into his page and posted the video there themselves, clearly hoping to shock his family and friends. It did – although it also proved that he was still alive.

Whoever had posted the video of Hill also had access to Hill's phone. A few days later, while taking the train to London for an update from the Ukrainian embassy, Candice received a strange text message, a series of morbid emojis showing skulls and Grim Reapers. Messages then arrived saying that if Hill's family did not pay 250,000 euros ransom, he would be killed by 25 May. A photo of a Russian bank card was also sent.

The Foreign Office had sent down a team of ransom experts from Scotland Yard, who'd advised Candice to simply ignore the messages. That was easier said than done. Whoever had the phone had accessed all Hill's photos, found some intimate photos of Candice and sent them to every one of the contacts on Hill's phone. It was a cruel, humiliating trick, routinely inflicted by Russians on captured Ukrainians. Candice had only found out from a friend, who'd received one of the photos and asked: 'Do you know they've got these images of you?'

It would later turn out that the demands were being made not by Hill's interrogators, but by one of the Russian squaddies who'd captured him, who'd stolen his mobile and was trying to make some money on the side. Even the Kremlin had not approved. After learning via diplomatic channels that ransom demands had been made, officials in the DPR jail had told Hill they were trying to track the miscreant down.

After all they'd been through, Candice felt he was being selfish to want to go back. She also knew that he was stubborn, and that if his mind was made up to go back out again, no amount of talking would change him. Besides, in the gloomy state he was now in, he was no better than he was before the war started. He'd promised it would be a short tour, just enough to chase his demons away, and that he'd be back to see his son for his birthday in three months' time. If this was what it took to get the cheerful Andrew back, so be it.

25

IN HIS ANCESTOR'S FOOTSTEPS

'In a war, there is often a place for mad people.'
General Montgomery, 1942

After the Russians' retreat from Kherson in November 2022, Jack Knight had returned to Britain, pondering his next move in life. He'd found a job as a warehouse technician for Amazon – similar to his old gig at Ocado, only rather than being the nation's grocer-in-chief, he was keeping it supplied in books and gadgets. It paid £75,000 with overtime, but it was often 12-hour shifts, sitting alone. Much of which he spent listening to the different voices in his head, arguing about whether to go back to Ukraine.

One voice told him it was time to call it a day. Sure, the Kherson offensive had been a damp squib. No chance to win a Victoria Cross like his great-great-grandfather's. But he'd done his own small bit, endured some scary moments without bottling it. Why not quit while he was ahead, and in one piece? Unlike those two other volunteers he knew, who'd recently both lost a leg?

The other voice, the gambler seeking one more hit, told him to go back. He couldn't stop thinking about Ukraine anyway, for better or worse. When he'd first come back to the UK, he'd gone for a break to Center Parcs, only for the landscaped woodlands to remind him of the frontlines around Kherson. He found himself scanning the trees for good recon points. In the bar, he'd worked out the best defensive spot if Russian troops were to storm in.

Then, one evening in the summer of 2023, he'd been sat at his work desk, when Daniel Burke, his old commander in the Dark Angels, had messaged him out the blue from Manchester.

'Hey, pal, I am getting a flight tomorrow to Spain, picking up a vehicle there and then driving to Ukraine. Are you coming?'

A few days later, he'd joined Burke in Spain, and they'd driven to Ukraine together in a Mitsubishi L200. It had felt good, an old team back on the road, driving up through France, across the Swiss Alps, on to Poland. Then, in Ukraine, they'd parted company. While Burke was now launching a new humanitarian venture, the Dark Angels' Rescue and Recovery service, Knight wanted to fight again. This time, to see proper combat, the kind that had eluded him before. And now, there was a volunteer unit promising that in spades.

* * *

Chosen Company, a new unit commanded by an ex-US serviceman named Ryan O'Leary, was an attempt to re-establish the reputation of foreign volunteers in Ukraine. The aim was to create an elite group of experienced, disciplined warriors, specialising in the toughest frontline infantry work. As the name implied, only a chosen few would get to wear the Chosen patch. Recruitment criteria was strict. No combat virgins. No Screamers – and, yes, references would be checked. No drinking, especially while on duty. No part-time soldiering, spending one week on the frontline and then three weeks partying in Kyiv. And no whining if things got tough. Applicants were explicitly warned that service in Chosen carried a high risk of being seriously injured.

It was just what Knight and many others had been looking for. By the time he joined them in mid-2023, Chosen's ranks had already swollen to nearly 50 fighters, making it one of the largest foreigner units in Ukraine. They were attached to the 59th Motorised Infantry Brigade, considered one of the more battle-hardened of Ukraine's armed forces. Already, Chosen's appetite for trouble had earned them respect among their Ukrainian peers, who also saw them as slightly mad. But parts of the frontline needed people like that, the more the better.

The 59th were based in the Donbas, where the Russians had already spent a year waging a titanic battle for the town of Bakhmut. A drab salt-mining settlement, Bakhmut was home to only 70,000 people, and of little real strategic value. Yet the Kremlin had thrown everything it could into capturing it, using a sledgehammer approach that relied on crude superiority of munitions and men.

Russian artillery batteries had pounded Bakhmut with up to 20,000 shells a day, five times what Ukraine could reply with. Hundreds of thousands of Russian troops were poured in, including units of ex-jailbirds offered a pardon in exchange for military service. The 'Storm-Z' units, as they were known, allowed Putin to fill his depleted army ranks and solve Russia's prison overcrowding problem at the same time. The Kremlin's cynical calculus was that few convicts would survive to enjoy their freedom. Storm-Z units were used for so-called 'meat wave' assaults – blind charges at the Ukrainian positions, hoping to overwhelm them by sheer force of numbers alone. Even a Ukrainian machine-gunner could only pick off so many, and in the process they also gave away their positions. While Russian meat wave casualties were horrendous – sometimes 1,000 dead a day – the tactic slowly captured ground.

In May 2023, Russian forces finally took Bakhmut, raising their flag over what was now just a sprawl of bomb-wrecked tower blocks. President Putin issued a message of congratulations, neglecting to mention the fearful price that had been paid. An estimated 25,000 Russian lives had been lost, making it one of the bloodiest urban battles since World War II. All for a town that reminded the average British volunteer of somewhere like Scunthorpe. Among Ukrainian forces, Bakhmut become known as 'The Meatgrinder', a nickname that soon spread to the entire Donbas frontline.

The technology race on the battlefield made the fighting even harder. Whereas once the Ukrainians had enjoyed superiority with drones, now the Russians had caught up, deploying tens of thousands of them. Both sides were also using new explosive-carrying First-Person-View kamikaze drones, or FPVs, which allowed the operator to fly a bomb directly into a target. Social media was now full of clips of FPV drones chasing individual soldiers across the battlefield like birds of prey, hovering over their victims and then swooping down for the kill.

* * *

In July 2023, Chosen planned an operation to take some Russian positions in a village outside Donetsk called Pervomaiske. It had been fought over ever since the separatists had seized Donetsk in 2014, with most of it razed to the ground. Its rubble was now covered in chest-deep weeds and grass, from which the odd roofless cottage protruded.

Scattered everywhere were Russian POM-2 anti-personnel mines that had been dropped in by rocket or helicopter. When a

POM-2 landed, six stabilising legs popped out, along with four thin nylon cords that would eject out over a ten-metre radius. The weight of a boot on the cords would cause the mine to detonate, maiming anyone nearby. The POM-2s lurked amid the weeds and rubble like deadly spiders, waiting for the unsuspecting to stray into their web.

It was perilous territory to even tread in, let alone stage an assault. Brazen attacks, though, were what Chosen prided itself on, which had the advantage of catching the enemy by surprise. They'd already conducted a previous assault in Pervomaiske three weeks earlier, taking several Storm-Z positions. The key was all-out aggression, combined with meticulous planning. They'd spent days studying maps and drone footage, familiarising themselves with the Russian positions and trench layouts. By hovering the drones low, they'd also identified approach routes that were relatively clear of mines. The Russians – thinking, perhaps, that nobody would risk attacking – hadn't known what had hit them.

'Pervo 2', as the follow-up operation was called, aimed to apply the same formula again, securing a stretch of highway in the process. The entire company would take part in the attack – 42 Chosen members plus eight Ukrainians, fighting in three separate teams. Knight, as an ordnance disposal specialist, would stay at the rear, ready to clear the highway of anti-tank mines once secured.

As the days counted down to Pervo 2, nerves grew. So did the level of black humour. Chosen came up with their own version of the song 'Dumb Ways to Die', the soundtrack to an Australian railways public safety video that had gone viral a few years back. Where the original warned of the risks of walking on railway tracks or standing too near the platform edge, Chosen's take focused on the hazards ahead in Pervo 2:

Dumb ways to die
So many dumb ways to die
Getting shot by sniper in the head
Stepping on a mine and blowing off your leg
Dumb ways to die
So many dumb ways to die ...

Pervo 2 began just before dusk on 29 July, and ran into trouble almost straightaway. Over the radio at the rearward position, Knight could hear the sounds of fighting and cursing. It sounded like they'd encountered far heavier opposition than anticipated. Certainly more than just an unsuspecting Storm-Z unit.

Within ten minutes, reports of wounded came in. First five, then nine, then eleven. Then it got hard to keep count of. The Russians were hitting them with everything they had: mortars, Dropper drones, FPV drones, machine-gun fire. Accurate, disciplined machine-gun fire. Not the spray-and-pray chaff of the Storm-Zs.

On the camera feed from a Ukrainian drone, those at the rearward position could see groups of injured comrades lying in the tall grass. The drone was close enough to show their faces, staring skywards, wondering if help was coming. It was already clear that the operation was unlikely to succeed. If an attack force took more than about 30 per cent casualties, it usually struggled to do its job. Knight turned to Chosen's commander, O'Leary.

'We're not going to be clearing any mines today,' he said. 'Let me form a casevac team.'

Knight teamed up with Wayne Hallatt, a Canadian ex-infantryman, and two others. It would be nearly a kilometre's walk to where the first group of four injured lay. The key would be to stick to the routes over the rubble, where mines could at least be seen fairly easily, and avoid the long grass, where they couldn't.

Knight went through his usual mental routines he practised to keep calm.

#1 Remember, you're well-trained – better than those Russians probably are.

#2 Be your own best mate. Advise yourself the way you'd do if it were him out there, not you.

Even without the mines to worry about, the going was tough. No flat ground, just undulating rubble, every step a potential ankle-breaker. They also knew that two of the injured would have to be stretchered back. There was only four in the casevac team, when normally a stretcher team would have at least six. Knight had done stretcher-carrying exercises during his days with the Royal Engineers, remembering it as the toughest of all basic infantry training. Just brute strength, agony on the arms even if you did it regularly.

The first stretcher casualty was a big guy, maybe 16 stone. By the time they got him back to the rearward position, they were soaked in sweat, arms numb. There was no time to rest. On the next trip out they got clearance from O'Leary to ditch their weapons and ammo to lighten their load. The task right now was casevac, not combat. If they had to return fire, they could grab weapons from the injured.

The next group of casualties were 400 metres beyond where the first group were. They'd been hit by salvoes of air-burst mortar fire, raining shrapnel down on everyone. Two of them – ex-US Marine Lance Lawrence and ex-US Army paratrooper Andrew Webber – had suffered catastrophic injuries. A medic, Tango, had tried to save them, despite being wounded himself, but the pair had died where they were. Tango was now stuck there with the two dead men and two other casualties, one with tourniquets on both legs and an arm.

Knight, Hallatt and four Ukrainians pushed their way

towards the group, trying to stick to the 'Proven Route'. That was the path already trodden, the one least likely to contain landmines. Theoretically, anyway. In this weed-logged, unsteady ground, it was hard to see where their feet were even treading, let alone what might lurk under the rubble. Plus, when under fire, it was better to dive into the long grass for cover than stay in the open as a target.

One of the Ukrainians was walking five metres in front of Knight. Briefly, he vanished in a small puff of grey smoke, with a bang no louder than a firecracker. When the smoke cleared, he was on the ground, his head bloody.

Oh shit …

'Nobody move, stay where you are!' shouted Knight.

The landmine had sprayed shrapnel into the Ukrainian's face, although he was still breathing. For now, anyway. Overhead, Knight could hear two drones circling, tiny dots in the air about 30 metres above them.

'Are those friendly or enemy drones?' he asked over the radio.

'One is friendly, the other is enemy. You need to get away. *Right now.'*

The enemy drone was a spotter, not a dropper. That gave them about four minutes before artillery started coming in. They pulled back 100 metres, taking the injured Ukrainian with them. He seemed to be missing half of one eye, although they were lucky he could still walk. The anti-personnel mines were designed to cripple their victims, forcing comrades to have to stretcher them off the battlefield.

When the enemy drone vanished, they pressed on again towards the second group of casualties. By now it was nearly dark, so they could barely see where they treading anyway. The five casualties were concealed in a patch of grass. Lawrence and Webber's bodies were lying to one side. The three still alive –

Tango the medic, a soldier call-signed Bubbles and a rifleman call-signed CeeBee – thought they were about to die too. CeeBee, who had a wound to the neck and both legs tourniqueted, was staring up at the sky, thinking about the phone call his family would get.

As they started stretchering him back, he went into hypothermic shock, his body temperature plummeting. Somewhere at the rearward positions, Knight remembered seeing a thermal blanket amid someone's stash of kit. He ran ahead to get it, leaving Hallatt to look after CeeBee on his own.

Weaving his way along the proven route, Knight heard another two sharp cracks, more shouts of injured men. Some Ukrainians who'd been stretchering Webber's body had tried to take a short cut through the long grass, hitting more anti-personnel mines.

Fuck's sake. Why can't people stick to the fucking proven route?

He grabbed the thermal blanket, made his way back to Hallatt and Ceebee, then went to investigate, following the shouts of pain in the dark. The four Ukrainians were in a patch of long grass about 15 metres off the proven route. Two had badly injured legs, the other two were scared to move in case they set off another mine. Some other mug was going to have to go in and rescue them, before the two wounded bled out. Some other mug like him.

Taking a deep breath, Knight plunged into long grass himself. Fuck mine clearance protocol. Fuck everything he'd ever learned at bomb disposal school. His old instructors would have had him secure the route in first, probing his way step-by-step, with a torchlight. Rescuers weren't supposed to take risks, lest they end up needing rescue themselves. His old instructors, though, had never been in a minefield full of weeds in the pitch dark, with Russians bearing down on them, and drones that would drop grenades on anyone with a torchlight.

He trod through the grass blindly, every step feeling like it might be his last. Somewhere in the back of his mind, he could hear one of his instructors yelling. *'What the fuck are you doing, Private Knight, you stupid cunt?'* He ordered the Ukrainians to follow him out the exact way he'd come, giving one of the injured a fireman's lift. Somehow, nothing went bang.

Meanwhile, Hallatt was still with CeeBee, lying on top of him to try to keep him warm. The pair were huddled against the wall of a ruined cottage, which pinged occasionally with machine-gun fire. At one point, Hallatt made out Russian voices behind him, perhaps just 20 metres away. If they heard CeeBee's moans of pain, that would be it.

He still had no weapons, but grabbed a couple of base-ball-sized rocks. The moment the Russians came into sight, he'd hurl one at them. They'd think it was a grenade, and would instinctively dive for cover. That might give him a chance to rush one of them, grab his weapon and go down fighting. Then he heard some commotion elsewhere and the voices faded.

When Knight returned, they stretchered CeeBee back to the rearward position. By the time they got there, it was 2.30 a.m. They'd been out for nearly eight hours. Donut, another Chosen fighter, gave Hallatt an unexpectedly hard hug when he saw him.

'What's going on?' Hallatt asked.

'You're alive!'

'Er ... yeah ...?'

'We thought you were dead!'

'Ah, no. Sorry to disappoint. You want me to go back out there?'

* * *

Pervo 2 was Chosen's bloodiest mission so far. As well as losing Webber and Lawrence – two of their best soldiers – 26 out of 40 Chosen soldiers suffered injuries. The consensus was that it could have been worse. They'd staged a fighting, tactical retreat, stopped the enemy over-running them and retrieved all the casualties, including the two KIA. They debriefed over the following days, working out lessons learned, analysing good calls and bad calls, going through GoPro camera footage and swapping horror stories. One soldier told how a decomposing Russian corpse, left rotting in Pervomaiske since God knew when, had been hit by an artillery shell, spattering him with putrefying flesh. Another discovered that a piece of shrapnel had gone through one of his testicles. In some of the GoPro footage, soldiers could be seen crouching right next to landmines, unaware of how close they'd come to setting them off.

Tango the medic, who'd been with CeeBee, Bubbles and the two KIA, told how at one point he'd heard voices coming their way, and assumed it was a party of Russians. He'd put a fresh magazine in a rifle, pulled the pin from a grenade and warned his comrades to expect the worst. 'This could be it, boys,' he'd said. Instead, it had been Knight and Hallatt's rescue party.*

---

* In July 2024, Chosen Company was the subject of an article in the *New York Times* alleging that some of its members had shot and killed Russians troops who were wounded or attempting to surrender during combat. Citing claims by two former Chosen members, it said that a Greek member of Chosen had shot a Russian soldier while he was injured and pleading for help, and had thrown a grenade at another Russian who had his hands raised in surrender. Chosen's commander, Ryan O'Leary, said that at the time the Russians had been killed they still posed a potential threat and could have fought back. It was further alleged that on a leaked log of a Chosen group chat, a Chosen member had made reference to prisoners of war being shot during an operation in October 2023. Chosen claimed this was a joke that had been taken out of context.

A few weeks later, Knight and Hallatt were told they'd been nominated for a Ukrainian medal for their rescue efforts while under fire. The Medal of the Cross of the Brave, it was called. Or, as some of Knight's old army instructors would probably have put it, the Medal of the Cross of the Fucking Insane. It wasn't quite how Knight had imagined distinguishing himself on the battlefield – plunging through minefields, casting caution to the wind. But it was still in the spirit, hopefully, of his VC-winning ancestor, Private William Young. Treading in his footsteps, you could say. Bloody dangerous footsteps some of them had been too.

26

ENEMY WITHIN

Zaporizhzhia, eastern Ukraine, summer 2023

In mid-2023, Ukrainian forces launched a summer counter-offensive that they hoped would win the war. The plan was to assault the Russians along a 400-mile stretch of eastern Ukraine, from the Donbas west to Zaporizhzhia. Spearheading it would be new Nato-trained units, using modern Western tanks that outclassed the Russians' ageing T-72s. It was a bold, ambitious strategy, a head-on charge at the Russian positions. But after the successful north-east counter-offensive and the Russian withdrawal from Kherson, Kyiv felt it could do anything. With a determined push, the Russian lines would hopefully collapse altogether.

This time, however, it was the Ukrainians' turn to over-reach. Thanks to dithering in Western capitals over the supply of the new tanks, Russian forces had months to prepare defences beforehand. At the front's western edge around Zaporizhzhia – where the counter-offensive planned its main thrust – the Russian general Sergey Surovikin built an 80-mile-long obstacle course of minefields and tank traps. The Surovikin Line, as it became known, was the most formidable fortification built in Europe since World War II.

Within days, the Ukrainian force had got bogged down in Surovikin's minefields, far thicker and deeper than any of their

Nato trainers had imagined. Western leaders who'd hoped the counter-offensive would showcase their military hardware saw it lying crippled in fields, then paraded as trophies by jubilant Russian troops. After just a fortnight, US officials were briefing that the counter-offensive was a failure.

President Zelensky put a brave face on it, reminding his Western critics that real-life war wasn't like a 'Hollywood movie'. He questioned whether Nato forces would have done any better – especially without air superiority, which left the Ukrainians vulnerable to Russian helicopters. By August, though, there was no denying it had failed. Even the most successful Ukrainian units had only advanced a few miles.

Watching the counter-offensive from the sidelines was Daniel Burke, the founder of the Dark Angels, who'd decided that his fighting days were now over. The former Para had been a valued mentor to less experienced Legionnaires, thanks to his willing-ness to admit novices into his ranks. But when Russian forces had withdrawn from Kherson, they'd taken with them the Angels' first real opportunity for a serious battle. Like a band whose breakthrough tour had been cancelled, individual Angels drifted away, teaming up with pals who might hook them up to action elsewhere.

Burke wasn't surprised that his men were 'unit shopping', as it was known. He couldn't simply redeploy the Dark Angels to some brand-new frontline overnight. Doing that required a whole new process of contact-building, seeking out friendly Ukrainian commanders receptive to having foreigners on their patch, who wouldn't just use them as cannon fodder. Besides, he himself was tired of commanding a volunteer army over whom he had no real authority.

Back in the Paras, there'd be a whole chain of command above him, plus a burly sergeant or two behind him. Here, he was a lone Caesar, relying on force of personality alone, with no sanction against insubordinates except to kick them out of the unit. God only knew what ructions he might face if something went badly wrong on the battlefield. He also had no way of vetting his fighters' backgrounds. A case in point was a Finnish volunteer call-signed Joker, a former MMA champion who'd been a popular member of the Angels. He'd been wounded in the counter-offensive, and had since been named by Finnish police as the leader of a major drug gang.*

Burke's new project was Dark Angels' Response and Recovery, or DARR. A smaller, tighter outfit, doing just frontline casevacs, be it for civilians or military. With the Kherson front now quieter, he'd relocated up to Zaporizhzhia, where a friend had found him a peppercorn-rent flat in an old Soviet housing block. DARR wasn't fully operational yet. Right now, it wasn't much more than just him, a couple of Mitsubishi L200s and a new website, parts of it showing the Dark Angels' past exploits. But it was already bringing in donations of medical kit from around the world.

All he needed now was a military unit to team up with, who could also sort out the frontline paperwork. Talks were under-way with a volunteer unit serving with Ukraine's 78th Gertz Regiment, which was involved in the counter-offensive. He'd helped repatriate a unit member who'd been hospitalised in Zaporizhzhia, and met a few of his comrades in the process. They were still working out whether they'd be a good fit for each other, but there was the potential for a productive relation-ship. The Gertz would get DARR as a bespoke casevac service. DARR, in turn, would get the chance to do the kind of mercy dashes that kept the donations coming in.

---

* Joker, aka Jimmy Immonen, was later jailed for 13 years on drug traffick-ing, firearms and assault charges.

Meanwhile, there were worse places to be based than Zaporizhzhia. A nice big city on the River Dnieper, quiet enough for some of its restaurants and bars to be still open, but only an hour's drive from the counter-offensive frontlines. Plenty of scope for DARR's new search and rescue missions. Before the summer was out, though, Burke would be the subject of a search party himself.

* * *

In mid-August, word went around on the Legionnaire's WhatsApp groups that Burke had gone missing from his flat in Zaporizhzhia. He'd spoken briefly to his brother online in Manchester mid-morning on Friday 11 August, saying he'd call him later for a proper catch-up, but hadn't been heard from all weekend or on the Monday. For a gregarious soul like Burke, normally in regular contact with home, that was out of character.

The last person to claim to have seen Burke alive was an Australian-Algerian fighter named Nourine Abdelfetah, a member of the volunteer unit attached to the Gertz. He said he had met up with Burke on the Friday to practise some combat medical drills, and that they'd driven in one of Burke's Mitsubishis to a rifle range outside Zaporizhzhia that afternoon.

Abdelfetah said he'd driven Burke back to his flat around 5.30 p.m., his companion having complained of a stomach bug. Burke had told Abdelfetah he could borrow his L200 for some errands, saying he was unlikely to need it that weekend. When Abdelfetah had tried to return the car on Sunday, he'd been unable to rouse Burke on the phone. Abdelfetah had then rung his unit commander, a Welsh volunteer named James Sutton, who was in Lviv recovering from a battlefield injury. Sutton told Abdelfetah to check Burke's flat, where there was no sign of him. Sutton had then rung the police in Zaporizhzhia, who told him to file a missing person's report.

At first, nobody was too worried. The assumption was that Burke had probably just gone on an all-weekend bender, behaviour not unknown within the Legionnaires' ranks. Perhaps he'd hooked up with some woman, or perhaps he was crashed out on some Ukrainian pal's settee, recovering from a mammoth hangover. Ukrainians, after all, put even Britons in the shade at drinking, imbibing vodka in volumes that British livers were unused to. That might also explain why he wasn't answering his phone, which could easily have gone missing in action.

By the end of the week, the bender theory was ruled out. Even Burke, who was known to like a drink, wouldn't have gone boozing for days on the trot. A drunken misadventure couldn't be ruled out, but no hospital, police station or morgue had reported a body being found.

Might he have taken his own life? Behind his rugged ex-Para persona, Burke was, like many volunteers, prone to bouts of introspection, wondering if he was on the right path in life. But he'd seemed his usual cheerful self while talking to his brother on the Friday morning. Plus his rifle – the obvious way out for a depressed soldier – was still in his flat. So too was his laptop and other possessions, which seemed to rule out robbery.

That left the question of foul play. Some wondered if Burke's media profile might have led to him being kidnapped by pro-Russian sympathisers. Yet for all the talk of Russian saboteurs roaming Ukraine, there was little sign of such cells in operation. Even if there were, they'd have more important targets than a lone Legionnaire. They'd have also had to smuggle him back to Russian-held turf across the world's most contested frontline. Had they pulled that off, they'd have been parading him on social media by now.

Perhaps he'd simply got in a bar brawl with some Ukrainians, who'd got carried away and then hidden his body somewhere. Yet any serious scrap – and Burke would probably not have gone down without a fight – would have caused a commotion. Some bartender or passer-by would have seen something.

Finally, there was the possibility that some other volunteer had killed him. In his time leading the Dark Angels, he'd had a few fall-outs – sometimes personality clashes, sometimes rows over funds raised through the Dark Angels' website. But to the best of anyone's knowledge, he'd had no running feuds, no social media spats, no online challenges to pistols-at-dawn. If some steroid-fuelled hothead had got Burke in their sights, they'd kept it quiet.

* * *

Two weeks after Burke vanished, the Parliamentary offices of Boris Johnson and several other senior British politicians received a round-robin email about Burke's disappearance. The email's slightly rambling tone, combined with the scatter-gun approach, suggested an author who was not a trained lobbyist.

Sent: Monday, 21 August 2023, 2:23:53 PM
Subject: URGENT – DANIEL BURKE
Dear Sirs & Madams,
I write concerning Daniel Burke. The chances of Daniel being
alive at this time are very slim to none, the information we
have suggests.
I and others have made statements to police to help if we
can, fortunately they seem to be a smart team and expressed
their determination to find Daniel.

We all think that his disappearance is as a result of murder, and my reason for writing is that (some of the suspects) are Brits, either directly involved or complicit in Daniel's disappearance ... It seems that these people are quite callous. Groping for Daniel's property and knowing where his money is their sole concern.

Most foreign fighters here are people that can't live in the general population very well, they are often violent drug & alcohol abusers, and most definitely suffering PTSD.

I'm concerned that with the 'fog of war', and the fact that the Armed Forces of Ukraine are most grateful to decent, effective foreign fighters, this will overwhelm the investigation into Dan's disappearance.*

The email's author was Steve English, a retired British engineer who'd been visiting Ukraine since before the war. He'd begun working with aid convoys after the start of the invasion, during which he'd got to know a number of Legionnaires. He helped them with logistics occasionally, at the same time maintaining a certain distance. While many volunteers were clearly brave, committed guys, some struck him as dangerous chancers. They seemed to fight each other as much as the Russians, and when they weren't on the battlefield spent their time drinking, woman-ising and bullshitting.

He liked Burke, who was at least a doer as well as a talker, although he'd sensed the former Dark Angels leader was struggling to find a new role for himself. Whenever the pair met, Burke would complain about his old comrades having scattered elsewhere, and about other volunteers letting him down. Despite that, DARR seemed to be off to a promising start, from what

---

* Letter edited for brevity.

English could see. Burke's flat in Zaporizhzhia was warehousing about £40,000 worth of high-quality medical kit, with two Mitsubishi L200s parked outside. Burke had said that a mystery benefactor in the US, a millionairess he identified only as 'Steph', had sent over $8,000. That, English feared, was what lay behind Burke's disappearance: $8,000 was a lot of money in Ukraine, especially if it became a regular payment. Enough, possibly, to make him a target.

English wasn't the only person whose thoughts were moving that way. After Burke had been reported missing, a help group had been set up on Signal, a secure messaging app widely used by Legionnaires. Burke's family in Manchester had been on it, as had a few ex-Dark Angels, plus Sutton and Abdelfetah, the two volunteers who'd first raised the alarm.

The purpose of the Signal group was to pool any information that might be of use to the Ukrainian police. But it had quickly dissolved into acrimony. Other group members claimed that Sutton and Abdelfetah seemed more interested in Burke's property and vehicles than whether he was still alive. A dispute broke out over who owned one of the Mitsubishis, with Sutton saying that Burke had sold one of them to his unit. Perhaps Sutton felt he had no choice but to raise the matter, especially if the vehicle was needed at the frontline. But other Signal group members thought it suspicious. Heated messages had been exchanged, insinuations made. Sutton and Abdelfetah then left the group in protest, which merely agitated the others further. Did the pair have something to hide?

English had tried to keep an open mind. He too, though, felt mystified by aspects of Sutton and Abdelfetah's behaviour. On the Monday after Burke had disappeared, Sutton had arrived in Zaporizhzhia, where the police wanted him to make a statement to back up the missing person's report. The charitable explana-

314

tion was that Sutton was simply eager to help the police with their inquiry. To English, it seemed a little *too* eager. The alarm had only been raised the day before, when Sutton had still been in hospital in Lviv. Why drive 15 hours straight to Zaporizhzhia to make a police report, when there was still a chance that Burke might resurface at any moment, badly hungover or fresh from a one-night stand? Did Sutton know something that others didn't? Sutton also seemed keen to get hold of contacts for Steph, Burke's mystery US benefactor. Was that to let her know what had happened, and thank her for her support? Or was it to ensure her money kept coming?

Perhaps he was getting paranoid. When someone simply vanished, it was easy to see motives for foul play everywhere. Especially here in a warzone, where guns were plentiful, and money and equipment very short. Burke's Mitsubishis alone, English knew, were like gold dust on the front. Some Legionnaire might have killed him over them alone, figuring that the local police had more to worry about than some dead foreign volunteer.

The Ukrainian cops, though, weren't quite the deadbeats that some foreigners presumed them to be. They'd opened a formal investigation into Burke's disappearance, and seemed to think something had happened to him up at the Zaporizhzhia frontlines. It might have been some accident, or it might have been something more sinister. The frontlines were good places to get rid of someone. The sound of gunfire didn't draw attention. And there were vast, empty stretches of mine-strewn no-man's-land to bury a body in, which might be out of bounds for years to come.

By the end of August, nobody seemed any the wiser. Nearly three weeks had passed since Burke's disappearance. His parents in Manchester were in despair. They were used to their son's adventurous, peripatetic ways, and had worried plenty when he was fighting in Syria and stuck in Wandsworth prison. This, though, was almost worse than being told he'd been killed in battle. Burke's father, Kevin, a retired lorry driver, issued a desperate public appeal for information.

'We want the investigation to be kept going as much as possible, and I would love to see a British police investigation too,' he said. 'If anyone has information, please come forward. We want to know where Daniel is.'

Burke's father seemed unlikely to get his wish. Having warned its citizens to stay away from Ukraine, the British government was not going to send Scotland Yard to comb the frontlines. Nor could the British embassy help much. They were on a skeleton staff, and had to get security clearance just to travel anywhere east of Kyiv.

English feared that if there was no breakthrough soon, the local police would quietly shelve the case. He sent his email to every important figure at Westminster he could think of: Boris Johnson, Defence Secretary Ben Wallace, Foreign Secretary James Cleverly and the Tory MP Adam Holloway, an ex-soldier who'd made several fact-finding visits to Ukraine since the war started.

English reasoned that the British government wielded a certain clout in Kyiv, thanks to its generous weapons support. If British politicians were made aware that Burke might have been the victim of skullduggery, perhaps they'd lean on Kyiv to get to the bottom it.

Burke's disappearance was picked up by British newspapers, several of which had interviewed him during his time with the Dark Angels. Meanwhile, in the WhatsApp groups of the volunteers' fraternity, online sleuths chewed endlessly over various lines of inquiry, scraps of which leaked from the police investigation.

It emerged that Abdelfetah had been questioned in detail by police about his claim to have dropped Burke back off at his flat on the Friday afternoon. Detectives had unearthed CCTV footage showing Burke's Mitsubishi being driven back through Zaporizhzhia. But it was Abdelfetah at the wheel, with no sign of Burke. Why was that? Abdelfetah said that because Burke had been feeling ill with a stomach bug, he'd been lying down in the back seat. Few volunteers bought that explanation. Burke was an ex-Para, not a car-sick schoolkid. Feelings began running high. Burke was a mascot for the volunteers' cause. If the police didn't take action, they would. Abdelfetah received text-messaged death threats. So did Sutton.

Burke's supporters hoped the media attention would keep up the pressure on the police to act. But the 'Ex-Para missing in Ukraine' headlines also cast a harsh light on the whole Legion setup and its lack of proper vetting. All kinds of unsavoury characters appeared to be roaming around, carrying weapons they'd never be allowed back home, and were now turning on each other.

For the Tory MP Adam Holloway, who raised Burke's case with the Ukrainian government during a trip to Kyiv, it was no surprise. He'd witnessed the influx of volunteers while visiting Ukraine at the start of the war, and had advised the Legion to recruit some British or American ex-sergeants to weed out the undesirables. It seemed his worst fears had come true. 'Daniel Burke had a brave and noble record,' he told journalists.* 'But any war can also attract those with psychiatric problems and people who just want to kill.'

Feeling he was the victim of a witch hunt, Sutton fought back. Contacted by reporters to get his version of events, he claimed

---

* Interview with author.

he'd been the victim of 'rumours and conspiracy theories'.* All he'd done, he said, was report Burke missing on the Sunday afternoon, having been told by police that without a formal notification they couldn't investigate. He said he'd travelled from Lviv to Zaporizhzhia to help on the ground, given that Burke's family were thousands of miles away. Instead, he'd found himself accused of a cover-up.

'I just tried to assist as I was able to speak with people and I'm in the country,' he complained. 'But unfortunately that seems to have backfired. I just hope that we can get some answers soon and we can all get back to normality, and hopefully Dan is alive and well.'

Sutton said he'd never even met Burke in person, having been hospitalised at the start of the counter-offensive in June. The pair had had some correspondence about DARR signing up to the 78th Gertz, but that was it. Had there been some issue over vehicles or money? Yes, Sutton said, he'd paid some money to buy the older of his two Mitsubishis off him – a 20-year-old model that had since broken down. He had a proof of purchase to show for it. But if asking to keep the car was going to create bad feeling, then he wasn't bothered. It wasn't much money anyway. Abdelfetah likewise protested his innocence, saying he was 'as clueless as anyone else'. 'I don't really give much thought to the armchair detectives,' he added.†

The inquiry seemed at a dead end. Burke's friends tried to dig into Sutton and Abdelfetah's backgrounds more, to see if they had any skeletons in the closet. In ex-military circles, there was always a friend of a friend who could either vouch for someone, or say to avoid them. Nothing much came up.

---

* Ibid.

† Ibid.

Sutton, apparently, had served in the British Army, leaving in 2010 to work in private security. Abdelfetah was a civilian but had fought Isis in Syria. Beyond that, all anyone could glean was that the pair had been through tough times together in the counter-offensive. During the assault in which Sutton had been shot, Abdelfetah had apparently rescued him. All the more reason, some reckoned, for Sutton to back Abdelfetah up. If you owed someone your life, you also owed them your silence.

*   *   *

A month after Burke was reported missing, Ukrainian police found a body in the countryside outside Zaporizhzhia, near the rifle range that he had visited with Abdelfetah on the Friday he'd last been seen. In the summer heat, the corpse had badly decomposed. The physical description the police had of Burke – including the YPG tattoos on his forearms – was not enough for identification. DNA tests would be required. But there seemed little doubt it was him.

Once again, the online sleuths went into overdrive. For those convinced that Burke had died at Abdelfetah's hand, the discovery of the body appeared to prove that he'd lied. Had he not claimed, after all, to have driven Burke back from the range that afternoon, his comrade lying ill in the back of the car?

The whodunit was also picked up by a prominent military YouTuber, Matt Williams, an ex-Australian infantryman who did a regular talk show on the war. The conflict had inspired its own entire genre of YouTube armchair generals, broadcasting from spare rooms and man-sheds worldwide, of whom Williams was one of the more credible. He'd spent six months in Ukraine at the start of the war, and now had more than 150,000 followers, including many Legionnaires. Within their world, he had more clout than CNN. Unlike mainstream media, he was also unconstrained by libel laws, and not afraid to air the theories being bandied around about Burke's death.

Two days after Burke's body was found, Williams' show, *Willy OAM*, broadcast an anonymised letter from one of Burke's friends. It pointed the finger at Abdelfetah again, and claimed that Sutton, who by then had stopped answering calls from journalists, was covering up 'the truth'. Sutton then broke his silence to give his own version of events on Williams' show the very next day. He refused to be interviewed directly, doing only an online Q&A, in which he claimed 'the truth' was more extraordinary than anyone had imagined.

He said that when he had first arrived in Zaporizhzhia, he too had wondered if Abdelfetah had anything to do with Burke's death. 'I looked him in the eye and asked: "Did something happen? Was there an accident?",' Sutton told Williams' show. 'Are you telling me the truth?'

'As God is my witness he looked straight back at me, and with no signs of any kind of anxiety, said: "Nah, mate, nothing. I dropped him off to his apartment and that's the last I'd heard of it."'

Sutton said he warned Abdelfetah that as the last person to see Burke alive, the police might seek to interview him as a potential suspect. Abdelfetah had seemed entirely unconcerned, saying it would give him an excuse to have some time off from the frontline, sleeping in a decent bed. His attitude struck Sutton as somewhat naïve. But it hardly seemed like the response of a guilty man. Over the following days, Sutton said, he did his own detective work, attempting to establish if Burke had enemies. Several ex-Dark Angels claimed that Burke had promised them salaries from the funds he was receiving online, but that they'd never been paid. Sutton had reasoned that a money dispute was the most likely explanation, and felt obliged to stick up for Abdelfetah.

One thing, with hindsight, had struck him as odd, which was some text messages Burke had sent to Sutton's own phone on the Friday afternoon, after he'd supposedly been dropped back off at his flat. While Burke normally sent voice messages for anything longer than a few words, these text messages were several sentences long. They also started with 'Hey mate' – a greeting Burke never used, but which was Abdelfetah's customary address.

Might Abdelfetah have sent them from Burke's phone to make it look like he was still alive? Sutton had found that hard to believe. Abdelfetah was only 25, still baby-faced, not much more than a kid really, always in awe of more experienced hands. He just didn't seem capable of killing a fellow volunteer in cold blood, let alone covering up his tracks afterwards. When police had hauled Abdelfetah in for questioning, though, Sutton had begun to have second thoughts. It was one thing to stand by a comrade. It was another thing to be accused of covering up for him.

Then, one afternoon in September, he'd had a phone call with Abdelfetah that he'd 'never forget'. Abdelfetah, he said, had confessed to shooting Burke with an accidental discharge of his weapon at the shooting range on the Friday afternoon. The pair had been practising the use of 'Buddy Straps' – a sling that allowed a soldier to carry an injured comrade like a rucksack. During the practice, Burke had told Abdelfetah off for letting his rifle point in his direction. Abdelfetah insisted the weapon had its safety catch on. Then, to demonstrate, he'd pointed the gun at Burke and pulled the trigger.

'It was not on "safe", it was on full auto,' Sutton told Williams' show. 'Apparently one round hit Dan in the side of the head and Dan had fallen to the floor.' Sutton said that Abdelfetah had realised Burke was mortally wounded, but that one of his hands was still 'twitching'. Abdelfetah then fired a second shot into Burke's head to put him out of his misery, and then buried the body near the shooting range.

Sutton hadn't taped the phone call, so had no proof it had taken place. He did, however, provide Williams with some screenshots of some later Signal exchanges between him and Abdelfetah, which appeared to corroborate what had been said.

Thu 14 Sept

Abdelfetah: I don't know what to do. I'm sorry, I'm really sorry.

Sutton: You've fucked me Adam. The world will know soon enough. You didn't tell me the truth but you could have just told me not to get involved. I've defended you through it all. No-one will believe I didn't know. I'm in utter shock. You're a cunt mate. I doubt I'll forgive you but for now you need to look after yourself. Fucking retard.

Abdelfetah: I'm really sorry, I promise I'll clear your name.

Sutton: Did you use his (Burke's) phone on the 11th?

Abdelfetah: No, I threw it in a field at night while doing 100 (km) on the Friday night and the keys.

Sutton: I don't understand why you kept up the lies Adam. You went back to the apartment. You told me the following week to look in the woods around his apartment.

Abdelfetah: I'm sorry I don't know what to say. I killed someone and didn't know what to do. I'm really sorry. If I can ever make it up to you I will.

Sutton: You could have just thrown him in the truck and drove 1,000 miles an hour to the nearest hospital. Accidents happen. It could have been explained.

Sutton said he'd handed the screenshots of the Signal conversations to the police. He doubted, though, that he would ever be able to fully clear his own name.

'I'm always going to have the stigma and theories that I must know (something),' he told Williams' show. 'I don't blame people … if I was outside looking in I'd have the same theories too.'

Over the following days. Williams' interview with Sutton – headlined 'Accessory to Murder or Innocent?' – was the talk of the Legionnaire social media networks. It took the concept of trial by media to a new level – a witness first sticking by his friend, then spotting holes in his story and finally claiming to have extracted a confession. Much of Sutton's account was hearsay, but the screenshots of the Signal exchanges bore an avatar that several Legionnaires recognised as Abdelfetah's Signal account. Unless Sutton was an IT mastermind, the screenshots would have been hard to fake – especially to standards that would fool a police investigation. Williams reminded his YouTube viewers to keep an open mind. But he warned that whoever the culprit was, it threatened yet another blow to the Legion's already tattered reputation.

'I could really see this being like the last straw for Ukraine, and them just saying "fuck it, we're collapsing the entire Foreign Legion",' he said.

Many of Williams' listeners were sceptical about Abdelfetah's purported claim to have shot Burke by accident, saying it raised as many questions as it answered. Not pointing a gun at someone was the cardinal rule of weapons safety, drilled into even the ineptest Legionnaire from day one. Would Abdelfetah really have been that amateurish after 18 months in Ukraine? Also, if Burke had told him off for doing it, would he really have pointed his weapon at him and pulled the trigger? That could have earned him a punch in the face.

'*I would lose my shit if someone pulled the trigger at me even if it was empty, safety on and no pin,*' one viewer of Williams' show wrote in the comments section. '*What a bs (bullshit) excuse.*'

The following week, Ukraine's National Police said they had opened 'criminal proceedings' into Burke's death. A statement said that 'as a result of investigative actions carried out with the participation of Nourine Abdelfetah, the body of a presumably dead volunteer was discovered in one of the settlements of the Zaporizhia region.'*

The language was cautious officialese, but implied that Abdelfetah had led police to Burke's body, which had been inside a concrete drain near the rifle range. The police statement also said the case was now being treated as 'intentional murder'. They declined, however, to specify whether Abdelfetah was a suspect. Nor was he detained. Instead, he was told to remain at a hotel in Zaporizhzhia pending further inquiries.

For some Legionnaires, no further investigation was necessary. Death threats against Abdelfetah continued. At least one hot-headed online sleuth circulated the name and address of his hotel. A few days later, it emerged that Abdelfetah had fled. His whereabouts were now unknown.

---

* Statement to author.

27

THE LEGIONNAIRE
IN THE LAKE

Kramatorsk, eastern Ukraine,
summer 2023

In the Donbas countryside west of Bakhmut was a vast reservoir, so big it was nicknamed the 'Kramatorsk Sea'. It stretched for eight miles through meadows and marshes, and was a haven of tranquillity on the frontline's doorstep. Despite the distant boom of artillery, anglers still fished on its shores, enjoying a few hours where the only battle to worry about was with a crafty trout or carp.

In June 2023, the reservoir's anglers made a catch that reminded them that, even here, there was no escaping the war. Floating amid the reeds at the lake's eastern end was the body of a soldier. How he had ended up there, nobody knew, although it seemed to have been no accident. His hands were tied behind his back with a set of plastic zip-cuffs.

Such discoveries weren't unheard of in this corner of Donbas. At the beginning of the pro-Kremlin uprising in 2014, several local towns had briefly fallen under separatist control, during which numerous people had been abducted and never seen again. Some were left in woods or buried in shallow graves, others dumped in the reed beds of local waterways.

This corpse, though, looked no more than a few days old. And it was not that of a Ukrainian, but a foreigner. Local police identified him as Jordan Chadwick, 31, a British volunteer with the International Legion. He was a former member of the Scots Guards, famous worldwide for their red tunics and black busby hats, and had been in Ukraine for nine months.

News of Chadwick's death wasn't reported until early September, and was overshadowed by the hue and cry over the disappearance of Daniel Burke, whose body was found a week later. Yet it confirmed a grisly rumour that had been doing the rounds on the Legionnaire gossip circuit. The story went that some British volunteer – nobody knew who – had got killed in an altercation of some sort, with his body being quietly dumped in a river. As with much gossip on the Legionnaire rumour mill, there was a strong chance it was bullshit, and most people had paid it little attention at the time.

What news coverage there was of Chadwick's death shed little further light. The discovery of his body was first reported by the BBC, in a short news story that highlighted the intriguing detail about his hands being tied, but offered no explanation for what had happened. Nor was there much comment from his family in his home town of Burnley, Lancashire. They had learned of his death from the British police in late June, and appeared to be in shock. The BBC report included a brief statement from Chadwick's mother, Brenda, the language of which suggested the hand of a police family liaison officer.

'His passion to support freedom and assist others with his skills led him to leave the UK and travel to the Ukraine in early October 2022. Although we are extremely proud of his unwavering courage and resilience, his death has been devastating. No words can be found to describe the loss of such a short life.'

Unlike Burke, Chadwick was not a prominent figure on the Legion circuit. He was, by some accounts, a troubled soul, who at one point prior to going to Ukraine had been homeless, living rough in Burnley. There was no Instagram account showing him on the frontline, no GoFundMe page asking for donations. But the outfit that he fought with, the 50-50 Assault Group, already had a certain swashbuckling infamy. Like Chosen Company, the 50-50 styled itself as a go-to unit for Legionnaires seeking hardcore combat, its very name a reference to their appetite for risk. The men who wore its patch had a reputation for taking on missions that others wouldn't do, and for letting off steam afterwards with heavy drinking and the occasional punch-up. Ukrainian command generally turned a blind eye. After a year of war, committed fighters were becoming thin on the ground. Especially those willing to work in places like Bakhmut, where the 50-50 had spent much of the summer.

Like many volunteer units, the 50-50 showcased its battlefield exploits on an Instagram page, which it also used to raise funds. In the wake of a comrade's death, such a page would often feature an online tribute. The 50-50 page had nothing, nor did the unit issue any statement addressing what had happened. In the absence of any explanation, plenty of theories were bandied around on Legionnaire WhatsApp groups. As with Burke's death, none entirely added up.

One theory was that Chadwick had been taken prisoner and killed by Russians. Any Legionnaire familiar with the area where his body was found could discount that. The Kramatorsk Sea reservoir was nearly 30 miles east of the nearest frontlines outside Bakhmut, and had never been part of the combat zone. Perhaps he could have been killed by pro-Russian locals, who might also have known their way around the remote roads near the reservoir. But much as some Donbas residents did have pro-Kremlin sympathies, they stuck mainly to spying. Locals would also probably have known that the lake was used by anglers, and that a corpse would not go undiscovered.

As with Daniel Burke's death, the speculation then moved to a run-in with his fellow volunteers. 50-50's reputation as a bunch of no-holds-barred bruisers offered fertile territory. One theory was that there'd been a punch-up, possibly over a battle-field mishap, or possibly just a personality clash. Once again, the military blogger Matt Williams's YouTube show became a sounding board for those claiming to be in the know.

One informant messaged Williams's show to say that Chadwick had died during an SAS-style 'selection' ritual, involving waterboarding. He named the culprit as a British soldier said to be an ex-member of the French Foreign Legion. Chadwick's body had then been dumped in the reservoir, perhaps to make it look like he'd drowned. The informant said the police had analysed the water inside Chadwick's body, and had realised it was different to that in the reservoir.

Another informant messaged Williams's show to claim that the waterboarding had been done not as part of a 'selection' ritual, but as a punishment for stealing. The source said it reminded him of mercenaries in Africa in the 1960s and 1970s, when commanders had sometimes disciplined their own troops in brutal fashion.

'Blokes who steal kit, you bin them and you get them out, you don't murder them. The former French Foreign Legion guy is implicated but there's certainly more involved. Nobody will sit and let someone do that to them without others holding them down.'

The police response to Chadwick's death did little to quell the speculation. Detectives in Kramatorsk told reporters that they had questioned Chadwick's teammates about the incident. Their conclusion was not murder, but accidental misadventure.* They

---

* Author interview with police investigating Chadwick's death.

said that on the night of Chadwick's death, the team had been drinking together at the house they were billeted in when a quarrel had broken out. The argument, bizarrely, was not about something on the battlefield, but the comparative performances of the British and US armies in Afghanistan. Chadwick had apparently become violent, to the point where his teammates had restrained him with plastic cuffs. They'd then kicked him out of the house, telling him to 'go away and never come back'.

The house, police said, was in a village just next to the Kramatorsk Reservoir. Their hypothesis was that Chadwick – distressed and perhaps disorientated – had then somehow strayed into the reservoir itself, where his body had been found a day or two later. Whether he'd wandered in deliberately, or stumbled in drunkenly in the dark, was unknown. Either way, he would have struggled to swim with his hands tied behind his back, and the recorded cause of death was drowning. Murder had been ruled out, the police said, as there were no signs of injuries that indicated a struggle. All his 50-50 teammates had been questioned, they added, but as witnesses rather than as suspects. No arrests had been made.

Some observers were inclined to believe the police version of events, which struck them as just mundane enough to have the ring of truth. Tempting as it was to speculate that Chadwick was the victim of murder most foul, real-life tended to be more humdrum than that. Yet on closer examination, the police account raised as many questions as it answered.

Would a responsible volunteer unit really let a distressed, angry soldier go wandering off into the night on his own, hands tied behind his back? Why not simply zip-tie his ankles as well, or tie him to a post or tree? By letting him wander off round the village, they also risked him drawing attention from locals, who might complain to 50-50's superiors. And did the absence of injuries on Chadwick's body really prove that he had simply wandered into the lake of his own accord? Might he not have been frog-marched there at gunpoint?

It didn't take a conspiracy theorist to suspect a cover-up was going on, or that at the very least the Ukrainian authorities had little incentive in getting to the bottom of it. The war in Bakhmut that 50-50 were involved in was the most intense combat of modern times, a battle for Ukraine's very existence. Every soldier willing to take part in it was precious. Jailing any of them over some squabble that had got out of hand would not be a good use of resources.

Besides, stories of blind eyes being turned to felony were increasingly common on the frontlines. Some stressed-out bunch of troopers coming to blows, someone getting killed, some commander quietly forgetting about it because there were bigger priorities right now. Such cases never made the news, because it was in no-one's interests for them to do so. As it was, Chadwick's death got limited coverage, mentioned mostly just in passing in articles about Daniel Burke's disappearance. Perhaps if his family had spoken out, as Burke's had, things might have been different.

Yet as autumn beckoned, both cases vanished from the headlines. The world's attention was on the bigger picture in Ukraine, on how the counter-offensive was faltering, not on the messy, unsolved mysteries surrounding two dead volunteers. In any other circumstances, the deaths of British citizens in such murky circumstances would have been big news, especially if the culprits remained at large. In the world of the Legionnaires, however, an untimely demise was simply deemed an occupational hazard – on or off the battlefield.

PART IV

'BRAVERY IS IN OUR DNA'

Grief and loss, epilogue

28

THE GOLD STAR FAMILIES
OF UKRAINE

By the end of 2023, the war once again began to tilt in
Russia's favour. Kyiv's much-vaunted summer counter-
offensive had failed, pushing barely ten miles into the Surovikin
Line. Meanwhile, on 7 October, Hamas gunmen massacred
nearly 1,300 people in Israel, re-igniting war in the Middle
East.

The death toll in what Israel called its own 9/11 equated to
just a couple of bad days on the Donbas frontlines, yet immediately it was clear to Ukrainians that events 3,000 miles away
would mark a new phase in their own conflict. No longer would
Ukraine be the sole priority in Western leaders' foreign in-trays.
Instead, it might come to be seen as just another intractable
foreign war – far bigger than most, but still best brought to an
end regardless of the rights and wrongs.

Already, that was the view of supporters of Donald Trump,
whose re-election campaign included a pledge to force Kyiv to
the negotiating table by cutting military funding. In December
2023, a faction of pro-Trump senators delayed the passing of a
$60 billion US aid bill, holding up Ukraine's weapons lifeline.
Their intent was partly to browbeat Joe Biden's government
into tougher immigration controls on the Mexican border,
which they regarded as America's own 'invasion'. But it led to

Ukraine running low on artillery stocks, costing Kyiv hard-won territory on the battlefield.

The faction were condemned by many within their own Republican camp, who accused them of hijacking Kyiv's plight for domestic politics. Among the correspondence the faction's senators received was an impassioned letter from Jon Frank, of Orange County, California. An ex-US Marine, retired US Marshal and lifelong Republican voter, he begged them to think again.

'Since the Civil War, we have never had to fight for survival and have the option to walk away from war without consequence to our citizens, yet we still fight for others. Ukraine is fighting for its life, but it is America who ensures the free world lives. We are demanding that Ukraine fight our way by "using 16 oz gloves" while the Russians fight with "brass knuckles". Our Cold War is their hot war. They are fighting our fight, the least we can do is give them ammo and the permission to use it in the most effective manner to survive.'

Frank wasn't just writing as a patriot concerned about America's place in the world. At the start of the war, his son Ian, a former US Marine himself, had enlisted with the International Legion, fighting everywhere from Irpin to Bakhmut. He had acquired a reputation as one of its best, bravest fighters – always leading from the front, be it charging a Russian trench or rescuing comrades from trouble. The war, though, was no respecter of talent or valour, nor did those fighting it get to choose how they died.

Ian had been killed not on the battlefield, but on a rare night off-duty at the Ria Pizza restaurant in the Donbas town of Kramatorsk. As one of few decent eateries still open, it was packed most nights with soldiers, civilians, foreign aid workers and journalists. That had brought it to the attention of a local Kremlin spy, who passed its coordinates to Russian forces.

Just after 7.30 p.m. on 27 June, as Ian was eating with comrades, a Russian Iskander hypersonic missile – a 21-foot rocket big enough to carry a nuclear warhead – was launched at the restaurant. It took off behind Russian lines, climbed close to the edge of the earth's atmosphere, then plummeted at five the times the speed of sound, depositing nearly a tonne of explosive on the restaurant. The blast killed Ian and 14 others, including 14-year-old twin girls, and left 60 injured. The attack was condemned internationally as a war crime, with President Biden branding Putin a 'pariah around the world'.

Ian's body was interred five weeks later at California's giant Riverside military cemetery, alongside veterans from World War II, Vietnam, Iraq and Afghanistan. In a message from Ukraine early in the war, he had told Frank not to bother bringing his body back if he was killed, and urged him not to 'make a fuss' if the worst happened. That was easier said than done. While Ian had long accommodated himself to the possibility that he might die in Ukraine, his father hadn't. He'd followed the war closely, monitoring the frontlines he knew his son was fighting on. On four occasions, when Ian had gone out of contact for a long period, he'd become an anxious mess. Then had come the call from the US State Department, three days after the pizza parlour bombing, to say that Ian and a comrade were among the dead.

It was a call that no family, no matter how steeped in military tradition, ever wanted to receive. Six months on, Frank still wasn't doing well. He'd quit his post-retirement job as a security consultant, finding it difficult to be around people. He and his wife were long divorced, making the sense of bereavement lonelier still. He now found himself part of a new, extended family – the growing fraternity of Americans who'd lost a loved one on Ukraine's frontlines.

Since World War I, Americans who lost a family member during military service had been known as Gold Star Families, the name taken from the gold-starred flag that many flew in their front gardens. It was a symbol of honour that nobody wanted, displayed to show they had made the ultimate sacrifice. But while the Gold Star was normally something to be publicly proud of – worn on a lapel pin, posted on a Facebook page – those who'd lost loved ones in Ukraine often kept it quiet. They feared harassment, not just online from Russian trolls, but also from a growing minority of fellow Americans, who'd bought into Trump's idea that Putin was a man to admire, not loathe. It was estimated that at least 50 American families had lost loved ones fighting in Ukraine, although the real figure was possibly higher, because many felt obliged to keep it secret.

Frank had seen hostile comments posted on news articles about his own son's death. People wrote that his son 'had no business' in Ukraine, and that the invasion was to teach the West's 'wealthy Davos class' not to meddle in Putin's backyard. But the harassment could be more than just gross insensitivity. Some families had been sent graphic photos of their son's corpses. Others attracted the attention of Kremlin troll factories, bombarding them with death threats and scam calls. Normally, Gold Star Families were a powerful public voice on US military policy: in the case of Ukraine, they were muted.

Frank, for his part, no longer cared about keeping a low profile. He was proud of his son, and wanted America to learn who Ian was, and why he'd quit a comfortable existence in the US to give his life in a far-off conflict. After all, it was only thanks to the war that he, as a father, had really learned who Ian was himself.

* * *

Ian was born and raised in California, in a household of three boys and two girls. With his older brother a star athlete, and younger brother suffering health problems, he was a classic middle child, getting less attention than his siblings. He didn't seem to need it, however, or want it. He was a good school student, becoming the first in his family to go to university, and a champion wrestler. He was also self-effacing to a fault, never talking about his achievements, uncomfortable even if others did. He squirmed during college graduation photos, and cringed when his proud father posted a YouTube video showing his son's wrestling triumphs. *'To whom it may concern, I do not condone this video,'* he wrote in the comments section.

On leaving school in 2009, he'd joined the Marines to help pay for college, specialising as a communications operator, but left after six years. Unlike his father, he'd never really taken to the Marines' boisterous culture, with the 'Hooah' battle cries and buzzcuts. Most ex-Marines lost no opportunity to tell people they'd served in America's elite infantry unit. Ian kept it quiet.

He then career-surfed, interning as a schoolteacher, working for Microsoft and serving three years as a US Park Ranger, before moving to Philadelphia to work as an Immigration and Customs Enforcement agent, tracking down fugitives and escorting prisoners. He won the Distinguished Honour Graduate award at the Federal Law Enforcement Academy, something his family would only learn of after his death, when they found a certificate at his home.

Despite being known in the Frank household for a certain deadpan humour, Ian had a serious side, and a streak of conservatism not common in Americans his age. In his spare time, he took long backpacking trips to Europe, pursuing an interest in the family's distant roots. He added the Italian name Tortorici to his surname in honour of a great-grandfather, and embraced Orthodox Christianity, with its more muscular, traditional interpretation of the faith. His travels also took him to Eastern Europe and eventually Ukraine, where the family had distant ancestry. There he met a girl, Nadia, who like him was quiet, religious and conservative in outlook. Ian was her first boyfriend.

In December 2021, as Russian troops began massing on Ukraine's borders, Ian announced he was planning another visit, somewhat to his father's bemusement. Wasn't Ukraine the place that the Russians were surrounding, Frank asked? His son seemed unconcerned, leaving Frank to assume that he was perhaps planning a farewell visit, maybe to wrap things up with Nadia.

Then, at the height of the siege of Kyiv in mid-March of 2022, Frank got a message from his son saying he was in the capital. As ever, he made it sound like nothing.

'Just in Kyiv. Helping out a bit.'

'Come on, son. The Ukrainians are gonna lose this war. It's going to be really bad. The Russian military is as big as ours, and they use terror tactics too. Come home now, while you can.'

'I'll be safe, Dad. I'm not gonna do anything dangerous or stupid.'

Frank presumed Ian might be working at a humanitarian aid station somewhere, where his field medic training as a Marine would be handy. Then, later in March, Ian sent him a cryptic photo, showing a Russian military comms device, one clearly captured somewhere in Ukraine. In the photo's background was a pair of soldier's boots. Frank recognised them as a pair that Ian owned. Was he now fighting?

He got his answer in another photo a few days later. It showed Ian in a shabby Legionnaire's uniform, sporting a gun and a big grin. For once, the son who always hated having his photo taken was smiling for the camera, like he meant it. Ian had not, however, turned into an overnight Instagram warrior. He told his father that the photo was for his eyes only. No-one else was to know he was fighting. That included his mother – who wasn't even aware he was still in Ukraine, and thought he was on a special long-term work assignment.

From then on, the photos and messages became more regular. Ian was serving as a machine-gunner, just as Frank had been in the Marines. One video he sent showed a horrendous firefight in a treeline, bullets flying everywhere. Ian told Frank that he had fired on an enemy machine-gun position, which had then fallen silent. The son who'd been so taciturn before was suddenly opening up, proud of what he was doing, keen for his father to know.

Frank was proud too, if worried sick. He was buoyed by how upbeat Ian's messages sounded, but in early June one arrived that left him cold. Ian told him he was going into battle in the Donbas town of Severodonetsk, the scene of the war's fiercest urban combat yet. Up to 100 Ukrainian soldiers were dying there every day. Ian made it clear, in typically deadpan fashion, that he might end up among them.

'Won't be a message for a while, Pop.'

'Son, please stay safe and make contact again as soon as you can.'

'I will and if I don't make it back, don't make a fuss and make sure nobody goes online about it. I asked to be buried here. You have two more sons and grandchildren so everything will be okay. Also please tell Taylor (Ian's younger brother) *that if he marries that Chinese girl, I'm going to haunt him.'*

Frank didn't hear from him for the next fortnight, most of which he spent worrying. He'd seen what the loss of a son in combat could do to a parent. Two workmates had had sons in the Marines at the same time as Ian, one dying in Iraq, the other in Afghanistan. He now faced that same prospect himself, in a conflict with a far higher fatality rate than America's recent wars. In July, he urged Ian to come home. 'It's six months now, you've done your share', he told him. Ian's reply was slightly curt. He'd only done four months, not six, he said. And anyway, he'd now be staying until the war was over.

Where his son's sudden zeal for Ukraine's cause came from Frank had no idea. Ian had never been political before, beyond complaining sometimes that in modern-day America, with its tribalism and culture wars, everyone had to be 'on this side or that side'. In his message about going into Severodonetsk, though, he did say that he was going 'for our people'.

Frank reasoned that 'our people' were the Ukrainians, whom Ian felt some kinship to via the family forefathers. In that very first photo he'd sent of himself in uniform, he'd joked that some of the Ukrainians he was serving alongside were old grandpas – long-lost cousins, perhaps, of his ancestors. More specifically, 'our people' meant Ukrainians like Nadia, who Ian now planned to marry. The couple planned to become farmers in rural Ukraine, a corner of the world still sheltered from modernity, where the traditions they both cherished still prevailed.

*　*　*

Frank knew by now that some of Ian's comrades would never be coming home. While scrolling through news coverage of Ukraine, he'd see reports of Legionnaires being killed, and sometimes recognised their faces from photos that Ian had sent previously. Then in December 2022, Frank learned that Ian's 16-man team only had six people left. Ian himself was trying to rebuild it, having stepped into a new role as a commander.

Frank sent him cold weather gear for the winter, along with two medals of St Michael, a patron saint of soldiers, that he himself had worn on duty.

The one consolation was that he finally felt like he was really getting to know his son. The boy who'd always been polite but reserved was treating him almost like a brother-in-arms, discussing military tactics, asking for advice on leadership. Some of his new recruits were too impatient, Ian complained, wanting to fight without training properly. Other were indisciplined, drinking too much. This from the kid who'd always rolled his eyes at the Marines' regimented lifestyle, who got into trouble for having long, messy hair.

There was still some of the old Ian there, determined to play everything down. While other Legionnaires gave themselves macho call signs, his own was 'Clown 1'. Yet his father sensed a steely inner warrior coming out, who relished combat in a way that even many US Marines didn't. He seemed to grow bolder on the battlefield, telling his father that he insisted on being point man during attacks on enemy trenches. He asked Frank to send him a new US Marine camouflage flameproof combat shirt, saying the old one had got stained with blood. When Frank had asked whose blood, he'd replied: 'Not mine.'

Ian seemed to live a charmed life. Latterly he was serving with the 50-50 Assault Group, who by that time were suffering up to 80 per cent casualties, yet Ian regularly walked away unscathed from firefights that left others dead or injured.* He was wounded only once, hospitalised for ten days due to

---

* Ian knew the 50-50 member Jordan Chadwick, who was found dead in a reservoir just days before Ian himself was killed. It is unclear whether the two served alongside each other, as the 50-50 was composed of two squads, or whether he was aware of what happened to Chadwick.

concussion from a landmine blast, after an 18-hour battle in which he'd saved a teammate's life.

Then, just three days after he'd asked for the new combat shirt, Ian had been killed while on leave. The seasoned combat veteran, who'd done 16 months in the worst hotspots, felled by a missile from the sky as he dined off-duty with civilians, women and children, at a pizza parlour 40 miles from the frontlines.

Frank, who was following events in Ukraine as closely as ever, saw the news as it broke. He knew Ian was off-duty in Kramatorsk, and messaged him repeatedly to check he was okay. He got no response. A few days later came the call from the State Department. Also learning of the news was Ian's mother, who was still unaware he was in Ukraine. Ian hadn't wanted to her worry.

* * *

Ukrainian military funerals were no longer big public affairs because of the risk of attracting Russian missile attacks. Ian's took place at a small church outside Kyiv, the mourners limited to fellow Legionnaires, his girlfriend Nadia and a few local townsfolk. Also there was Frank, who'd travelled to Ukraine to meet Nadia and the soldiers who Ian had spent the last year and a half with. It was an open casket service, which Frank wasn't expecting, but Ian's face looked good. A Ukrainian commander presented Frank with Ian's posthumous combat merit medal. When the service ended, soldiers queued up to shake his hand.

Then they went to a restaurant in Kyiv, where a dozen of Ian's comrades shared memories of him. It had never crossed Frank's mind that his son would exaggerate his exploits on the battlefield, but if anything it sounded like he'd played them down. Ian's comrades described battles they'd fought in with him, illustrated by terrifying GoPro footage. They described a man almost without fear, still keen for more when everyone else was exhausted and losing their minds. And yes, who never made a big deal of it. As they put it, Ian could have fought at Iwo Jima and said it was boring, nothing much.

It was still the height of summer, and Kyiv's bars and restaurants were full of people, some partying loudly. The bacchanalia left Frank somewhat disconcerted. Was this what his son had given his life for? So that Ukrainians far from the frontlines could act like there was no war on? Nadia, Ian's girlfriend, sensed his angst. She told him that she'd once been out in Kyiv with Ian during similar scenes of revelry. She asked Ian if he found it upsetting to see people enjoying themselves, when so many of his comrades had been killed and wounded. He'd shaken his head. 'I fight because I can and it's the right thing to do,' he said. But it made him happy to see people out enjoying themselves, pursuing their way of life. That, he said, was the whole point.

29

A BEER IN THE GARDEN

County Durham, summer 2024

Christopher Perryman's parents spent most of the war largely free of the worries that stalked other families with sons volunteering in Ukraine. He'd told them he was just helping out with training, and nothing in the photos he sent home caused them to think otherwise. Rather than the riverine battles around Kherson, there were pictures of him enjoying life far from the frontlines. Life as a military instructor in Ukraine, it seemed, offered plenty of opportunities for R&R – canoeing, playing in gardens with stray dogs, the odd session of darts.

It was a white lie, told primarily for his mother Dorothy's peace of mind. His brother, a fellow ex-Fusilier, knew what he was doing out there, so too did an uncle. He would have told his father, Tony, too, who was likewise ex-military, but didn't want him to have to keep it secret from Dorothy.

As time had gone on, however, both Tony and Dorothy had sensed a degree of mission-creep. When Christopher had come home at Easter 2023, he had a gash to the head and a finger bandaged up. It was injuries he'd sustained while serving on the river islands near Kherson, where the Russians had surrounded the OP and nearly captured him. He told his parents that he'd been in a road accident, driving without a seatbelt on. They weren't convinced. A couple of times, when it had come up in conversation, Dorothy had caught looks being exchanged between Christopher and the menfolk in the know. 'What's going on?' she'd asked. *Nothing, nothing.*

Neither she nor Tony were born yesterday. They realised that their son was closer to the action than he was saying, but understood why he was being coy. Probably just wanted to spare them the angst they'd gone through when he was in Iraq, when they'd lived in fear of a knock at the door from someone in uniform bearing bad tidings. And, perhaps, to spare himself the third-degree that his dad, who'd served in Northern Ireland in the Troubles, would have given him if he'd known he was fighting. The lengthy pre-deployment checklist ... Have you got this, have you done that, have you checked your life insurance? Had you made provision for your son? *Yes, I know, but just in case ...*

Then, at 3 a.m. one night in October 2023, they'd had a knock at the door of their home in County Durham. It was the grandparents of Perryman's girlfriend, who lived nearby. They'd had a call from one of his comrades in Ukraine. Christopher was dead. No further details had been released, only that he'd been killed in action.

It left them in bits. Never mind all the planning for the worst, never mind that three generations of the family had served, nothing could have prepared them. Casualties were always something that happened to someone else. What were the odds, Tony asked himself? Hundreds of thousands of soldiers fighting out there, only a few thousand of them foreigners, and his son ended up among the handful killed.

Perryman's body was returned home to County Durham five weeks later. Large numbers of fellow ex-Fusiliers turned out for his funeral, his coffin draped with a Union Jack. The proceedings were also broadcast live via video link to his old comrades in Ukraine. Tony expected a courtesy call from a senior Legion officer at some point, expressing his condolences and giving some details about the circumstances of his son's death. Standard procedure in the British Army. The call never came. Once again, the Legion's fallen weren't getting the after-service they should have had.

Instead, his parents had to wait for answers until the following summer, at the formal inquest into Perryman's death at a British coroner's court. Even then, the coroner, Nicholas Graham, said the Ukrainian military had supplied only sparse details of the operation that Perryman had been on. All the court knew was that he'd been killed on Snake Island, a rocky outcrop in the Black Sea near Odesa. It had been made famous at the beginning of the war, when a Ukrainian soldier there told a Russian warship commander to 'go f yourself' rather than surrender. Perryman had suffered fatal chest injuries from an artillery strike. He had died almost instantly. The coroner noted that Perryman's parents were sat in court, and that they'd been unaware that he'd been involved in combat. 'I don't know if you approved of Christopher's actions,' he told them. 'But he clearly felt this was a cause that he wanted to risk his life for.'

Did they approve? Of course not. They'd lost a son. Were they proud of him? Absolutely. He'd died protecting people from bullies, doing the job he'd wanted to do since he was a boy. The same job, indeed, that had made it so hard to re-adjust to civvy street after leaving. Tony had had similar difficulties after leaving the army, where he'd served in the Royal Corps of Transport. But it was even harder for 'teeth arm' soldiers like his son,* who'd served in combat specialist roles. They were trained

---

* 'Teeth arm' soldiers are troops directly engaged in fighting. 'Tail arm' soldiers are support personnel such as logistics, medical and transport staff.

as fighting men, and they couldn't settle. It was like telling a Premier League footballer to spend most of their career on the subs bench. They wanted to get on the pitch, to see a return on all those hard years of training. Which was why these men ended up back in hotspots around the world, doing bodyguarding work, training armies, guarding diamond mines. Or fighting other people's wars.

It was also why Christopher was still roaming the world aged 38, coming home to roost every so often at his parents' place. The Man in the Loft, they nicknamed him. Now there no more, but still present in photos and mementoes around the house. Especially in the garage and the garden, where he liked to spend time, and where his parents remembered him best.

Tony and Dorothy had one favourite photo of him framed in a piece of slate. When they sat out in the garden, they would put it next to them on the table, with a bottle of Christopher's favourite Budweiser beer. The garden also had a pot with a memory rose, sent by a well-wisher and fed with Christopher's ashes, which produced fine yellow blooms.

Some of their mementoes of Christopher were now also with his son, ten years of age when Christopher had gone to Ukraine. When the boy had visited his grandparents, Tony had taken him up to Christopher's old loft room, and they'd gone through his possessions together, assembling a box of his medals and old military paraphernalia. Christopher had gone to Ukraine knowing he might never see his son again, aware that as he grew up he might come to understand his father's decision, or might not. As of yet, the boy kept his thoughts to himself.

30

HOMES FOR HEROES

In mid-August 2024, President Zelensky announced that all Legionnaires and their families would be entitled to Ukrainian citizenship. 'Every warrior who defends the Ukrainian state deserves recognition,' he declared. 'This applies, in particular, to those of our soldiers – Legionnaires – who currently have the citizenship of other states. They deserve to be our citizens.'

To many Legionnaires' families, this was a less-than-tempting offer. Few were delighted that their loved ones had volunteered in the first place. Fewer still would relish the prospect of relocating to a bankrupt, war-ravaged ex-Soviet nation, still embroiled in Europe's bloodiest conflict since 1945. Even if some kind of peace deal was reached with Moscow, there'd be no guarantee that it might not flare up again.

Yet among the volunteers, the take-up rate for citizenship application forms was considerable. For many, Ukraine had been both a war and a romance – not just the kind that occasionally blossomed during R&R in bars in Kyiv, but a love affair with the country itself. Yes, it was a wreck, yes, it had a psychotic neighbour and, yes, its language was bloody hard to learn, especially for those who'd struggled with basic literacy at home. But for the average ex-soldier, it met many of life's basic requirements.

Welcoming, friendly people. Decent food and plenty of booze. Beautiful countryside, especially if all the landmines could be removed. Hot, tough women, who didn't mind men being men, but took no shit either. And a culture that was gallant and gutsy, that still paid due to military values, that saw combat veterans as the nation's saviour, not some embarrassing relic to move on from. On street corners, there were billboards celebrating soldiers' sacrifice. On trains and buses, posters declared 'Bravery is in our DNA'. As one British volunteer put it, that was a lot more inspiring than 'See It, Say It, Sorted'.

More prosaically, Ukraine was also cheap as chips. Twenty thousand pounds could buy a cheap flat, or a cottage in the countryside with a few acres. For many younger volunteers from Britain, where a foot on the property ladder was now all but impossible, that was a potential dream come true. Not only was Zelensky offering a home for heroes, but he was offering one they could afford.

Among those debating a move to Ukraine was Stephen Wilson, the former Royal Engineer from Rochester. He'd quit fighting in April 2023, and had found work back in Britain, clearing old World War II bombs from the proposed site for the new Sizewell C nuclear power plant. It was well-paid, but it wouldn't last for years – unlike the same job in Ukraine, where it was going to take decades to clear all the minefields.

It wasn't just about the money. Ukraine reminded him of the Britain he grew up in – a Britain which, to his mind, no longer existed. A Britain where old ways were still upheld: not just respect for the military, but for family and tradition, where a man and woman were still king and queen of their house, where neighbours still looked out for each other. Where white, working-class men weren't regarded as some benighted indigenous tribe.

Ukraine had changed him for the better, he reckoned. He was more reflective, more grounded. Less anxious to prove his manliness, less likely to get into fights (unless someone really deserved it). Sure, most other folks back home still thought he was crazy, the more so if they knew what he'd done in Ukraine. But it had given him the sense of purpose he'd craved. It was where he'd been at his best, where he'd had to be at the top of his game just to stay alive. Now that he was back in Britain, with all the safety nets that life had to offer, he could feel himself getting stagnant. Many other Legionnaires felt the same way.

Indeed, it was possible that the war had done more for the Legionnaires than the Legionnaires had done for the war. For all the talk of 20,000 volunteers applying to join, less than half that number were thought to have actually turned up. Many of them then quit – some after the bombing at Yavoriv, some because of the lack of organisation and some because the frontline, when they finally reached it, was not what they expected. Sitting around in trenches being hit by artillery from miles away, with no facetime with the enemy, was not for everyone. Nor, conversely, was doing the headlong trench charges that the likes of Chosen Company specialised in, which carried far too much risk of injury or death.

Those who stuck it out realised there was no such a thing as a 'Goldilocks' war, neither too safe nor too dangerous. Volunteers had to adapt to the battlefield, not the other way around. But it still meant that the Legion's ranks probably never swelled beyond a few thousand at most, many scattered in small, ad hoc units along the vast frontline. By way of comparison, some 35,000 foreigners joined the International Brigade in Spain – and roughly the same amount volunteered to fight for Islamic State in Syria and Iraq. The Legion's contribution was therefore way too small to be a game-changer. As one analysis

351

by the Danish Institute for International Studies concluded: 'It remains unclear whether the strategic benefits of such recruitment efforts ever came to outweigh the costs.'

Rather, the main contribution was symbolic, showing that the world stood with Ukraine in its darkest hour, and that if foreign governments weren't willing to put boots on the ground, ordinary citizens were. For the average Ukrainian, the sight of foreigners coming to do more than just aid work, being willing to fight and die alongside them, was a huge morale boost, a sure sign that right was on their side. Zelensky, the master showman, was often said to have created the Legion as a PR gesture to the wider world, but perhaps its more important impact was on Ukrainians themselves. The average citizen didn't witness the Legion's dark side – the Screamers, 'roid ragers and fantasists, or the tensions that sometimes flared between the Ukrainians and the foreigners in the field.

The more experienced Legionnaire units also doubtless made a difference, if only at the tactical level – a successful recon here, a position taken there, a sound judgement call that saved some lives. And despite the high drop-out rate, many Legionnaires – including novices like Douglas Cartner – stuck it out, heading home occasionally to tend to their affairs, then returning for more.

A significant number, too, paid the ultimate price. While the Legion, like the rest of Ukraine's armed forces, never disclosed overall casualty figures, there were unofficial counts based on news reports of individual volunteers' deaths. These put the number at around 500, including around 50 Americans and 20 Britons. The true figure may well be higher, given that many fighters – especially those from countries that forbade service in Ukraine – kept their involvement secret. Either way, it suggests an attrition rate comparable to Ukraine's own military, who had lost 43,000 soldiers out of nearly a million active personnel by the close of 2024. It is also not far short of the estimated one in five International Brigade volunteers who – in Hemingway's words – became 'part of the earth of Spain'.

While those who became part of the black, rich soil of Ukraine were fewer in number, historians will still record them as one of the biggest international mobilisations since World War II. Those same historians may also ask, however, how much bigger and more effective the Legion might have become with proper organisation. Had it been better run – perhaps with discreet, arm's-length help from Ukraine's allies – there might have been less chaos, fewer bad headlines about idling in bases or being used as cannon fodder. Rather than shrinking and fracturing into myriad tiny units, the Legion's numbers might have grown to 50,000 or 100,000.

Indeed, many volunteers were surprised the numbers weren't higher, given the global goodwill Ukraine enjoyed. In the words of Andrew Webber, the ex-US Army paratrooper killed while serving with Chosen Company, it seemed just the kind of war that most soldiers really wanted to fight – a full-on, kinetic conflict, where their skill set would be stretched to its limit, and where there'd be no agonising over whether it was right to be there. As he once texted to a friend: 'It surprises me that there isn't, like, fuck tons of US military West Point people here. It's a free war with a fairly clear bad guy.'*

With bigger numbers and better commanders, the Legion could have fielded large, foreigner-only battalions, sidestepping the language and cultural barriers that made it hard for its smaller units to fit into Ukrainian command structures. Had it attracted more of the elite Nato-trained veterans that Zelensky

---

* 'Andrew Webber's forever war', *Business Insider*, 27 October 2024.

first aimed the Legion at, it could have been a formidable fighting force, winning significant battles on its own. Or, in the words of former British Army officer Richard Johnson, a force that did not merely nibble at the Russians, but chomped.

Putin would of course have tried to discredit it as a CIA- or MI6-sponsored mercenary force, but with volunteers from 50-plus countries that would have been a hard sell. The symbolism of such a Legion liberating towns or villages would have been potent PR, and a rallying cry for others to join in. Nor would every recruit have to be an ex-Para or Green Beret. As the war has ground on, what Kyiv has run shortest of is not weapons or ammunition, but ordinary infantry, whose main contribution is simply being willing to stand their ground. With nearly 400,000 wounded on top of the 43,000 killed, the long queues that once formed at every Ukrainian recruitment centre are no more, forcing President Zelensky to introduce unpopular conscription measures. The Kremlin's calculation is that, sooner or later, Ukraine will simply run out of soldiers to fight with.

In a sense, of course, Ukraine has already won. The moment Putin gave up on his siege of Kyiv, his stated objective to topple Ukraine's government had failed spectacularly. Everything since then, including the horrendous 'meat grinders' to claim a few benighted towns in the Donbas, has been an exercise in saving face. The botched invasion has also bound Ukrainians together like never before, healing the very divisions that Putin hoped to exploit, creating a sense of identity and national pride that previously didn't exist. No other modern nation has faced Russia down in such fashion before, let alone given it such a bloody nose.

At the time of writing, Europe is watching anxiously as new US President Donald Trump threatens to force Zelensky to negotiate a truce with Moscow. With Trump threatening to cut off Kyiv's weapons supply, and Ukraine's military-age population exhausted, Zelensky may be tempted to swallow his pride and comply. Whatever peace that might buy, however, could be short-lived. Many Western capitals fear a truce will simply tempt Russia into further aggression in the coming years – perhaps against Ukraine again, but perhaps this time against Europe, which the Kremlin may now see as easier prey. With the possible exception of the Baltic nations and Poland, which have long and bitter memories of life of Russian occupation, most European nations seem woefully unprepared.

In Britain, senior generals have been queuing up to warn that after 80 years of peace the country has forgotten what real war is. They doubt that Britain's under-equipped, understaffed armed forces would last more than a few weeks against a battle-hardened Russian army. And they question whether the civilian population would rise to the challenge – as Ukraine's has – if asked to take up arms to defend their land.

All the more reason, perhaps, to value the experience of those Britons who have volunteered in Ukraine, who know what twenty-first-century warfare against Russia is like, with its artillery barrages, meat-wave assaults and ever-evolving drone threat. For a regular army that has never encountered such foes, might the volunteers not be a valuable teaching resource? To date, though, there is no sign of Britain's Ministry of Defence attempting to tap into their hard-won knowledge. Of all the volunteers interviewed for this book, only one reported being asked to talk to serving soldiers about their experiences, and that was an informal invite from a comrade in his old regiment.

Why the reticence? The MOD declines to elaborate, saying it cannot discuss 'defence intelligence matters'. One reason may just be old-fashioned Whitehall rigidity: having discouraged British citizens from volunteering in Ukraine, it cannot be seen to show an interest in what they have learned. Another might be institutional pride. Many Legionnaires are from the lower end of the armed forces echelons, or, like Douglas Cartner, amateurs who learned on the job. A professional army that considers itself the best in the world might not consider them ideal guest lecturers. Yet in a wartime setting, it is amateurs who have to step up and learn on the job, just as they've done in Ukraine. Indeed, when Britain formed its two-million strong Home Guard to fend off the threat of Nazi invasion, one of its better platoon commanders was George Orwell, by then battle-hardened from his days in Catalonia, where he too had started out as a rookie.

The skills Legionnaires have learned during their time in Ukraine present risks as well as opportunities. Many have acquired familiarity with all manner of weapons, explosives and drones, in combat conditions that few other soldiers have endured. They often went to Ukraine to fill a lack of purpose in their lives, which might haunt them again on return home, making it easy to drift into trouble. Given the number with chequered pasts, the script for some might be less *The Deer Hunter*, and more the film *Kill List*, with its war-traumatised ex-squaddies as hitmen-for-hire. Most are also resigned to their home countries greeting them with shrugs of indifference rather than as returning heroes. As of 2024, there are no invitations to receptions at Downing Street, no students' unions renaming wings in their honour, no guest invites onto *Strictly Come Dancing*, or even *SAS: Who Dares Wins*.

Nor, despite its support for Ukraine's cause, does the British government have any plan for a public memorial to the fallen. Tony Perryman, whose son Christopher's name would be among those etched on it, would like to see one, but doubts it will ever happen. The Christophers of this world, he laments, are not seen as Orwell-style heroes, or even ordinary soldiers, but as mercenaries and thrill-seekers, who do what they do either for money or kicks. As long as that perception lingers, he says, public support for any kind of monument will be limited.

The mercenary tag, though, is not how it seems. Yes, the Legionnaires were paid – if they had proper contracts – but not very much. Maximum pay was around £70 per day – less than a McDonald's worker in Britain – and only while on active combat duties. Volunteers like Perryman, who had come to Ukraine from the global bodyguarding circuit, could earn ten times that per day in Iraq or Somalia, usually for a fraction of the risk. For all the reasons, good and bad, that volunteers might have fought for – principles, adventure, redemption, bragging rights – money probably was the least likely. Instead, they see themselves as new pieces on the chessboard of global conflict – freelance freedom fighters who act not for the money but for the cause. Or, as some jokingly put it: 'Minimum wage mercenaries'. And whatever the Ukraine war's outcome, they may not have fought their last battle.

In an ever less stable world, their WhatsApp networks could mobilise again wherever the fight seems right. Fighting Kremlin proxies around the world, perhaps, taking on a resurgent Isis or helping Taiwan fend off an invasion by China. Because for all its horrors, for all its hardships, for all its death and danger, war for many of them is business mixed with pleasure. And as President Zelensky said when he created the Legion, the Legion was not just about fending off Russia's invasion of Ukraine, but about defending a 'global order of law, rules and peaceful coexistence'. Of standing up to be counted, to ensure a decent future for kids and grandkids. And, of course, having a few good war stories to tell them too.

EPILOGUE

The updates below were written in the spring of 2025, when newly elected US President Donald Trump was promising to broker a ceasefire between Ukraine and Russia. Events may have moved on since.

The funeral of former Dark Angels leader Daniel Burke took place in March 2024, at a packed crematorium in his home city of Manchester. A large cortege drove there from his family house in Wythenshawe, joined en route by others who had gathered at his local pub. At the service, the 300-strong crowd swelled with mourners from further afield: old army pals, fellow Legionnaires, friends from Syrian Kurdish groups and grateful representatives of Manchester's Ukrainian community.

Nearly six months had passed since Burke's death, with the man accused of shooting him, Nourine Abdelfetah, still at large. Ukrainian police had by then formally identified Abdelfetah as the suspect, but his whereabouts remained unknown. Fellow volunteers believed he'd left Ukraine altogether, and had gone back to either Australia or Algeria, where he had family roots.

It hurt Burke's family all the more to bid farewell to him not as a warrior fallen in combat, but as a victim of a senseless killing by someone on his own side. But at the service, there was no mention of how he had died. Instead, the focus was on the life he had led. The army-mad young lad growing up in Wythenshawe, who covered everything in camouflage, and nick-named his local woods as Congo 1 and Congo 2. The soldier with a conscience, troubled that he couldn't do more for the war-orphaned kids he saw in Afghanistan. The freelance free-dom fighter, serving in Syria, wrongly banged up in Wandsworth, soldiering on to Ukraine. The local hero round Wythenshawe, whose pub stories put everyone else's in the shade, who urged folk not to whinge about their 'First World problems'.

'Many of you here today have told us that there are women, children and men in the world who are living better lives today because of things that Dan did,' Burke's older brother Chris told the service. 'What's happened is devastating, but we'll always love him and be proud of him.'

Mindful that their brother would not have wanted everyone to sit around being miserable – let alone without a drink – the mourners were then invited to raise a glass in his honour at the wake. Despite the tears on the day, Chris knew his brother regarded death an occupational hazard of his career as a roving warrior, and that however it came he'd prefer it to a life work-ing 9–5, dying peacefully aged 80. Heartbreaking as it was, he would never have done things any other way.

* * *

The first few weeks of Alex Drueke's return home from captivity were joyful, euphoric and something of a blur. Emotionally, he felt fine, supremely happy to be alive. Functionally, he was a mess, like his brain was on buffering mode, downloading months of trauma it had previously suppressed. By night, there were bad dreams. By day, there were flashbacks. He didn't even feel safe to drive.

At his local Military Veterans' clinic, they put him on an anti-nightmare medication, and also spotted a fracture in his jaw. They put that down not to the constant beatings in captivity, but to the force with which he clenched his teeth while being electrocuted by Dead Eyes.

He tried a trauma therapist, only to decide in the end that the best counsel he might seek might just be his own. Rather than long afternoons sat on a shrink's couch, he spent long nights sat on his back porch, beer in hand, cigarette in mouth, the last four months slowly processing in his head. Just like his decision to go to Ukraine in the first place, it wasn't the most conventional approach to therapy, but it seemed to work.

He had no regrets, felt he'd faced down not just his demons from Iraq but also those that came to test him in Ukraine. And for every sleepless night, every queasy flashback, there were moments of pure joy at simple things. Like walking his dog Deisel, or sitting over a home-cooked dinner with his mom. In the bad old days of his PTSD, he'd often pondered killing himself. Now, having had others threaten to do that for him, life felt very precious.

Not all his therapy sessions were solo. Sometimes he'd sit up late with his mother, who struggled at times too. Luckily, they found a handy pick-me up, one that didn't come from a bottle or a shrink's prescription pad. Instead, whenever the mood got low, they'd look at each other and joke: 'We beat the KGB!' If they could survive an encounter with an organisation dedicated to breaking souls, they could survive anything.

Aware of just how lucky he had been, Drueke used his profile as an ex-PoW to advocate for Ukraine's plight. He gave interviews to newspapers, TV channels and podcasts, reminding

Americans that the war was still going, of the importance of keeping the weapons tap on. He did speaking engagements, addressing foreign policy forums, community groups, church halls in deepest rural Alabama, anywhere he could spread the message. He adapted a talk for high schools – toned down on the gore, but still livelier than the average civics class.

Together with his fellow captive Andy Huynh – whose wedding he attended as best man – he also met members of Congress in Washington. Huynh's Congressional representative told them that when news had broken of their capture, he'd had 16,000 emails and calls in a single day. He'd had no choice but to put it at the top of his in-tray, raising the PoWs' case at the highest levels. Drueke often mentioned that in his speaking engagements, citing it as proof that America's much-maligned democratic system still had life in it. 'Use your voice to talk to your representatives about Ukraine,' he told his audiences. 'Because I can tell you, the system still works. Otherwise I wouldn't be here talking to you.'

Whether the voice of a lone ex-Legionnaire made much difference was another matter. Drueke had always voted Republican, seeing it as the party that cared most about law and order in the world, that was prepared, when needed, to act as its policeman. Now, with Donald Trump at the party's helm, it was retreating into isolationism, just as the US had done before World War II. Trump's return to power in early 2025 left him profoundly worried, not just for Ukraine's future, but for that of America and the wider world.

Keen to reacquaint himself with the people who had made him feel so welcome, Drueke also made return trips to Ukraine, doing humanitarian work, fundraising and conduct under-capture training. One day – he wants a few years' rest first – he also plans to walk the entire Appalachian Trail.

*   *   *

After returning to Ukraine, former PoW Andrew Hill was despatched to Kupiansk, in Ukraine's north-east, spending two months in muddy, water-logged trenches. There were gun battles most days, and a narrow miss with a tank round. But by soldiering standards it was manageable, and enough to restore his confidence. When he returned to Plymouth that December, as promised, for his son's birthday, he was no longer gloomy, wondering whether he had lost what it took to be a soldier. Unorthodox as it had been, the Man Up school of therapy, to face down his demons, had had the desired effect.

Once back in Plymouth, he retrained as an HGV driver, after finding scaffolding too hard on his bullet-wounded arm. Meanwhile, he began telling his children about the horrors he went through as a PoW. On a trip with them round Devon's former Dartmoor Prison, now open as a tourist site, he told them how its spartan Victorian cells reminded him of those in his jail in the DPR. Dartmoor, he noted, still looked rather more comfortable.

*   *   *

Henry Stevens continued to serve in Ukraine as a drone pilot, although no longer with Boxer, the German paratrooper who was his long-time partner in combat. In March 2024, while Stevens was running a drone training programme away from the frontlines, Boxer was killed by a 155 mm shell during a mission near Bakhmut. As Boxer himself had told Stevens, when artillery came in, there was nothing you could do except pray that it missed.

Stevens was devasted by the death of his friend, who'd been his mentor on the battlefield. He could have interpreted it as a sign that it was time to quit, and return to his off-grid cottage in Germany. Instead, it doubled his resolve. Rather than carrying on with drone training, he returned to active frontline duties. It wasn't about revenge, simply determination to see the war won. Besides, by then, he was used to losing comrades – to the point where he was wary of becoming close friends with anyone on the frontline. As he'd learned the hard way far too often, companionship one day could mean grief and loss the next.

He now fought mainly alongside Ukrainians, avoiding fellow foreign volunteers. Far too many were cowboys and fantasists, whose only real cause was themselves. A case in point was a fellow American, Ryan Routh, who'd got in touch with Stevens one day, offering to supply drones and boasting of connections in high places, which had come to nothing. The next time Stevens had seen Routh's face was on the news in autumn 2024, when he was arrested for attempting to assassinate Donald Trump at his golf course in Florida. In Routh's case, it turned out that even the Legion had rejected him for service.

Part of Stevens wondered if Ukraine might have been better off had Routh succeeded in killing Trump. Now, he saw Ukraine's fate being left to the whims of an ignorant narcissist, not much more in touch with reality than his would-be assassin. Trump, he sensed, had no idea of how many Ukrainians would fight on regardless, whether Washington gave them weapons or not. Stevens vowed to be among them, no matter how badly the war went. If Kyiv fell to the Russians, he'd serve as a partisan, helping to wage the mother of all insurgencies.

Germany, where he'd spent most of his adulthood, no longer felt like home. He'd return to his eco-cottage every so often, wandering around the overgrown garden, selling honey from his beehives to finance his next stint in Ukraine. Today, though, Germany felt too cossetted, too insulated from the horrors unfolding 1,000 miles further east. If Stevens heard anyone complaining about the cost of supporting the war, or rising living costs, he'd make his feelings known.

'Here you are in a safe country with a good job, enough to eat, no worries about drones or cruise missiles crashing into your house. Yet here you are, complaining that you can't afford more than one fucking holiday abroad this year! Read a history book, realise what Putin and Russia is. We either pay a bit in money to Ukraine now, or we pay in blood ourselves later.'

That was usually enough to shut them up.

* * *

Within months of coming home to Middlesbrough, James Durose returned to Ukraine, missing the excitement of combat. He fought through the early spring of 2023, once again on a steep learning curve. Temperatures in the trenches dropped to minus 20 degrees centigrade, and with the trees bare there was no cover from the mounting FPV drone threat. He was now fighting in the Donbas, where the frontlines were visions of hell: corpse-littered landscapes, burned-out vehicles with charred skeletons behind the wheel, the smell of fire and death. In one notorious hotspot outside Donetsk, his unit pulled back from an operation, fearing they'd been sent on a suicide mission. A few days later, another unit were sent instead, suffering seven casualties out of nine. One fighter's body was left trapped in no-man's-land, used for target practice by Russian troops.

It was a slow, grinding war of attrition, with none of the lightning advances that Durose remembered from his days during Operation Claw. He also realised that not every

Ukrainian shared his fighting spirit, after being assigned to a unit who spent most of their time sitting terrified in the trenches. Durose later learned that they were part of a 'disciplinary squad', where the army sent soldiers who did not want to fight. They were baffled by the foreigners who had come to fight of their own free will.

In the end, it was love, not war, that brought his time in Ukraine to a close. Among the donors to Durose's GoFundMe page was a Texan woman, with whom he started to correspond. Romance blossomed, and he invited her to Ukraine, where they spent the Christmas of 2023 together in Lviv. The prospect of returning to the winter frontline did not appeal, so he followed her back to New Mexico, where the pair got married and had a son in early 2025. Despite the locals struggling with his Middlesbrough accent, he was happier there than in his home town, with no reputation to live up to, and no drug gangs on his tail.

He remembered Ukraine as an important crossroads in his life, where for once, he took the right turn rather than wrong one, and his days with the Carpathian Sich as some of the best in his life. He also hopes one day for a reunion, toasting Craig Mackintosh and Jed Danahay, his fallen comrades.

* * *

John Harding, the former Azov fighter and veteran of the siege of Mariupol, found it hard to re-adjust to life in Britain after his time in Russian captivity. He ended up living with his sister in Luton, a city that fell short of his cultural expectations. It had no decent bookshop, and if he wanted the kind of theatre or concert venues he'd enjoyed in Mariupol, he had to travel into London.

In time, even trips to London became difficult, after he suffered crushing chest pains one morning, and was rushed to hospital with a heart attack. Doctors later told him it was not his first heart attack, but his second, the first probably taking place during his time as a PoW. Harding put it down to the 20-minute beating he took during his early days in captivity. With hindsight, he recalled suffering exactly the same chest pains while lying in his cell afterwards. A less fit and robust man might well have died there and then.

Now 63, he continues to struggle with infirmity, although his thoughts are for other Azov comrades, some of whom remain in captivity. He passes his time reading books on philosophy and human rights, while debating how to spend his retirement. For someone who spent many of his happiest years as a wandering warrior in Syria and Ukraine, Britain doesn't offer many obvious options. 'I don't want to sound ungrateful for the fact that I've been freed,' he jokes to friends. 'But I do sometimes wonder – what the hell am I doing here?'

* * *

Jack Knight, the former Royal Engineer from south London, continued to serve in Ukraine into 2025. Just as he credited his early days in the army with being the making of him as a youngster, he credited his time in Ukraine with being the making of him as an adult. With hindsight, he regarded his decision to quit his warehouse job at Ocado as the most important call of his life. He feels no desire to return to the UK, where he could never afford a home, and may settle permanently in Ukraine, clearing ordnance like his old comrade Stephen Wilson. With a third of Ukraine's landmass currently contaminated with mines – an area bigger than England – there is plenty of work to go around.

* * *

Richard Johnson, the former British Army captain, left the Legion in the late summer of 2022, but remained in Ukraine. He set up a consultancy in Kyiv supporting foreign firms wishing to set up business. He remained a close supporter, however, of both the Legion and the wider Ukrainian armed forces, continuing to act as a sounding board on military matters. In recognition of his services on the frontlines in Mykolaiv, he was awarded the HUR medal second class from Ukraine's spymaster-in-chief, General Kyrylo Budanov – the first foreigner to receive the honour.

* * *

After returning to Scotland from his first stint in Ukraine, self-taught fighter Douglas Cartner spent the next year working as a mechanic in Edinburgh. Unable to afford the city's high living costs, he saved money by sleeping in his car. After months living in a foxholes, it felt almost palatial. Much as he tried to put thoughts of Ukraine behind him, he missed it greatly. When he looked at photos of himself from his time out there, he saw a different man, smiling far more often than he used to. In January 2024, he decided to return – rowing with his family again, but this time parting on better terms. He promised to stay in touch more regularly, sparing his family the stress of weeks incommunicado.

Like his fellow Carpathian Sich fighter James Durose, his second stint in Ukraine brought different challenges. Drones had transformed the battlefield dynamics, leading him to pine for the simpler days of gunfire, tanks and artillery. Some of his

Ukrainian comrades showed signs of war fatigue, their foxholes smelling of vodka and marijuana. He stuck it out, however, and now thinks he may one day buy land in Ukraine, pursuing a long-held dream to be a smallholder. Britain, he says, no longer feels like a happy place, its people at odds with both government and each other, feeling powerless to change anything. If Britons can go to Ukraine and make a difference, he sometimes wonders, why can't they do it at home too?

*   *   *

Damon Adams, the owner of the army surplus store that features in the opening chapter, began doing aid deliveries himself in March 2022, and to date has done 18 trips to Ukraine. Meanwhile, he continues to see a steady flow of would-be Legionnaires at his shop. He estimates that over the last three years around 60 people have passed through his doors en route to Ukraine – some despite his best efforts to dissuade them. A number have been killed or injured.

ACKNOWLEDGEMENTS

Among my collection of souvenirs from reporting trips around the world is an old boarding pass for a flight to Ukraine. A Ryanair flight stub is not the kind of thing most people would bother keeping, but this one has a certain significance. Flight FR1642, arriving at Lviv at 8.20 p.m. on 23 February 2022, was one of the very last into Ukraine before the outbreak of war closed the airspace a few hours later. Fortunately, this was one of those rare Ryanair flights that arrived on time – had it not been, we might have been sharing the skies with incoming Russian missiles.

Arriving at my hotel that night, I remember thinking that nothing much was going to happen. At the time, nobody thought Vladimir Putin would be crazy enough to invade. The expectation of the *Telegraph*'s foreign desk, who had sent me there, was that Putin would, at most, despatch a few more tanks into separatist-held republics in the east, sabre-rattle a bit, then leave it at that. My instructions were to hang around for another few days, reporting on what foreign correspondents refer to as a 'diplomatic climbdown' story.

As we now know, it didn't quite go that way. I was in Ukraine for the next month and a half, most of it spent reporting from Kyiv while it was under Russian siege. It was chaotic, exhausting and occasionally frightening, but I am still indebted to the foreign desk for sending me there, to cover one of the most significant events in early-21st-century history. Thanks to the then foreign editor, Memphis Barker, and his ever-capable team for all their support on that trip, and the dozen or so I have made since. A special note of thanks should also go to the succession of Ukrainian translators whom I worked with while there, particularly Eugene, whose calm unflappability was the perfect disposition for those long, hard weeks on the road. After clocking 100,000 miles with me and other *Telegraph* journalists (Ukraine is a huge country), he left us at the end of 2023 to volunteer at the front – good luck there, mate, and stay safe.

I mention the foreign desk first, because without their sending me to Ukraine, I'd probably never have bumped into any Legionnaires, and wouldn't have had the idea for this book. But many others also helped out – be it with insights and knowledge, or introductions into a world that is often wary of outsiders. One was Royal Marine-turned-documentary maker Emile Ghessen, whose own 2017 documentary, *Robin Hood Complex*, tells the story of Western volunteers fighting for Kurdish YPG forces in Syria. That episode in some ways foreshadowed the creation of the Legion in Ukraine, and if you haven't seen it, the documentary is well worth a watch. Also helpful with introductions was Daniel Ridley, a former British soldier who served with the Ukrainian army before 2022, and who now runs the Trident Defence Initiative, offering private training for Ukrainian forces.

Like those 1,000-mile crawls from Lviv to Donbas, the process of writing a book is always a long, tiring journey, and my thanks go out to those who helped me reach the end. My agent James Spackman helped shape the idea for the book and succeeded in tempting Joel Simons at HarperCollins into publishing it. As well as making some very deft editing calls, Joel came up with the 'The Mad and the Brave' title, which I think sums things up well (and was certainly better than anything I'd managed to think of). A shout also goes out to Joel's colleague Gaurika Kumar, who helped things run smoothly day-to-day, and project editor Simon Gerratt, who cast his eagle eye over the finalised manuscript.

At home, my partner Jane was a tower of strength, putting up with my long absences in Ukraine, and the even longer spells holed up in my study writing. My children Robyn and Daniel also had to put up with an absent father (much as they professed not to care, the cheeky gits). Jane also had the unenviable task of critiquing the very early drafts, which were far from polished, and listening to me moan when all seemed to be going wrong, as it always does at certain points when writing a book. Also kind enough to give me feedback on early drafts were two old journalist pals, Lisa Mitchell and Ian Evans, whose only reward for ploughing through hundreds of pages of rough-cuts was a bottle of wine in the post.

Finally, I should thank the volunteers themselves who appear in this book – and in some cases, their next of kin – who put up with many hours of interviews, sometimes in difficult circumstances. Many others were equally generous with their time, but for various reasons their accounts did not make the final cut. Sometimes this was due to lack of space and at other times it was simply because I lost contact with them. Most volunteers are, after all, peripatetic, freewheeling souls. Keeping in touch with curious journalists is not among their strongpoints. So, for all those who vanished off the radar, I hope you're doing well, and perhaps we'll meet again one day for a beer. After all, if you're reading this, it proves you're still alive.

Very last of all, a thanks to all the countless Ukrainians I have met over the past three years, whose courage and spirit is proof that despite Mr Putin's best intentions, there is still hope for both Ukraine and humanity. Without their hospitality and friendliness, this would have been an even tougher war to cover than it has been. I hope to return one day to report on the outbreak of peace – when Ukraine's Legionnaire allies can lay down their weapons, and when those budget flights into Lviv might finally resume.